Brothers in Sport
RUGBY

Charlie Mulqueen

MERCIER PRESS
IRISH PUBLISHER – IRISH STORY

MERCIER PRESS

Cork

www.mercierpress.ie

© Text: Charlie Mulqueen, 2011

© Foreword: Keith Wood, 2011

ISBN: 978 1 85635 826 2

10 9 8 7 6 5 4 3 2 1

A CIP record for this title is available from the British Library

Printed and bound in the EU.

CONTENTS

FOREWORD

THERE HAS always been a sense of family in rugby. Indeed, I suspect in many ways it has been the sport's biggest recruiting tool. And even though I followed my father in wearing the green jersey of Ireland and the red jersey of the Lions, his was not the biggest influence on my career.

The dulcet tones of Bill McLaren commentaries in the late seventies always led to very competitive games in the garden with my older brothers. Gordon and John were my heroes, the people I always wanted to emulate. There was never going to be any doubt that I was going to make the trek to St Munchin's to follow in their footsteps and to play rugby. I even joined Bohemians as a scrawny twelve-year-old scrum half before I bulked up and made the transition to a totally different area of the rugby pitch!

But it was in the games in the back garden where their influence found fertile soil. Skills were honed, mental games enacted. I was toughened up. My first injury was a chip and chase that ended up with a dive and a dislocated jaw in the rockery. A quick trip to the doctor and then back out for a rematch after dinner. As if I had a choice!

I am reminded of those times when I see my own three sons kick the lard out of each other in the garden. Their drive and determination are something to see and give me an insight into my own development as a brother and as a rugby player. For some brothers, this early competition leads to extraordinary results.

From those early days back in the 1920s when the many brothers who represented their country first came to prominence, to the unparalleled modern achievements of the Wallaces, Charlie has, with his usual skill, brought these stories to life. Each chapter is a story in itself and each story is part and parcel of what we are all part of – the rugby family.

KEITH WOOD

Former Ireland captain, twice Lions tourist
and IRB World Player of the Year 2001

INTRODUCTION

ONE OF the many delightful features of Irish rugby is that it is a thirty-two-county activity that enables one in the course of a long and enjoyable career to visit many parts of the country and meet a whole series of fascinating characters.

The challenge presented by a book of this nature comes in highlighting the achievements of brothers who have achieved distinction on the rugby field but who have not necessarily represented their country in the international arena. In this professional age (since 1995), the scene is inevitably dominated by the exploits of the Irish team, with the provinces on a slightly lower rung of the ladder and the clubs somewhere further down the order of significance. After that there are the schools and the junior clubs spread out the length and breadth of the country, without which the steady and essential flow of talent would not be forthcoming.

Within these pages you will encounter rugby players who haven't played for their country and in some cases never got close to doing so. But in consort with their siblings and with the massive support of their parents, relatives, clubs and friends, they gave selflessly of their time, energy and ability to shed lustre on the Irish rugby scene.

Indeed, without the family connection, one wonders just where Irish rugby would be today. A wonderful tradition was born in 1878 when F. Schute (Wanderers) was capped against England and was followed by his son F.G. Schute (Dublin University/Trinity), who lined out against South Africa in 1912. The flow after that of son following father into the green jersey was relatively steady. In 1884, W. Collis from the Wanderers club was capped against Wales and forty years later, his son W.R. Collis (Harlequins) made the first of his eight appearances in the green jersey against France.

The numbers playing rugby back in those days was relatively small, but as the game grew in popularity, the challenge for Irish team places inevitably intensified and accordingly the opportunities for different generations of families to wear the green were reduced. However, a tradition had been set and as the years went by, new records were inevitably created, some of which may never be broken. When Noel F. Murphy lined out for the first of his ten caps, against England in 1930, he could hardly have foreseen that he would be followed by his son, Noel A., who earned the first of his sixty-four caps in 1958, and grandson Kenny, who represented his country on twelve occasions from 1990. To underline further the family's magnificent contribution to the game, Noel F. (1960–61) and Noel A. (1998–99) were both elected president of the IRFU. Noel A. twice toured with the Lions, in 1959 and 1966 in Australia and New Zealand respectively, and coached the 1980 side in South Africa, as well as coaching and managing several Irish teams in the course of a magnificent and far-reaching career.

The Murphys remain the only father, son and grandson to have played for Ireland although Keith Wood, who so kindly contributed the foreword to this book, may have something to say on that score in a few years time! G. Collopy (Bective

Rangers), first capped in 1891, was followed in 1914 and 1923 respectively by his sons W.P. and R. Collopy (also Bective), while the illustrious McKibbin family from Belfast matched this achievement some years later. H.R. McKibbin (Queen's University and Instonians) made his first appearance in 1938 before being emulated by his offspring C.H. (Instonians) in 1976 and A.R. McKibbin (Instonians and London Irish) a year later. Harry McKibbin, CBE, LLB, served as president of the IRFU in 1974–75, and also played in all three Tests with the Lions in South Africa in 1939 when a student at Queen's University. He revisited that country as assistant manager of the Lions in 1962.

The tradition of three brothers playing for Ireland began in 1880 when A.J. Forrest of Wanderers was capped against England and was followed in time by E.G. and H. Forrest (also Wanderers). This has now happened on eleven occasions. The latest to achieve this distinction are the Wallaces – Richard, Paul and David – who have gone a step further, entering the *Guinness Book of Records* by becoming the first family to also provide three members to Lions touring teams.

Will that achievement ever be equalled or even bettered? Records, as we know, are made to be broken and sometime in the future that may well come to pass. However, the advent of professionalism in 1995 makes that eventuality all the more unlikely. Either way, the family connection has served Irish rugby well and long may this desirable trend continue.

Here is the full list of the brothers, fathers, sons and grandsons who have played for Ireland (with the date they were first capped):

THREE BROTHERS

E. Doran (Lansdowne) 1890
G.P. Doran (Lansdowne) 1899
B.R. Doran (Lansdowne) 1902

A.J. Forrest (Wanderers) 1880
H. Forrest (Wanderers) 1893
E.G. Forrest (Wanderers) 1897

T.A. Harvey (Dublin University) 1900
A.D. Harvey (Wanderers) 1903
F.M.W. Harvey (Wanderers) 1907

T.R. Hewitt (Queen's University) 1924
F.S. Hewitt (Instonians) 1926
V.A. Hewitt (Instonians) 1936

W.E. Johnstone (Dublin University) 1884
R.W. Johnstone (Dublin University) 1890
R. Johnstone (Wanderers) 1890

S. McVicker (Queen's University) 1922
J. McVicker (Collegians) 1924
H. McVicker (Army) 1927

D.F. Moore (Wanderers) 1883
F.W. Moore (Wanderers) 1884
C.M. Moore (Dublin University) 1887

J. Pedlow (Bessbrook) 1882
T.B. Pedlow (Queen's University) 1889
R. Pedlow (Bessbrook) 1891

D.J. Ross (Belfast Albion) 1884
J.P. Ross (Lansdowne) 1885
J.F. Ross (NIFC) 1886

T. Smyth (Malone) 1908
W.S. Smyth (Collegians) 1910
P.J. Smyth (Collegians) 1911

R.M. Wallace (Garryowen, Saracens) 1991
P.M. Wallace (Blackrock College, Saracens) 1995
D.P. Wallace (Garryowen) 2000

TWO BROTHERS

C. Glynn Allen (Derry, Liverpool) 1890
C. Elliott Allen (Derry, Liverpool) 1900

George R. Beamish (Coleraine and RAF) 1925
Charles E. Beamish (Coleraine and RAF) 1935

S. Best (Ulster, Belfast Harlequins) 2003
R. Best (Ulster, Banbridge) 2005

H. Brown (Windsor) 1877
T. Brown (Windsor) 1877

S.J. Byrne (Lansdowne, UCD) 1953
F. Byrne (UCD) 1962

W.P. Collopy (Bective Rangers) 1914
R. Collopy (Bective Rangers) 1923

M.P. Crowe (Lansdowne) 1929
P. Crowe (Blackrock College) 1935

M. Deering (Bective Rangers) 1929
S.J. Deering (Bective Rangers) 1935

C.J. Dick (Ballymena) 1961
J.S. Dick (Queen's University) 1962

M.G. Doyle (Cambridge University and Blackrock College)
1965
T.J. Doyle (Wanderers) 1968

S.H. Easterby (Llanelli, Scarlets) 2000
G.W. Easterby (Ebbw Vale, Ballynahinch, Llanelli,
Leinster) 2000

Con Feighery (Lansdowne) 1972
Tom Feighery (St Mary's College) 1977

E. Galbraith (Dublin University) 1875
R. Galbraith (Dublin University) 1875

W. Gardiner (NIFC) 1892
F.T. Gardiner (NIFC) 1900

L.H. Gwynn (Dublin University) 1894
A.P. Gwynn (Dublin University) 1895

J. Heron (NIFC) 1877
W.T. Heron (NIFC) 1880

W.R. Hunter (CIYMS) 1962
L. Hunter (Civil Service) 1968

P. Kavanagh (UCD) 1952
Ronnie Kavanagh (UCD, Wanderers) 1953

F. Kennedy (Wanderers) 1880
J.M. Kennedy (Wanderers) 1882

J. Lyttle (NIFC) 1889 J.H. Lyttle (NIFC) 1894
L.M. Magee (Bective Rangers, London Irish) 1895 J.T. Magee (Bective Rangers) 1895
E.H. McIlwaine (NIFC) 1895 J.E. McIlwaine (NIFC) 1897
H.R. McKibbin (Queen's University, Instonians) 1938 D.E. McKibbin (Instonians, London Irish) 1950
C.H. McKibbin (Instonians) 1976 A.R. McKibbin (Instonians, London Irish) 1977
R.J. McLoughlin (Gosforth, Blackrock College) 1962 Phelim McLoughlin (Northern) 1976
R.B. Montgomery (Queen's University, Cambridge University) 1887 A. Montgomery (NIFC) 1895
H. Moore (Windsor) 1876 W. Moore (Queen's University) 1878
Jack O'Connor (Garryowen) 1895 Joe O'Connor (Garryowen) 1910
K.P. O'Flanagan (London Irish) 1947 M. O'Flanagan (Lansdowne) 1949
T.O. Pike (Lansdowne) 1927 V.J. Pike (Lansdowne) 1931
M. Ryan (Rockwell) 1897 J. Ryan (Rockwell) 1897
D. Scott (Malone) 1961 R.D. Scott (Queen's University) 1967
D.E. Spring (Dublin University, Lansdowne) 1978 R.M. Spring (Lansdowne) 1979
G.V. Stephenson (Queen's University, United Services) 1920 H.W. Stephenson (United Services) 1922
R. Stevenson (Lisburn, NIFC, Dungannon) 1887 J. Stevenson (Lisburn, NIFC, Dungannon) 1888
F.O. Stoker (Wanderers) 1886 E.W. Stoker (Wanderers) 1888
R.B. Walkington (NIFC) 1875 D.B. Walkington (Dublin University) 1887
Joseph Wallace (Wanderers) 1902 James Wallace (Wanderers) 1904

W.A. Wallis (Wanderers) 1881
A.K. Wallis (Wanderers) 1892

FATHER, SON AND GRANDSON

N.F. Murphy (Cork Con) 1930
N.A. Murphy (Cork Con) 1958
K.J. Murphy (Cork Con) 1990

FATHER AND TWO SONS

G. Collopy (Bective Rangers) 1891
W.P. Collopy (Bective Rangers) 1914
R. Collopy (Bective Rangers) 1923

H.R. McKibbin (Queen's University, Instonians) 1938
C.H. McKibbin (Instonians) 1976
A.R. McKibbin (Instonians, London Irish) 1977

FATHER AND SONS

W. Hallaran (Dublin University) 1884
C.F. Hallaran (United Services) 1921

A.D. Clinch (Dublin University, Wanderers) 1885
J.D. Clinch (Dublin University, Wanderers) 1924

W. Collis (Wanderers) 1884
W.R. Collis (Harlequins) 1924

S. Deering (Bective Rangers) 1935
S.M. Deering (Garryowen, St Mary's College) 1974

B.O. Foley (Shannon) 1976
A.G. Foley (Shannon) 1995

T.R. Hewitt (Queen's University) 1925
D. Hewitt (Queen's University, Instonians) 1958

S.T. Irwin (Queen's University) 1900
J.W.S. Irwin (NIFC) 1938

P.F. Murray (Wanderers) 1927
J.B. Murray (UCD) 1963

F. Schute (Wanderers) 1878
F.G. Schute (Dublin University) 1912

B.G.M. Wood (Garryowen, Lansdowne) 1954
K.G.M. Wood (Garryowen, Harlequins) 1994

* * *

THIS BOOK would never have seen the light of day were it not for the help and support of its central characters who are warmly thanked for their support and interest. But there are many others deserving of my freely expressed gratitude and appreciation. My great friend and colleague Edmund Van Esbeck was typically generous with his advice while his many histories of the Union and the various clubs around the country were nothing short of priceless when doubts needed to be assuaged and facts checked. My thanks, too, to another denizen of the press box, Sean Diffley, and indeed those other journalists whose work helped me to piece all the diverse strands together.

And, of course, I am deeply grateful to that prince of rugby hookers, Keith Wood, for his foreword.

RICHARD, PAUL AND DAVID WALLACE

Paul Wallace was my player of the series.

Lions captain Martin Johnson after the Lions beat world
champions, South Africa, on the 1997 tour

ELEVEN FAMILIES HAVE provided three brothers to the Irish rugby team – but only one has also produced three Lions tourists. That unique honour rests with the Wallaces – Richard, Paul and David – whose achievement is all the more remarkable in that it has happened in an era when competition for places at the highest level of a major professional and international sport has never been greater. Indeed, when David was first capped against Argentina in 2000, the 'Wallys' were bridging a sixty-four year gap since V.A. Hewitt, the third of the famed Belfast clan, wore the green jersey for the last time in the game against Wales in 1936.

By the end of the 2011 RBS Six Nations Championship, the Wallaces had accumulated 146 international caps between them – Richard: 29, Paul: 46 and David: 71 – a staggering number for members of the same family and one unlikely to be surpassed. Furthermore, Paul played in all three Tests in the victorious Lions tour of South Africa in 1997 and David did likewise in the less successful trip to the land of the reigning world champions in 2009. And when the fifteen-year European Rugby Cup 'Dream Team' was chosen in 2009, David was there along with fellow Irishmen Geordan Murphy, Brian O'Driscoll, Ronan O'Gara and Anthony Foley. However, the list of achievements by the Wallace brothers goes a whole lot further than that.

* * *

MICHAEL WALLACE started to play rugby from an early age with Cobh Pirates and later with CBC, Clongowes Wood College and London Irish. It was, perhaps, inevitable that he would pass on his love for the sport to his four sons. This was not as easy a task as it might appear at first sight, as in their formative years Richard preferred hurling and David was happier watching television! However, eventually dad Michael and mum Gretta were to be rewarded for their perseverance, dedication and sacrifice, as their offspring went on to reach a pinnacle in rugby that no other family has so far approached.

As the Wallace boys were growing up, their parents moved between Cork and Limerick on a couple of occasions and so they split much of their time between the Cork Constitution and Garryowen clubs. Henry is the oldest of the four Wallace boys and although he displayed considerable promise in his younger days, he gradually drifted away from big time rugby, despite having featured on the first ever Irish Colleges' side with Richard. There wasn't much of the oval ball stuff when the family settled in the lovely village of Adare in County Limerick, a period in his life that Richard particularly enjoyed.

'Henry got involved in rugby before me and I started at the age of nine at Garryowen, but I gave it up and instead played hurling with Adare CBS,' he explains. 'I was handy enough and I loved it, but after sixth class, we moved back to Cork and into an environment that didn't have any hurling at all. My parents later returned to Limerick and at the time I had finished my second year in college in Cork and all I really wanted was to be a pilot. I also needed a roof over my head and decided I would try flying out of Shannon and that's what I started doing with the intention of taking out a commercial pilot's licence.

'I asked the guys in Cork Con who I should join and they said Garryowen. I was very lucky. They were short in a few positions in the centre and wing, and I got into the team pretty quickly and we had a lot of success. We had a number of good coaches in Garryowen and I think we were the first to bring in professional coaches, Nairn McEwan and a succession of guys like Murray Kidd and Andy Leslie after that. They were all very good, positive influences on me, bringing with them a lot of expertise from the southern hemisphere and a more professional way of thinking about the game. They were very, very helpful.

'Garryowen's success – we won two All-Ireland Leagues and I got to see plenty of the ball and scored a good few tries – led to a call-up to Munster after a few years and then into the Irish scene. I would never have thought I could achieve anything like that. And then came the Lions call in 1993 … I had originally been put on a shortlist and went off to play World Cup sevens with Ireland in Scotland and we had a very successful campaign. We were actually beaten 21–19 by a conversion in injury time by Australia in the semi-final. We went bloody close. I had a good campaign and that maybe pushed me up ahead of Simon [Geoghegan], who would have been close to the Lions call as well, and probably got me on the plane. Fortuitous again, I suppose, but that's the way the cookie crumbles at times.'

Interestingly, the sevens game was right up Richard's alley and he went on to become Ireland's record try scorer in the abbreviated game, with ten to his credit. In fairness, though, his call-up by the Lions was earned on the back of a lot more than that, his progress highlighted by outstanding performances on the wing for Garryowen, for which he scored many important tries, and Munster, whom he helped to defeat the then world champions, Australia, at Musgrave Park in 1992. He earned his first Irish cap against Namibia in 1991 and later made his mark with Saracens in the English Premiership and in the Heineken Cup, where he played alongside brother Paul. He was a strong running, fleet-footed and elusive wing, who had the happy knack of scoring tries when they were most needed. When Ian Hunter of England was injured in the early stages of the 1993 Lions tour of New Zealand, Richard was the obvious replacement, having been a little unlucky not to be chosen in the first place. However, Ieuan Evans, the brilliant Welshman, was one of the game's outstanding wings at this time and the No. 14 jersey was always going to be his property.

It was a good tour, though, and having lost the first Test, the Lions levelled the series before going down in the third. Richard fully justified his place, scoring a typical try in the victory over Taranaki on a day when another Irish replacement, Vinny Cunningham, scored on a couple of occasions. However, he has less happy memories of the day the Lions lost to a Waikato side containing a former Garryowen team-mate, the formidable second-row Brent Anderson, and another man with close Garryowen connections, back row forward John Mitchell. Rhys Ellison, who later joined Shannon and played in Europe with Munster, also helped to beat the Lions that day.

'It was fantastic to be called up to play for the Lions,' says Richard. 'I never really expected to be picked for Ireland, and the concept of playing for the Lions, well you might as well have asked me to be an astronaut in outer space. It was certainly an amazing experience and to wear a Lions jersey was something else. Ieuan Evans and Rory Underwood were the first choice wings and were more or less unmovable, so Tony Underwood and myself formed the mid-week pairing on the wing. I thought I did reasonably well but unfortunately the wheels came off the mid-week team midway through the tour for any number of reasons. It became a bit dysfunctional at times. There are always fellows disappointed at not getting on the Saturday team but it all depends on how it's managed by the management, and in my inexperienced opinion at the time, it wasn't handled very well at all.'

Richard Wallace's career ended when he broke his ankle playing for Saracens on a frozen pitch in the north of England on 10 January 1999, a date that comes instantly to his mind because 'it was just before my birthday and it was a game that should never have been played in the first place. Beforehand, François [Pienaar, the Saracens captain and the man who led South Africa to the World Cup in 1995] asked us all whether we should play and I was the only one to put up my hand and say no we shouldn't. Sod's law dictated that I was the only one to be injured and funnily enough, much the same later happened to Paul.

'I was fortunate in that, unlike him, there was no collateral damage, although I did go back into training on the premise that it was healing when it wasn't. I didn't realise that until a good friend, Nigel Roe, came back to Saracens and looked at the x-rays and he just said, that's still broken. The insurance company's doctor then advised me that I shouldn't play again. I had just closed the door of his surgery and was halfway down the steps on to the street when the flying school rang and said someone had just pulled out of the first course in six weeks. They offered me the spot and I just thought, one door closes and another opens. In 2001, I joined CityJet and I've been there ever since, a great company to work for.'

As Richard's career was ending, Paul and David were emerging as major forces in the game. True to the unassuming nature of the family in general, Richard insists that he doesn't regard being one of three brothers from the same family playing both for Ireland and the Lions as 'any great achievement'. But it is, of course, very special.

'I'm excited at seeing these two brothers go on and do so well,' Richard says. 'They have both had fantastic careers. Surprised? No, not all. The only thing that surprised me about Paul is that he converted from a wing-forward playing for Cork Con to next year playing at senior level as prop for Crescent College. It was a bit of a surprise that he could do that, but once you saw he could do it, you assumed he was going to be able to do a lot more. I had played with Paul at Munster and at the time he got the Lions call-up we were in Saracens together and I played there with him for quite a while. His dedication to training and his commitment was so fantastic that I wouldn't have expected anything less from him.

'I regret not having seen much of David when he played at school because I was playing professionally myself, but I do remember going to Thomond Park to watch him in a Schools' Cup match and I was very taken by how at home he seemed to be on the pitch and how comfortable he was in his surroundings. That was always a sign to me of a player with a lot of potential. He has realised that potential big time. Again, he's very dedicated to his preparation and his training and has a great attitude towards life, his family and his job as a rugby player. It has stood him in great stead all through and he's such a great character. He's easygoing, he can take the good with the bad and be very philosophical about it.

'I remember a few years ago there was a lot of comment in the press about him not being picked by Ireland and so on. I talked to him around the end of that time, just before he broke back into the side and asked him if he was a bit put out that he didn't appear to be getting a look-in. And he replied, "No, I'm not fit enough yet, I'm not ready enough yet and when I am, they'll pick me." All through my career, I remember guys, myself included, might have moaned at not being picked here and there, so to see his attitude being completely the opposite – when he was good enough, he'd be picked again – I thought that was wonderful. And he would have told me exactly how he felt. I'm not a bit surprised at what he has done.'

* * *

BORN IN Limerick, David spent much of his early life in Cork before returning to Limerick, attending Crescent Comprehensive College, playing for Garryowen and then Munster, Ireland and the Lions, marrying Aileen and settling in the Treaty City.

'We were living in Adare when I was born and I remember Henry and Richard playing hurling when we lived there,' David recalls. 'We then went to Monkstown and we were all going to Cork Con for rugby. I was maybe as young as six and didn't really like it at the start. I was probably a bit lazy and preferred watching television on Saturday mornings. I spent probably two or three years going for the sake of it and at one stage stopped altogether. I was quite young, playing under-12s, and probably hadn't much of a clue about what was going on, just going out there and running around.

'I don't remember a lot about those days in Con, but five or six years ago, Frankie [Sheahan] turned up at Munster training one day with a photo and it was amazing. I never knew that I had played with Rog [Ronan O'Gara], Frankie and Micko [O'Driscoll]. There were only twelve or so of us in the photo, but five or six went on to train with Munster. I remember Strings [Peter Stringer] and his brother, they were hard to miss as they were like twins. It was funny, as if we had known each other almost in a previous life.

'It was only when we moved to Limerick and I started going out to Garryowen that I got a taste for rugby. I was about eleven at the time. Henry was playing out there a little bit, Paul was playing Schools' rugby at Crescent and Richard was still at college in Cork. Paul was the one making progress at rugby. He was a wing-forward until he came to Crescent and it was in transition year that he was told they needed a prop and in he went. He made the Irish Schools in fifth year and so had two years in the team.

'I went to the games with my parents. I was only in sixth class and was in awe of these guys. I remember seeing Derwyn Jones in the clubhouse after the match against Wales. He was 6 ft 10 ins tall, a giant of a man, and for me at that age it was amazing. Also, the fact that Paul was playing for Ireland was huge. Soon after that, 1989 or so, Richard moved to Limerick having finished college, joined Garryowen and came through the ranks there quite quickly. The AIL [All-Ireland League] started [in 1991] and I went to watch Richie play. They were an amazing few years and really captured my imagination. I was at the first game up in Lansdowne Road against Wanderers. They were the team to beat and were hot favourites to win, but Garryowen beat them and that was the start of it. They were great times to watch those games and see Richard play. He was a prolific try scorer and that gave me more of a taste for it as well and was a huge influence.

'Paul had won a Munster Cup at Crescent [1990] and I had seen what it meant to the school; the buzz, the chanting, everyone dressed up, the paraphernalia, the flags ... that was amazing, I was thinking, imagine being out there. I remember thinking, how do these players go out and play in front of that crowd and in this passionate atmosphere? It was so daunting and left you wondering how they could do it. And yet I was on a cup-winning team at Crescent ... we beat Pres in the final, I think Hoggy [Anthony Horgan] and Frankie were on their team. We had guys like Bevan Cantrell, Ian Foley, Philip Duggan – not very big names maybe, but they were for me because they had also won a Junior Cup a few years earlier and I was only coming through then. For me, they were stars. I was captain the following year and we lost in the final to Pres. Rog and I were the opposing captains that day and it's something that we still have a slag about because winning a Schools' Cup is important all your life.

'The parents moved back to Cork and when I left school, I stayed with Garryowen. It was a bit of a nightmare logistically. The folks were living in Crosshaven and I was attending CIT [Cork Institute of Technology] and it was an hour from there on the bus. I had no car and I was thumbing lifts to get to Garryowen for training. College was missing out as I was also playing for Ireland under-21s and it was almost the same as it is for me now – away for weeks on end. There was no college, no study, going on for me in February and March. We had one famous 21s win over England in Greystones [1997] when we scored fourteen points in the last couple of minutes to beat them by a single point, something like 28–27, and I got one of those tries. They were very good times. It had started with Munster Schools although I never played for Ireland Schools. I got a trial – I ended up watching the first half and was told to do touch judge for the second!

'Making it into the Garryowen team around 1996–97 probably opened the door to Munster. The game was still semi-professional and I was lucky to start on a full Irish contract. There were only seven or eight of us full-time and we trained at night because the others were all working. I was twenty when I went on the Irish Development Tour to New Zealand. That was my first taste of senior Irish rugby and it was demoralising to be honest. I enjoyed the tour and I was delighted to be in a country so far away. It was my first tour and the rugby went okay for me, but it was very difficult for some guys and I think the morale was quite poor as well.

'In my first year, 1997, I didn't play great for Munster and only subbed in the Heineken Cup and it was around that time I was having a look at myself and wondering if I should be thinking of going somewhere else. I wasn't playing much, I wasn't starting with Munster, so I had a chat with Deccie [Declan Kidney] and he said, don't go but give it a lash instead. It was then that I really turned the corner in terms of going from amateurism to professionalism and actually copping myself on and working very hard. I had been on an Irish tour to South Africa [1998] but had picked up an injury in an earlier AIL semi-final against Young Munster and carried that with me, and I was probably a little unfit as well at the time so it was a poor tour for me.

'The following year I didn't make the Australian tour and that was probably a good thing for me. I almost started my pre-season at the end of the season before, had a really long blast at it, and got my fitness levels right up there. Fergal O'Callaghan came on board as well at Munster and so we had a fitness coach to help us get on top of those things and that was the year we made huge strides and got to the Heineken final [2000]. A lot of the younger guys came through and of course we beat Toulouse away in the quarter-final and that day the Munster thing really started.

'The weather was brilliant, the game was spectacular, the Munster followers were terrific, there might have been little more than 5,000 but it seemed like 50,000. It was just one of those days. You had a sense going into that season that the team was full of confidence, it was a case of why shouldn't we win it? We got to the final and lost to Northampton. It was probably one where we didn't perform as we should have and probably were overawed by the whole thing. It was all so new, 50,000 people were travelling and they were all looking for tickets … Twickenham packed to the rafters with 78,000 people or whatever it was … I think we just got out of our comfort zone and didn't focus on the game as much as we should have … if we had played like we did against Toulouse we would have won it, although the manner in which our supporters reacted and sang at the finish will live with us all forever. And I think we learned a lot from that day.

'We had some amazing matches in that campaign. We played Saracens twice and beat them by a single point in both matches. Rog kicked a conversion in the last minute in Thomond Park and there must have been 30,000 there that day. It was unbelievable and there will never be a game like it – the ball hit the post and went over. We were training there the following week and we all lined up behind the posts and we challenged him to do it again, trying to recreate it if you like, and didn't he do it, in off the post again!

'Paul came on for Sarries in both games and he did not like losing, especially to the younger brother. There was a brawl at one stage and it was funny, it was himself and Claw [Peter Clohessy] and I was first man up and thought, what do I do here, which of them do I hit? I just broke it up, I think. The away game was also fantastic because beating an English team on the road was special. Yeah, they were great games. There was huge belief in the team. Woody [Keith Wood] had come back to us and he copped a lot of us on in terms of not accepting certain things at training. The game was becoming more and more professional and guys were really working hard to be as good as they could be. Goal-setting started at the beginning of the season. Somebody said the goal should be to win the European Cup. There were a lot of laughs at that but if we didn't have belief then, the confidence developed as the season went on.

'We were deprived in the end by the width of a post and I scored a try in that final against Northampton. Funnily enough, I sometimes wish I hadn't. I don't know why. It's so long ago now to make a judgement on it, but you sometimes wonder if you might have taken your foot off the pedal on scoring the try … probably didn't but it's something you wonder about, you worry that it might have been the case.

'I also got my first cap in 2000 on a tour of Argentina. Paul was on that trip as well and we did play a good few other games together as well. Richard and myself also played together in 1998 – they were mid-week games and so weren't full caps – and I played with him in Garryowen, but the three of us never played in the same team.

'I got two caps on that tour and so I got off Axel's [Anthony Foley] one-cap-wonder team pretty quickly. I made the Six Nations the following season and Munster were still motoring well and we got to the Heineken final again in 2002 against Leicester and were beaten by a better team on the day. Maybe we didn't have the belief that we should have had to beat them. It was a bitterly disappointing day, the day that Neil Back flicked the ball out of Strings' hands. I was on that side of the scrum but I didn't see it happening … Neil Back was vilified for a while, but if it was a Munster player who had done it and it was the other way around, he'd have been a hero. If you get away with something like that, it's cheating but … Back probably did it because although it was a penalty and a sin binning offence, so what, they would still have won and if you win it, it will be seen as a good judgement call. No, I probably wouldn't have done it.'

In a high-contact sport like rugby, injury is almost guaranteed and David suffered with serious shoulder trouble in 2002 from which he took a considerable time to recover. He tried it out in club games at Garryowen and smiles at the memory of winning an AIL seconds medal as he worked his way back to fitness. He went on an Irish tour of the South Sea Islands and came in as a substitute centre against Samoa.

'I was nowhere near where I wanted to be,' he admits. 'I scored a try against Scotland [in 2003] and hoped that it might be enough to get me on the World Cup squad. I was probably still a bit off the pace and didn't make it, but I did get the call midway through. I was back in the squad the following season and Keith Gleeson, a very good player, broke his arm and that left me wondering if I might be next in line. I made my return and we won the Triple Crown by beating Scotland at Lansdowne Road and I scored an important try.

'They were great years for Irish rugby and not so bad for Munster either. 2006 was our third time reaching the Heineken Cup final and the feeling for me anyway was that we couldn't come away without silverware this time. We just had to win it, there was no losing it on our radar, but it was tough. We had to get a bonus point against Sale in Thomond Park to qualify from our pool and I scored the fourth try near the finish. That was another memorable and emotional Thomond Park occasion when, if you like, the fantastic crowd carried us over the line. We beat Perpignan in Lansdowne in the quarter-final and Leinster in the semi-final and then it was on to the Millennium Stadium and the final against Biarritz.

'It was an emotional day for all concerned. Deccie had come back that season and winning the Heineken Cup was known as the Holy Grail and it was something we had been trying to win for years … getting back there a third time in six years, it was a case of we have to do it this time. Strings' try swung it, the homecoming was amazing, so was that entire period, such a sense of achievement and then to back it up two years later was very special.

'I suppose those two finals and the Grand Slam as well, those three would be the highlights of my career, but it would be hard to pick one over another. I certainly enjoyed the Toulouse final in 2008. After the Biarritz final, it was more a sense of relief. After the Toulouse final, it was a case of having really enjoyed it. Beating Toulouse is a very special thing, as they have clearly been the best team in Europe over a number of years. Watching them at times, they were magnificent and to actually beat them, and beat them in the final, was huge, never mind winning the cup. That made it a bit more special.

'As for the Grand Slam in 2009, a lot of us had been in and around the Irish team, especially Drico [Brian O'Driscoll] and he stressed how much he wanted to get more silverware coming on the back of several Triple Crowns. We met in Enfield, County Meath, at Christmas time, soon after Deccie took over as head coach, and had a good chat. A Grand Slam was the team goal without actually writing it down. Guys spoke quite freely and openly, but I wouldn't call it home truths because that might give the impression that we were beating ourselves up over certain things and that wasn't the case. Munster had played New Zealand close to that meeting in an amazing match to mark the opening of the new Thomond Park stadium and I think that game had a huge effect on everyone who had seen the pride and the passion of the occasion and the whole spectacle. The boys led until the last few minutes and played out of their boots and with an unbelievable will to win. At the get-together, Rob [Kearney] kind of said, why can't we play like that for Ireland, not saying that Munster guys don't play like that for Ireland but that when we come together we should be playing like that. He wasn't really having a go at anyone. His point was that the pride and passion that Munster played with in that game was magnificent and we needed to repeat it for Ireland rather than just coming together and not being the sum of all the parts. I think it was one of the truths spoken at that meeting.

'There were some outstanding performances, like when we beat France in Croke Park and Jamie [Heaslip] scored a great try. And, of course, we were soon facing into the Grand Slam in Cardiff. I think we were afraid to talk about it until after we had beaten Scotland at Murrayfield. Any time we were asked, we said, next game, next game. Anything else is the easiest way to trip yourself up.

'And then it was the next game, the Grand Slam game … it was huge and captured the imagination of the whole country and of course it also meant an awful lot to the Welsh players as they were going for a Triple Crown. It was probably one of the toughest games I have ever been involved in. Both teams really went hell for leather at each other. It was tight all the way and we were a point behind until Rog got his drop goal … he has some balls, so cool in those situations, and you wouldn't want anybody else there at that stage of a game.

'For me anyway, coming to the end of the game there's a heightened adrenaline rush. The focus is on playing safe rugby in terms of, I don't want to knock this ball on, I won't take my eye off the ball and look for a gap, it's a case of catch this ball and carry it on and see what we can do from there. I will not say it's a case of not trying to make mistakes because then you are focusing on mistakes. You are just trying to do everything right as much as you can and hopefully then you will get the reward at the end of it. It's not like, oh, we have to score a try, we have to try this. It's just doing the little things as well as you can. It's cup rugby, you know.

'People will tell you how important it is for the nation, for yourself and your family, for the supporters, but you can't take in what it means to every single person in the country. Everyone has a different story and it has a different meaning to different people. You would nearly go mad if you were thinking all the time of the importance of it. You know it's special but you try not to think about how special and just try to do your job. It's a bit like when I was in primary school and I went to watch Paul in those finals and saw the passion and the excitement of the crowd and I asked him, how do you play in front of this? But that's the thing, you don't focus on that, you're concentrating on your job and you're nervous about your rugby and not the crowd. You try not to be over-awed by the occasion and too emotional about it and what it means to people and to us as players – just as maybe we were in the first European final. You are not focusing on what you should be focusing on and you can always enjoy that part of it afterwards.

'Anyway back to that day in Cardiff. After Rog's drop goal, it was a case of don't give away a penalty … don't give away a penalty, and then it happened. Your heart just sank, absolutely sank. It was like, all this hard work and now we are in the hands of somebody else's skill to see if he can kick this ball over and totally break our hearts with the last play of the game. You are now just a spectator. There's nothing more you can do. It's a horrible place to be. Did I think Stephen Jones was going to get that penalty? I probably wasn't allowing myself to think that way because that would be a horrible way of thinking. Instead, I was thinking, I'm under the posts here and my job is to catch the ball if it comes off the posts and to focus on whatever needed to be done. My back was to him but I might have been able to see a screen and I don't know if I actually watched him kicking it. After he did so, I was watching to see if it was going over and seeing a clock and it was red and Geordan [Murphy] was just under the crossbar and caught it. It was a case of get rid of it, get rid of it, time is up, time is up.

'You go from thinking, oh God, this is going to be horrible, to we've won it, we've won it, can there be anything as good as this … it's a flip of a coin when it comes down to it. The end of that campaign and the hard matches and all the fight to win those games and it came down to one kick of a ball. But that's sport, isn't it.'

* * *

PAUL WALLACE takes no exception to brother David's claim that he 'doesn't like losing'. He would regard anything else as a reflection on his competitiveness and it is obvious that Paul could hardly have made such a massive contribution to the Lions' outstanding victory over the Springboks on the

1997 tour without his total commitment to the cause. He got into the squad in the first place when Peter Clohessy's back injury ruled him out at the last minute. But Paul quickly set about establishing himself as the number one choice at tighthead prop and he wound up as one of only five players to play the full duration of all three Tests. That was all the more praiseworthy given that the position is arguably the most arduous and demanding in the modern game and that his opposite number was the giant Os du Randt, who had been expected to give Wallace a miserable time before the series started. Instead, it was du Randt who was taken to the cleaners, leaving two leaders of the tour to heap praise on Paul's contribution to a memorable triumph.

'He was my player of the series,' commented Martin Johnson, the team captain, nowadays head coach of England and most certainly not a man given to flattery. Another famous English forward of immense stature, Fran Cotton, was manager of the side and a player who had distinguished himself in countless games in the front row for England and the Lions. He stated that Paul Wallace was quite simply the 'cornerstone of the series'. The official Lions website reports that 'just as the result of the series was a surprise, so, too, were some of the selections that achieved it. Paul Wallace and Tom Smith emerged as pint-sized tormentors of the massive Springbok front row and Jeremy Davidson came through to partner Johnson at lock.'

Chris Hewett put Wally's contribution to the Lions' achievement in perspective when writing in the English *Independent*: 'Paul found himself going eyeball to eyeball with

Os du Randt, the unusually substantial World Cup-winning Springbok loosehead prop and one of the half dozen most revered figures in South African sport. When du Randt ran out of ideas against a man so small by comparison that he might have been a wart on his neck, it suddenly dawned on the home supporters that the tourists were deadly serious about not losing.'

When the touring party was announced, there was no sign of the name of Paul Wallace and looking back now, he readily concedes that his omission hurt and hurt badly. 'I was pretty peeved about that,' he says. 'I thought we had done very well and I always thought I was better than the other guys … especially Claw,' he laughs, before adding: 'Ah, well, Claw and I were two different players … I would think I was better than him and he would think he was better than I was. At the time, I was a young guy meant to head down to New Zealand with the Ireland Development squad when I got the call-up. Once we went into camp, I realised it was going to be very competitive. It was a case of do as well as you can, play as well as you can, and while I wouldn't be an arrogant person, I was always quietly confident in my own ability. Dai Young had played the two series before and Jason Leonard in the series before, so it was obviously a competitive position. But, as I say, I always believed in my own ability and just got on with it.

'We arrived in Umhlanga Rocks in Durban and I shared a room with Jason and he was a great roommate. He was an old legend of the game, he had roomed with Richie back in 1993 and we got on like a house on fire and still do. It all started from there – you get your chance and you try to take it. I was probably in one of the worst positions in that we had two guys who had played in the previous two series as Test players … three tighthead props, something you rarely get, it's usually two and a floater, so I was very much number three going out behind Jason and Dai. I didn't get many chances early on. I think I got five minutes against Border in the pouring rain and it was nearly a case of every third game. That's why the Clive Woodward thing of bringing fifty guys just doesn't work. Everyone has to have a fair chance and in today's short tours you don't have the ability to do that.

'We had a great mid-week side comprised mainly of Celts. The general expectation was that the Test front five was going to be the England front five. We had Tommy Smith, myself and Fester [Keith Wood] and even he was only half and half at that stage. He was probably the one Celt who might make it. Doddie Weir and Jeremy Davidson were in the second-row and we had a wonderful time on and off the pitch and created a close bond. And as opposed to what I hear from other tours, there was a great intermingling as well. Ian McGeechan [the legendary Lions coach from Scotland] had a great saying: "You win a Test match and forty years from now, you walk down a street and you see a guy on the other side, you just look at him and smile and that's all you need to do, you don't even need to go over and say hello. He'll know you know …" It was an amazing speech, a great speech, by Geech and really sticks in the mind. That's what it was like with everyone playing for each other.

'And, of course, you're always underdogs in South Africa no matter who you are. A couple of games went well. I would have been a technical prop where scrummage height is very important, Jason and Dai would have been bigger, stronger guys but wouldn't have been as technical. Jason was really a loosehead, not a tighthead, and I suppose that stood to me. You saw that in 2009 with Phil Vickery being picked ahead of Adam Jones, but then Adam was picked and things improved right away.

'Os du Randt says he's twenty stone, but I've played against plenty of twenty stoners and he's much bigger than that, up around twenty-three or twenty-four. He was very fit but when you're that kind of size and carrying … well, just look at it like this: I had the English back five, the Saturday back five, behind me and in the first two scrums I decided to go square, to power scrummage as they do these days. In the first, I was absolutely minced. In the second, I was absolutely minced. So I told myself, you're going to embarrass yourself here Wally, let's go back to basics and start scrummaging with your head. The most important thing about scrummaging is putting a loosehead in a bad position. It's not about power, yes, that is important, but the most important thing is putting him in a bad position. Jonno [Martin Johnson] still goes on about the biggest clap on the back he ever gave me; he said Wally gave us the right shoulder … because he was behind me in the scrum he says that, meaning that he was half to do with it. After that we probably got dominance, but in the first two we got killed.'

The knowledgeable ones in South Africa at the time believed Os du Randt was a superman when it came to the scrummaging art, but Paul Wallace stressed that a guy called

Garry Pagel was a tougher adversary. 'He played against Jason for Western Province and I had a couple of ding-dongs with him playing for Saracens against Northampton Saints,' says Paul. 'Now Os was a big, formidable man, but I think Pagel was an even better scrummager and when he gave Jason a hard time in a game about two weeks before the first Test, that probably gave me one step into the Test shirt. Pagel was a difficult opponent but Jason was a loosehead playing at tight.

'We played against Transvaal on a Wednesday and that was a big turning point. My biggest memory is of standing in a line-out in what was quite an aggressive game and I was up against an Argentinian, Roberto Grau, who ended up being my team-mate at Saracens. I was facing him down and going into a line-out and the next thing, bang, I got this smack on the back of the head. So I turned around to hit someone and the only person I could hit was my scrum half. What had happened was that this orange, the size of a grapefruit, had been thrown from the top of the stand and hit me on the back of the head. But we won that game and it was a turning point on the tour because the Lions had lost to the Blue Bulls on the Saturday. We then beat Transvaal on the Wednesday and the amazing thing was that when we came into the changing-room, and even though a lot of guys must have felt because they had lost on the Saturday that they were probably losing their Test places, there was sheer joy. And it wasn't put on, that was probably the most telling thing. When it came down to it, everything was about winning the series. Of course there were a few egos but not really, it was not about me, it was more about us.

'On the Wednesday before the first Test, the team was selected and it was a bit of a surprise that I got in and obviously I was delighted. We went training in Stellenbosch and halfway through it, Jeremy Davidson, one of my best mates, only goes and stamps on my knee and I swear to God, I couldn't walk for two days. I thought, that's it, I was picked and now I will never get to play for the Lions in a Test. I wanted a miracle. I have seen it happen to Brian O'Driscoll – these are injuries you shouldn't come back from and I really don't know how I came back from this one. I suppose it's the passion, and you are carried away with the atmosphere and everything … I actually cannot remember it hurting me. In the second Test it felt a bit better and I left the knee brace off. I think you forget about everything when you're in that atmosphere and it becomes painless.

'We were complete underdogs going into the first Test. As I say, even if you're the All Blacks, you are written off in South Africa. But we loved that … in Ireland we think we love being underdogs, but they love it in England, Scotland and Wales as well … it's amazing, they talk all about all these team-building corporate things; well, you go on a trip like that and you have guys from many countries and you throw them in together and you're really put to the pin of your collar. You go for it and in fairness amazing friendships come from it.

'The first Test we won quite clearly and deserved every bit of it. The second, I thought South Africa played all the rugby. We did not play particularly well, but we kicked our goals and they missed a lot. The South Africans say that, but then we had Neil Jenkins at fullback. He was a famous place kicker but wasn't a natural fullback and one of their tries resulted from a dropped ball by Jenks. But he absolutely nailed every place kick and the Springboks picked a running fly half, Henry Honiball. They claimed if they had had a kicker, they would have won. But if they had had a kicker, they wouldn't have had a running out-half like Honiball.

'Jeremy Guscott's drop goal meant that we had won the Test series in South Africa and after that we went up north to a place called Vanderbilt Park, because they had thought it would all come down to the third Test. Of course, we were out celebrating having won the Test series and to be honest, we were in the middle of nowhere and ended up in a sort of wooden shed built over a garage on a Monday night. And the guys in there, all in their army fatigues, couldn't believe we were the Lions – what the hell would you be doing here?'

It was probably a fair question. With the pressure now off, the Lions were thinking about going home as much as playing rugby and even though Paul insists they produced some of their best rugby of the tour in that third Test, the intent wasn't quite there and the Springboks enjoyed a measure of compensation for their series defeat as they won 35–16. The game contained none of the drama of the previous week when the Boks scored three tries to none but the Lions still prevailed thanks to five penalty goals by Neil Jenkins and the famous late drop goal by Guscott. Paul also claims that the Lions won the first Test clearly, but the margin in their favour was still just three points, 18–15, and the win owed everything to second-half tries by Matt Dawson and Alan Tait.

* * *

PAUL WILL be best remembered for his achievements on that tour, but he had many other strings to his bow and so it should not come as any surprise that he made his mark at the very highest level. He had a terrific Schools' career at Crescent College in Limerick with whom he won a Munster Schools Senior Cup medal and represented Munster and Ireland Schools for two years. He also played for Ireland at under-21, Students and Development grades and with such a pedigree, it was inevitable that he would go on to shine in the colours of UCC, Blackrock College and Leinster, leading to a first international cap on a tour of Japan in 1995 in a side that also contained his brother Richard.

Professional rugby was taking off and Saracens came calling in 1996. Paul joined a team full of high profile names like François Pienaar, captain of the South African World Cup winning team in 1995; Frenchman Thierry Lacroix, Scott Murray of Scotland and a whole host of English internationals including Julian White, Danny Grewcock and Richard Hill. Surprisingly, and no doubt frustratingly for their benevolent and sporting owner Nigel Wray, they didn't win a whole lot and their single point defeats by Munster in those two memorable games in the 1999/2000 season hurt more than a little.

'It was the October after the 1999 World Cup and there was a new coach at Sarries and he went with Julian White and David Flatman at prop ahead of Roberto Grau and myself,' Paul recalls. 'To be honest, it was a bit embarrassing not to start either of the two matches against Munster. We seemed to be walking away with the first but from nowhere Munster came back. I recall that they got a few lucky ricochets from kicks ahead, Mike Mullins in particular, but it just showed the fight that Munster had in them because they had to come back from at least fifteen points down and I think that day was the start of the whole Munster thing.

'Then we went over to Thomond Park and again we seemed to have it under control until there was that last-minute try by Woody converted by Ronan. It was an amazing day, although I think their win at Vicarage Road was the more impressive in that they were completely dead and out of the game. We felt so comfortably in control but then it just went bang, bang and of course the Heineken Cup is all about winning away from home. David didn't give me such a hard time, but a few of the others didn't spare us and obviously the slagging is all part of the game. A core of players from those games went on to do great things for Munster and indeed Ireland.'

Paul also had great respect for Ulster's victory in the 1999 European Cup and feels they didn't get their due credit for the achievement because the English clubs weren't involved. And it was in a game against Ulster for Saracens that he broke his ankle so badly that he was out of action for twelve months. It was an injury that was to bring a premature end to his career, although there were to be quite a few more high points before he was eventually forced to call it a day. He returned to Dublin and Blackrock College and Leinster, and rates his success in attaining a sufficiently high level of fitness to return both at provincial and international level as one of the biggest achievements of his career.

'I'm not sure I should have come back because it really was

a very bad break. I took a wrong angle on a frozen pitch and suddenly the foot was back to front. The ankle joint was pretty badly damaged. I had a few games with Blackrock, came in for the quarter-final of the Celtic League with Leinster and we went on to beat Munster in the final. That was a sweet one for us and for me especially coming back after the injury. Eric Miller was sent off early on and we had only a seven-man scrum and for us to get on top up front was a big plus for us. Leinster were always being written off at that stage, but they had a lot of really good and tough players and it was a time when a lot of great Irish players were coming through. I think a winning mentality was born in Leinster that day and probably that's when the Munster–Leinster rivalry, that had always been quite strong, really took off.

'I went on a tour of New Zealand that summer, something I was really looking forward to, as it's such a great rugby country and I hadn't toured there before. But it was probably the biggest disappointment of my career because I only got five minutes of the third match when I would have loved to play a lot more rugby. The plan was to make it to the 2003 World Cup and all was going okay until I played a game against Swansea. I made a break down the side line, when I felt my ankle go. I off-loaded the ball, went down, was taken off and though I went on to the end of the season, I had to call it a day, accepting that I probably should never have come back having gotten that injury. I was thirty-one and felt I had another five years in me, as a prop is only coming into his own at that stage. But I look at other guys who had to quit after a year or so of international rugby and feel I did all right.'

It was about then, too, that Sky television came calling. Paul travelled with Ireland to South Africa as co-commentator and after that it was a gradual progression and he is now one of the most respected pundits in the game. 'It's a great way to stay involved,' he says. 'I'm not a full timer, it's more of a pastime and of course it's great when the Irish teams are playing. I would have liked to get into coaching, but feel I don't have the time to give to it and being involved in the media gives you a good feel for the game. I felt I would like to go in there and do something that was completely unbiased. You always felt as a player that you'd like to see an ex-player come in and comment without any kind of favouritism.'

Perhaps he does suffer a slight conflict of interest when obliged to comment on the performances of his younger brother, although he is fortunate that David's standards have remained so high over a period of fourteen years that he has been given little or no reason to criticise! Paul points out: 'He is around the longest of any of the Irish side and you rarely hear mention of him unless he gets a man of the match award or something. Of course he's carrying the odd few knocks, but he has been as important as any player in the Munster and Ireland teams. In Saracens, we used to call Richard Hill the unsung hero and David is like that today. It's only when he has gone that people will really appreciate what a dynamic ball carrier he is and what he gives to a side.'

* * *

DAVID BECAME the third member of the Wallace clan to tour with the Lions and so created a rugby record of considerable dimensions. As becomes each of the brothers and their extended family, there was only a quiet pride taken in the achievement. The Wallaces are unassuming people who do not brag or shout about their achievements, but for now and the foreseeable future, they stand alone in the world game. David recalls how in 1997, Paul and himself were in camp in Limerick's Castletroy Park Hotel preparing for Ireland's Development tour to New Zealand when big brother Paul broke a major piece of news. 'I was going down to a team meeting in my gear and he was coming out of his room in his jeans and jacket and I said to him, "Come on Paul, we're meeting now" and he said to me, "Dave, I'm off to South Africa with the Lions." I was kind of sad in one way because I was looking forward to going on tour with him.

'Paul went out to South Africa and did unbelievably well. On return from our tour in New Zealand, those Lions Test games were on. Richard and I were on holiday down in Kinsale and watched the second Test together. We were probably sailing down there at some regatta and had a massive party and it was great fun. It was good to be with Richard as well for that ... we rang Paul soon after the game and were chatting to him and said, fair play, he had won a Lions Test series and also for the fact that he played so well, having at the start been a call-up for Claw.

'I wasn't surprised that Paul did well out there. He would have been a kind of sporting hero of mine since watching him win the cup at Crescent and playing Munster and Ireland Schools. Dad would obviously have been a huge, avid fan of rugby, going to games and bringing me along. Paul was a hero for me anyway and it was just a continuation of that. I had always had faith in him and why shouldn't I? He was up against Os du Randt and the way he handled him was brilliant. That whole front row were amazing – Paul, Woody and Tom Smith – not the biggest I suppose, especially when you matched them to the size of the South African front row. Like myself, he would have shied away from appearing on the famous video made about the tour; he probably saw the camera and went in the opposite direction! And yet, for a young rugby player to watch that video, it was like, oh my God, I want to go out and play rugby now. It was one of the best rugby videos ever.

'And then it happened for me. We were going out to Spala for the first Irish session when the call came. It was a three-week trip to the middle of nowhere in Poland and a lot of people hated me for avoiding that! I went out to Poland a couple of times after that but not for three weeks. We flew to Copenhagen on the way and I turned on the phone and Rog rang me to say, "Wally, you're coming out, are you, I was talking to a cameraman, and he told me." Then he hung up on me. I was wondering what this was all about. Strings had seen my reaction to the phone call and asked what was up. I said it was something about being called up to the Lions and no sooner had I said it than he told everyone else and suddenly I was up in the King's Chair … Frankie, of course, taking any chance to embarrass me.

'I was nervous until Briano [O'Brien, the then Irish manager] told me I was going out to Australia and I had to go and get a ticket back to Heathrow. But I had a big smile as I took phone calls from people wishing me the best and when I got out there they held a press conference because it was the first time that three brothers had been called out to the Lions. That was the cherry on the top because I hadn't really thought about that side of it. I arrived at 11 o'clock in the morning and came on for the last half hour of a match that started at 3 o'clock in the afternoon. Between getting halfway to Poland and then getting back to Heathrow and waiting around there for half a day before heading off for Australia, I had been on the go for forty-eight hours. There was a strange vibe when I arrived because one of the liaison guys who had been with the team died the previous day – he had a heart attack while out swimming. My second game was against the Brumbies and I scored and I was nearly called up for the second Test because Scott Quinnell had a knee problem. But that tour was a great experience and one that stood to me in years to come.

'My form and a few injuries meant that I wasn't really in the running for a Lions place in 2005. My confidence was down for a few years around that time and it was very frustrating but Deccie coming back to Munster was a big thing for me. He's a very good man manager and he gave me a new lease of life. We had the Heineken success of 2006 and 2008 and I still wanted a taste of the Lions. Tom Tierney and myself had gone out to Giles Warrington at UL around 2000 and said to him, look, we want you to give us a fitness programme. Before he did that he sat us down and gave us a chart, and we discussed fitness and strengths and he got us to grade ourselves. And then there were medium and long-term goals. At the time, I wasn't even starting for Munster so that was the first target, then playing for Ireland and after that the Lions and that's why I had that big smile on my face on that plane from Copenhagen because I had achieved all those goals. There was a huge sense of achievement.

'The success of Munster and Ireland's Grand Slam would have put me in the shop window going into the 2009 tour of South Africa, but you're never too sure what way it's going to go. I got the call and went out there. I played the first two Tests and came on in the third. It was disappointing in that I really felt we could, and probably should, have won the series. There was a feeling of maybe we left it behind us. You look at the individual games and what happened and you cannot say why we actually lost.

'I was a fully fledged Lion this time as against being on the periphery eight years earlier and I really wanted to give it a good lash. I suppose I did that to an extent in the way I approached it mentally and looking after myself. South Africa is like nowhere else in terms of rugby and it's a fascinating place to visit. You are thrown into the whole culture of their approach to the sport and they are memories you will have, not just as part of your career but as part of your life. Lions are treated as special sporting people on these trips.'

David Wallace was widely regarded as Ireland's most valuable and consistent player in the 2011 RBS Six Nations Championship. The statistics showed that he made forty-five tackles through the five games, never missing even one, and was particularly outstanding in the 24–8 defeat of England at the Aviva Stadium in his seventy-first game for his country.

* * *

WILL THE achievements of the Wallace family remain unique into the far distant future? Very probably, for it will be extremely difficult to find three other brothers who have the skill to represent both their country and the Lions. However, already there may be youngsters somewhere in these islands with their sights set on equalling or even surpassing the record who are thinking, if the Wallys could do it, so, too, can we. But don't bet on it!

DICK AND DONAL SPRING

I have the minister ... I have his head.

Clonakilty rugby player as he grappled with Dick Spring during
match against Tralee RFC

IN THE 1979 Five Nations Championship, Dick Spring played successive internationals for Ireland against France, Wales and England. And when Donal Spring was picked to line out at No. 8 against Scotland for the last match of the campaign, it looked as if brothers would appear together in the same Irish team. However, the selectors in their wisdom decided to dispense with Dick and replace him with Ulsterman Ronnie Elliott, who earned his one and only cap on that stormy afternoon at Murrayfield.

So an occasion that would have meant a great deal to the famous Kerry sporting and political family was not to be. The disappointment, however, didn't linger. Instead, all concerned reflected with deep satisfaction and a little understandable pride on all that had been achieved on and off the rugby, football and hurling pitches of the nation over a span of sixty years by this remarkable clan. And yet, it was hardly surprising that the sons of long serving TD Dan Spring should have been successful sportsmen given that he himself had won three All-Ireland football medals with Kerry. Apart from what Dick and Donal achieved as rugby players, Arthur, the eldest of the three boys, was an outstanding amateur golfer who went on to turn professional on reaching the required age and duly made his mark as a member of the European Seniors Tour.

* * *

DAN SPRING gave his sons two choices where their secondary education was concerned – St Brendans, Killarney, or Cistercian College, Roscrea. Dick is not quite sure why he chose the latter option, but anyway he went off to board at Roscrea which, at the time, was on the main road to Dublin from Tralee, and so his dad and his Labour Party TD colleagues, Steve Coughlan from Limerick and Paddy Tierney from North Tipperary, were weekly visitors on their way to and from Leinster House.

'I always regarded boarding school as a sportsman's paradise,' says Dick. 'If you enjoyed sport, you had it seven days a week. But there was very little rugby in Tralee and I refused to play it for the first two and a half years at Roscrea because I thought it was a very stupid game and could not understand it. Those were the days when the rugby ball was nearly as big as a football, it was not exactly the modern oval. I played hurling at Roscrea, but by November of my Inter Cert year, we had been knocked out of all the competitions, and Seán McCann, who is now chief of staff of the Irish Defence Forces, asked, "What are you going to do for the rest of the year, why don't you come out and try the rugby?"

They put me in the centre and the first pass I got, I kicked the ball over the bar. I didn't drop kick it and I was reminded, no, no, this is rugby, not Gaelic football. I played Junior Cup that year, but the big attraction of rugby from the point of boarding school was that you went up to Donnybrook and had hot showers and went to the Castle Hotel off Parnell Square and got a big feed – a lot more attractive than going to Abbeyleix and washing in a cold tap and basically washing the cow dung off you from the hurling field. In those days, I played with Mick Sherry and against Mick Quinn, who would later be team-mates at Lansdowne. We beat Newbridge one day having been 8-0 behind and got it back to 11–11 before being awarded a penalty just before the end. Our coach, Fr Kevin, who later became the abbot in the monastery, told me to kick to touch. I said no and instead kicked the penalty and we won – it was my first time ever getting a headline in the Irish media. The *Independent* the following day told its readers: "Spring kicks Roscrea to Victory".'

While rugby was quickly taking over as Dick Spring's number one sporting love, Gaelic football was still very much imbued in the family's DNA. His brother Arthur helped revitalise the Kerins O'Rahillys club and each of the brothers helped them to reach the semi-final of the Kerry Championship. They were undone by Shannon Rangers with Dick recalling: 'Donal was fullback, I was centre-back and Arthur was centre-field. I got one great example of Ogie Moran's ability as a sportsman in the game against Shannon Rangers. There are certain things you will always remember in sport. Ogie was about seventeen or eighteen, I was twenty-three or twenty-four and he was causing havoc. He was the kind of guy who turns up everywhere for the breaking ball and runs fifty yards before letting it off. So I decided I should try to slow this fellow down a bit and that a little bit of rugby was required. So I hit him a full frontal of a tackle – and the result was that I was on the ground watching Ogie soloing off with the ball. For a guy who was quite small, he was a phenomenal athlete, a great guy and a great friend over the years.

'I got a few runs in the National League and will never forgive President Childers for dying when he did. I was picked to play against Cork but the game was postponed because the president died the night before the game.'

On first arriving in Trinity College, Dick divided his loyalties between the Freshers rugby team and the Garryowen club in Limerick, before facing reality shortly after Christmas: 'It was Trinity or Garryowen and I made the wrong decision. I chose Trinity, we were quickly knocked out of everything and Garryowen won the Munster Cup!'

In truth, Dick arrived at College Park in an era when they lost four Colours matches in a row against their arch-rivals UCD. They even considered opening the club to non-students but all that was forgotten when the losing run was brought to an end under Dick's captaincy. An old friend, Mick Sherry, was his counterpart at UCD and in typical self-deprecating fashion he loves to recall the pen pictures from the match programme: 'Michael Sherry, educated Cistercian College, Roscrea; Dick Spring, attended Cistercian College, Roscrea.'

After his years at Trinity, Dick took what might be described as a sabbatical from the game of rugby and Ireland. 'When you're brought up in a political family, it's like being in a fish bowl and I wanted to get away,' he explains. 'I said I was going to New Zealand and when asked why, I said because I looked at the map and it is the furthest place from Tralee, County Kerry. I went on a tour of the United States with Public School Wanderers for three weeks and had no intention of coming back. I bumped into Gerry Power in a restaurant called the Mad Hatter and that's where I started working – a fitting job for a barrister-at-law! I did attempt to get to New Zealand and got as far as Colorado when I bumped into a certain young lady whom I had met in New York called Kristi Hutcheson – and the rest of that is history, too.

'I didn't want to play rugby in New York because my life had been all rugby for about ten years but the guy I worked for said, "Hey, buddy, you're playing." I opted for the wing and you do not see much of the ball out there in American rugby. Trouble was, the New York Rugby Club was going great, we were promoted to Division One and, unbelievably, I was offered a trial for the US Eagles. I did quite well and was then offered a place in the final trial out in Boulder, Colorado. So I said, "Fine guys, when is it on and who's paying the expenses?" But they replied, "You've got to pay your own expenses", so I said, "Guys, forget it." But it would have been interesting to see what happened …

'I came back and joined Lansdowne. My first year back was very poor and I was given the captaincy the following season and that was the start of three Leinster Cups in a row. Every week, Ned Van Esbeck used to give out in *The Irish Times* about Lansdowne playing boring, ten-man rugby. But we were very successful and I have always appreciated the support I got from guys like Paddy "Basher" Boylan, Vinny Becker and D. Power. Discipline was key. One day, Vinny arrived out and said he could not train because he had drunk a few pints to celebrate the birth of one of his children. But I told him that's no excuse and made him get out there – with all the imaginable consequences!'

* * *

'RUGBY WAS a very alien game when I was growing up,' admits Donal, the youngest of the three male Spring siblings. 'The first time I saw a rugby ball was when Dick was at school in Roscrea. Even though I would have been only nine or ten at the time, I remember a debate in the house as to whether he could play rugby because at the time the GAA ban was in existence. My mother comes from a very strong hurling family in North Kerry, the Laides – her brothers Dick and Pat had something like fifteen county hurling medals between them. We often think, in fact we know, that one of the attractions for her of the Cistercian College in Roscrea for our education was that they played hurling and no football. Rugby was never thought of, there was never a question of a Spring going to Roscrea and playing rugby.

'Dick played hurling for Kerry and I played hurling for Austin Stacks in the Kerry Championship and we all played football for Kerins-O'Rahillys. Arthur went to National School in Kilflynn and played hurling, Dick spent his summers out there and played hurling and I took up golf very young because Arthur had started playing it. My mother is from Kilflynn, it's about eight miles from Tralee, and we used to go out there to help with saving the hay and everything during the summer. They played no football, it was all hurling, with a team called Crotta O'Neills.

'To Dad, sport was always just a game. He regarded it as something you did as a pastime, he never looked upon it as a means to an end or an all-consuming thing, even though he had three All-Ireland medals and captained Kerry in 1940 and brought the Sam Maguire home to Strand Road. We were always Dan Spring's sons because he was a Kerry captain as much as he was a TD. All of us grew up with the one ambition – to play football for Kerry. Arthur won a minor medal in 1963, discovered golf at University College Cork and the rest is history.

'Dick took up rugby in his fourth year in Roscrea. He brought a ball home and it was the first time I had seen one. We weren't very popular with some of the locals. One day at the rugby club, the ball went into a garden and came out flat and it wasn't that it hit a thorn or anything like that. That went on quite a lot. In fact, one of my dad's greatest supporters and a great friend and character from across the road, Massie Moran, came into the house to my mother one day shortly after Dick started and told her he reckoned my father would lose his seat in the Dáil if Dick played rugby. That was the feeling at the time. You were letting the side down if you played foreign games. This was 1966 and remember the ban was still in existence. My mother always said, and this was before either of us getting a cap, that her children could play whatever game they wanted and she would be the proudest mother in Ireland if any of us ever got a cap.

'There were six of us in the family and the house was quite small. There were two rooms downstairs, my father's office and obviously the kitchen, and with six kids ... my mother was fanatical about education and was determined that we would all get a good education. To explain her own education ... she was sent to Mount Sackville in the Phoenix Park from a thirty-five acre farm in North Kerry. How they were able to do that is still a mystery to me. So she valued education very highly and trained as a psychiatric nurse. There was a tradition of Kerry people going to Roscrea. A very good friend of hers from Kilflynn, Eddie Hayes, had sent his children there and so Dick followed on.

'The president when I was there was a Kerryman, Fr Patrick, and also, of course, it was on the road to Dublin, which meant it was accessible for my dad when he was driving up to Leinster House. He was in the Dáil for an unbroken thirty-eight years, thirteen elections, some narrow shaves; not as narrow as some of Dick's, although not far off it. He was a trade union official and Kerry captain. I remember Con Houlihan writing one time that when he was running for the Dáil they were giving Dad as much chance of being elected as Scunthorpe had of winning the FA Cup. Con's father was one of his biggest supporters and was chairman of the Labour Party in Castleisland for many years. Dad was a very hard worker and had great support among the working people and the small farmers and that grew over the years because of the service he gave to the people. It was all done

on the kitchen table with my mother as his unpaid secretary.
My dad left school at twelve.

'My grandfather was in the psychiatric hospital in
Killarney because he was grazed by a bullet during the Civil
War. I don't think Dad was ever happy about it, but in those
days any kind of mental illness and people were put away, so
to speak. My mother was one of the nurses and met my dad
when he was visiting the hospital. My father used to joke
that just after Kerry had won an All-Ireland and he was a
TD, a patient came up to him and asked who he was. Dad
said he was Dan Spring and the patient said, "Jeez, you're
very bad, a guy down the way has just told me he was John
the Baptist!"

'My mother was very strong on mental health, she was
the chairperson of Kerry Mental Health for many years, she
had a big thing about people being treated correctly and
with respect and dignity. She helped a lot of friends and
neighbours over the years. She was like the local dispensary
without being in an official capacity. She delivered babies, she
laid people out, she was called upon for all sorts of things. A
great house to grow up in.

'Anyway, Dick went up to Roscrea and did well in rugby,
but by the time I got there, he had moved on to Trinity.
I think I played one game of rugby before going up there,
it was for Tralee under-12s or 13s against Listowel and we
drew 3–3. Billy Keane [son of John B.] scored a try for them
and I kicked a penalty for us. I had a fight with Billy that day!
At that time, my passion was golf and I was stuck between
two brothers, one of whom wanted me to be a golfer and the

other a rugby player. My summer was golf, it was rugby all winter. But in what should have been my last year in Roscrea, I got sick as a result, I think, of growing very tall very quickly and playing too much sport. Every morning in the winter, I was playing table tennis, then it was basketball, at lunchtime I was rushing out for a game of soccer, from 3–5 p.m. it was rugby until the athletics season came along, and when I got a chance I was out playing golf. I played everything from table tennis to golf to push penny, once there was a ball involved.

'Gaelic football suffered, even though I did play for Kerins-O'Rahillys in the championship. The club had gone down a lot and Arthur came back from England and kick-started it again. He got everyone involved in it and even Barry McGann [Ireland out-half from Cork Constitution] played with us for a while. If somebody had asked me at seventeen or eighteen which sport I'd have liked to stick at, it was golf. I was playing Senior Cup for Tralee. It's an addictive game and I was in my addictive phase at the time.

'The illness knocked me out for a while and I missed the first few months of school. I decided I wanted to go back for another year and my parents didn't mind, but at the back of my mind was the fact that the Irish Schools team was coming on for the first time the following year and I was young enough to qualify for the side. It worked out really well and certainly going to college a year later was very useful.

'I finished up captaining the Irish Schools team [in 1995]. The Leinster Schools trials went very well for me [the school is on the Tipperary–Offaly border and opts to play in Leinster]. The extra year gave me that little bit of a presence,

I'd played three senior years of rugby by this time as against two by most of the others. Leinster won the inter-provincial championship, including beating Munster 4–3 at Thomond Park when they ran the ball all day and we kept it tight – not the usual scenario at the time! Mossie Finn was captain of the Munster team and beating them was probably the reason I got the captaincy, along with the fact that in the final match against Ulster, Johnny Murphy from Greystones missed a stack of kicks and when it was 3–3 we got a penalty on the halfway line which Johnny didn't want to take, so I did and knocked it over and we won 6–3. It probably helped as well that I took on that responsibility.

'The captaincy was a great honour for a small school like Roscrea. Apart from Gavin Duffy from Mayo, John O'Connor from Ardfert and myself, Roscrea wouldn't have had too many internationals and we didn't have an awful lot of inter-pros either. So it was a great honour and boost for the school. The fact that Dick was my elder brother and captained Trinity and the Universities against the All Blacks, didn't do any harm either. Ireland lost 6–3 to England, but we didn't let ourselves down. My father's interest in my rugby career was so colossal that it was the first time he ever saw me play the game! The first thing he said to me afterwards was that you cannot catch the ball if you stand with your hands on your hips. A lesson learned.'

Donal moved on to Trinity and Lansdowne, and more significantly still to Munster and Ireland. He and Dick played many matches in the red jersey, but Donal was the only Spring in the side that so famously defeated the 1978

All Blacks at Thomond Park. Typical of so many of those who made legends of themselves that day, Donal simply smiles at the memory, readily admitting that it will always be one of the proudest moments in his life before remarking that 'few teams have dined out on one match as much and as well as we have'. It would be superfluous here to regale the reader again with the details of Munster's 12–0 victory (see the chapter on the Kiernan brothers) except to say that two towering Kerrymen, Donal Spring and Moss Keane, played vital roles in the victory. And it took a clever piece of foresight on the part of big brother Dick to ensure his own personal presence on the heaving Thomond Park terraces!

'I had a three-piece suit on me at the game because I was in court that morning,' Dick recalls. 'I had a few cases and I was determined they were going to be over by lunchtime. Tim Desmond was the judge, we used to call him "The Horse", and I'll never forget that day in court. There was a famous Kerry rugby solicitor, Donal Browne, a larger-than-life character who went to all the Munster matches and all the matches at Lansdowne Road. As I was leaving to go off and meet my parents and Kristi who were collecting me in Listowel, he didn't look at all happy and told me, "It's all right for you, you big b*****x heading off, but I have to stay here. Some effing footballer is putting in a licensing application for a pub." And do you know who it was – Paudie O'Shea. And the application was refused on that occasion!

'Anyway, we got to the match. My parents had seats in the stand and Kristi and I watched it from the melee in front of the stand. I was one of the 100,000 people who were there that day, prominently positioned as any aspiring politician would be.

'Of course, it was a great occasion for the family to be a part of that. Aren't they dining out on it ever since – including the subs! It was one of those days like the GPO in 1916 ... we were all there. And it reminds me of the story that Gary McMahon [a Kerry footballer] always told. He scored after thirty-seven seconds against Roscommon in the 1962 All-Ireland final ... he'd be sitting down watching every final since and when there was no goal after thirty-seven seconds, the kids would say, "Dad, your record is still intact." And, you know, I was on a plane to China when Munster nearly beat the All Blacks in the most recent game for the opening of the new Thomond Park – in a way you want to see Munster beating the All Blacks and on the other hand, the boys are on such a pinnacle that you wonder if it would all crumble. It wouldn't, of course, because they got such a good run off it.

'My dad would have got a huge kick out of that day. He didn't understand the finer points of the game but he did understand the social nature of rugby in comparison with Gaelic football. Himself and Mick Fitzpatrick, the father of the Ireland prop who played with me at Trinity, were guests one day under the old stand at Lansdowne Road where there was great hospitality. As they were leaving, my father said to Mick, "You would get nothing like this in the GAA", and nor would you. And then the All Blacks win ... he got great craic out of that.'

* * *

LITTLE MORE than three months after that famous occasion, Dick Spring was pulling on the Irish jersey for the first time against France in 1979. Brother Donal had played in the late, narrow and unlucky defeat by the All Blacks the previous November at Lansdowne Road, three days after the heroics at Thomond Park, but an injury sustained in the final trial ruled him out of the championship opener against France. In fact, Dick also came off the field in the same trial with a suspected fractured nose, but was still fit to line out against the French. The game ended in a 9–9 draw although as Dick puts it, 'It was there for the winning. I had a very good game and they were telling me I'd be on the Irish team for the rest of my life! Then it was on to Cardiff Arms Park. My big concern that day was J.P.R. Williams and making sure he wasn't coming into the back line and so on. Anyway, I got caught out of position, famously forgot to catch a high ball, Terry Kennedy let it bounce over his head, Colin Patterson failed to dive on it – and your man, Allan Martin, who got the touch down, was offside. We were beaten 24–21 and that was the highest number of points Ireland had scored up to then.

'I've tried to do things with the rest of my life to try and put dropping that ball in the shade a little bit, but of course it keeps coming up and so I have my own way of dealing with it! We could have won that match even though it was a very good Welsh team. I kept my place against England, and we won 12–7, only to be dropped for the Scotland game in Edinburgh and Donal was picked. They went to Murrayfield, the game was played in a gale and the guy who replaced me [Ronnie

Elliott] was never heard of again. Donal and I played together for Munster a few times and there's a photograph of a fight in a match against Leinster at Thomond Park in which I'm hiding behind my brother even though I had started it all! And when I was captain of Lansdowne, he was captain of Trinity, so we had a few outings against each other.'

On the day in 1979 after he had shared in yet another Lansdowne cup triumph, Dick received a phone call from the IRFU offering him a place in the Irish team travelling to Australia. It put him in a quandary for he had already recognised that it was time for a few career decisions. The local elections were looming in Kerry and spending six weeks in Australia didn't seem to make a lot of sense. So the Springs moved back to Tralee from Dublin, Dick was duly elected to the council and not long afterwards his father was persuaded – reluctantly – to stand down from the Dáil. Dick stood in his stead in the 1981 election and made it to Leinster House.

'I captained Tralee when I came back and we got to six finals and didn't win a single trophy and it really was a killer,' he recalls. 'The following season I was junior Minister of State for Justice and played in the two opening games of the season. We were playing Clonakilty one day in Tralee and got caught in a ruck and I heard one of the Clon guys shout, "I have the minister, I have the f****r, I have his head", and after two weekends of that, I said to myself, it's time to get smart around here and so I quit. But I still needed some sporting activity and so I started training to go on the marathon circuit and was doing ten miles a day no problem. But then I had a car accident on the way to Dublin, just beyond Nenagh. My state driver and myself, we skidded on black ice and went into a spin, hit another car coming the other way – one person in that car was sadly killed, two guards going down to Limerick to buy a greyhound … there was a county council worker's car parked on the side of the road and we hit that as well. To give you an idea of the impact, I was sitting in the front seat dictating letters and they found my dictating machine in a field forty yards away. I suppose I should have been killed but I somehow survived. Thank God for a big car and a safety belt.'

* * *

In spite of the momentous happenings that day in 1978, Donal Spring has invariably put the club at the top of his list of priorities and that is one good reason for an unreserved affection for both Dublin University (Trinity) and Lansdowne. He went from Roscrea to Trinity to study law and loved college life from the outset. He was enjoying a drink shortly after arrival when the team captain John Robbie whipped the glass out of his hand and told him he was in the side to play Terenure on the following day.

'We went out and beat the Terenure club side which was interesting, as we had never been able to beat their school side. It was an incredible campaign, I think we played twenty-three matches and lost only once and won the Leinster Senior Cup', he reminds you proudly.

John Robbie, of course, was an outstanding Schools' player and a year or two previously had helped High School to an unlikely Leinster Schools title. He went on to play for Ireland

and on travelling with the national side to South Africa some time later decided to settle there. He became a household name in the broadcasting world, railing in the apartheid days against the regime of the time. Nowadays, John is widely respected for his shrewd and honest reading of how the country has developed. In Trevor West's delightful history *150 Years of Trinity Rugby,* Robbie (who was a mere nineteen at the time) recalled that 'in 1975, DUFC had experienced one of the worst years in its history. People felt that Dick Spring's good Trinity side of 1974, when all the universities had been defeated, would perhaps be the last good Trinity side in history.'

It transpired, though, that four of the 1976 side, in addition to Ollie Waldron who had already been capped, went on to play for Ireland. Robbie explains what led to the seemingly miraculous resurgence that year.

'The arrival of several talented young students helped and we had the best and most organised coach in the country in Roly Meates,' he wrote. 'Can you believe that Roly packed more into an hour-long session at lunchtime than most sides achieved in a week? In Donal Spring and Mike Gibson, we had two six-and-a-half footers who could dominate the line-outs. It's hard to believe that Donal was a kid of nineteen, but he took on and beat the best at the front of the line-out and mixed it with the toughest.'

Having beaten Carlow, Lansdowne and Wanderers on their way to the final, Trinity were not given a hope against a Blackrock College side that contained internationals Fergus Slattery, Willie Duggan, Eddie Byrne and Ray McLoughlin in the pack. But the students won the cup after extra time in a replay with the following squad: T.R.W. Meates, coach; J.C. Robbie (capt.), A.J. Stewart, M.E. Gibson, B.S. Doyle, P.J. Boyle, D.P. Menzies, W.M.J. Ryan, S.W.J. Hughes, M.P. Fitzpatrick, R.E. Greenlee, J.P. Power, D.E. Spring, O.C. Waldron, C.J.M. Agnew and R.G. Greene.

Donal loved every one of his five years at Trinity and, as well as that remarkable cup success, happily recalls four Colours wins over UCD, including a rather tempestuous affair that led to the end of Colours matches being played at Lansdowne Road. Having finished college, he and his girlfriend, Geraldine, now his wife, decided to see a bit of the world and especially the south of France, where he played for a couple of seasons with Bagnères, a powerful force in the game there at the time.

'If I have one regret in sport, it's that I came back from France twenty times a better player than when I went out and was never recognised as such,' he maintains. 'Bagnères had three of the French team in their back line – Aguirre, Gourdon and Bertranne. They were a phenomenal side and had been in the French championship final in the previous two years. Unfortunately, after I came back, I just disappeared into the ether. My seventh cap against Wales in 1981 was my last. I don't know whether going to France cost me, but I didn't go to South Africa that summer which probably didn't do me any favours either. It was the apartheid issue and I spoke out against it, which most people didn't do. I felt very strongly about it. I had been to South Africa myself before then with London Irish and so I had seen it and knew what

I was talking about. A lot of bullshit was talked about sport helping the people, because the reality is that the bans on sport did far more good than actually going out there.

'I have been back and it's better in the sense that they have got their freedom, but I'm very disappointed with the government, that while they have taken away the racial ban they haven't taken away the inequality to any extent and that is hugely disappointing.

'Anyway, I came back from France and definitely feel that Irish rugby didn't get the best of me in the sense that I had been playing a different standard out there. Once I started work as a lawyer, my travels were over, but I wanted to continue playing. I loved France. I had met Jean-François Gourdon on a Wolfhounds tour and he invited me out for a weekend festival that was the equivalent of the Rose of Tralee. I had started going out with Geraldine and she thought going there was a great idea. Bagnères was about seven miles from Lourdes which also delighted my mother. She used to give my address to anybody going to Lourdes from Tralee so we had loads of visitors. It was probably one of the best things I have ever done in my life.

'I came back then and had a phenomenal run with Lansdowne. Once again, the club scene appealed to me as much if not more than anything else and we had super teams, winning three Leinster Cups and four leagues and would you believe it, even a Metro Cup. I went into coaching, did the Leinster 19s, Lansdowne, Belvedere – and Leinster for one match but resigned after a difficulty with the selection system. I never agreed with the five man selection committee but I was promised I could pick the team on my own. And when that didn't happen, I walked away.'

While acknowledging that the professional game is faster and better to watch, Donal is far less sure of the effect the intensity of the exchanges at the highest level will have on players in later life. He instances the tackle as a major worry pointing out that 'in my time a high tackle was one that got you around the chest, now they have to take the head off you before it's whistled'.

* * *

THE VISIT of President Bill Clinton to the famed golf links at Ballybunion is one of Dick Spring's favourite memories from his much-varied life, although the weeks before the big day in the early autumn of 1998 were not without their anxious moments. Dick recalls: 'When I went to Washington as Tánaiste, the format would have been for me to meet Al Gore. The vice-president meets the deputy prime minister, but every time I was there Clinton came into the room to say hello and spent ten minutes because of his interest in Northern Ireland and because we got on particularly well. It was also great from my point of view that we had access to the top. With all due respect to Al Gore, he was not overly concerned about Northern Ireland, whereas we had great friends in Clinton and George Mitchell. Part of the old banter was that he would say, when am I going to play Ballybunion, and I'd say, open invitation, you come and I'll probably be able to get you out on the course all right.

'He was due to play when he came on the first big visit

and was supposed to come to Ballybunion having visited Limerick. The game was set up for Saturday in Ballybunion: a great combination of Christy O'Connor and myself versus Tom Watson and Bill Clinton. But Jean Kennedy Smith [the US ambassador at the time] came into my office on the Tuesday and I knew by her demeanour. "Ambassador," I said, "you don't have to say it, Bill Clinton is not coming to Ballybunion." And she said, "Sorry Tánaiste, but troops in Germany are leaving for Bosnia at the weekend." I understood perfectly, the president could not be seen to be playing golf when sending out thousands of people on a mission so he had to go to Germany to meet the troops. In fairness, though, we met afterwards and he said, "I promised you I'm coming to Ballybunion and I will."

'By the time he actually got around to coming, I was out of office. It was my gig, if you like, when I was in power, but now I was on the periphery and so wasn't exactly calling the shots. So it was announced that Bill Clinton was coming to Ballybunion and immediately there was the question of who was playing and who was not. The first message to come from Washington was that Dick Spring was playing and we'll work out the rest later. The captain of Ballybunion at the time was a very good friend of mine, Brian McCarthy, and I told him if you do this right, you will be playing golf with Bill Clinton. Of course, the government had to be represented; they were not going to let Dick Spring walk down the first fairway with the US president, so Charlie McCreevy was chosen to represent the government. That fourball was proposed until one of the Americans came into Jim McKenna, the Ballybunion secretary/manager, on the Wednesday and said, "By the way, we have to bounce the captain." And Jim said, "Sorry, this is a private club and we can bounce the president if you want to say that." So a forty-eight hour row ensued about who should play, with me stuck in the middle of it. I didn't want to lose my connectivity with America or the White House and I didn't want to lose my standing in Ballybunion where I had been a long time life member.

'And then out of nowhere, Christy O'Connor appeared, he was to play with the president and I said, okay, and then there was a suggestion that the captain would play the front nine and Christy the back nine, all sorts of combinations. It got to such a stage that I asked myself, what in the bloody hell did I ever get involved in this for? It was more trouble than it was worth. Eventually, it was a fiveball: Bill Clinton, Brian McCarthy, Charlie McCreevy, Christy O'Connor and myself. There wasn't a match, really. Clinton is a solid golfer, I would say 12 to 14 handicap, and hits the ball very well, very straight, but he could not cope with the rough in Ballybunion. The 200 people or so in the caravan park at the sixth saw him get into the rough on the left and of course you go from there into the ditch on the right and they were getting into fits of laughter. There were about 2,000 people around the first tee but there was nobody else on the course and the television cameras were confined to the first and eighteenth holes.

'It was good fun. I have to say Bill Clinton was a very affable guy for the most powerful man in the world, very easy on the golf course and good company with a great sense of humour. He had Mick Scanlon, the senior caddie in the club, on the bag and at the first of the par fives, Clinton was up by Joe O'Sullivan's house on the right-hand side. The caddie gives him a three iron and he puts it up there, a pitching wedge from the green. Christy takes out a three wood and puts it on the green. So Bill said, "I didn't think I could get that far, why didn't you give me a wood?" And he took out another ball and put it on the green. He was a big man and big hitter.

'The occasion worked very well and a great time was had by all. It was a great day for Ballybunion. It was great for golf in Ireland and for the country as well.' The television cameras had a field day and reflected Ireland in a very positive way, much to the satisfaction of the former Tánaiste.

This was not the only match Dick Spring was to have with Bill Clinton. 'Having left office, he came back afterwards and played another round of golf with me in Ballybunion. Interestingly, we played the Old Course, came in and had our lunch and he said, "OK guys, you have a new course, let's go and see it." I'm happy with 18 holes so I said, "We'll play the back nine on the Cashen." We're coming up the 18th and I said I was getting a bit tired, and he said, "That's all right, if you guys want to go to the bar, I'll play the front nine by myself." We couldn't allow that so we played on for the 36 holes and I was wrecked for three days after it. But he was determined …'

This is just one of the many great stories Dick Spring recalls humorously and interestingly from his time as one of our leading politicians. The Spring dynasty in the Dáil is maintained these days by Arthur John, Arthur's son, who was elected in the 2011 General Election.

DIARMUID, ALAN AND EOIN REDDAN

Eoin Reddan was brilliant for us in the way he played.

*Ian McGeechan, Director of Rugby at London Wasps and
renowned coach of British and Irish Lions touring teams*

THE FIVE Reddan boys from the Dooradoyle-Raheen side
of Limerick were born into a rugby-mad family. Their
father, Don, a speedy, elusive winger, had played with
considerable distinction in his own day with Crescent
College, Old Crescent, Galwegians, Munster and Connacht,
and subsequently devoted a considerable amount of time
to coaching up-and-coming talent. Uncle Michael was a
distinguished referee and another uncle, Kevin Uniacke, was
also an outstanding player.

So it really was inevitable that Don's sons would play the
game with considerable distinction and that they did so was
largely due to the support they received from within the
family and the positive rugby ambience in which they grew
up. The eldest boy, Donal, a distinguished physician, and the
youngest Cian, had their ambitions thwarted by injury. A

burst spleen put an end to Donal's aspirations while Cian, who showed considerable promise in his school days, fell foul of dodgy knees. In contrast Eoin and the two older boys, Diarmuid and Alan, all followed in their father's footsteps by representing Connacht before and after the game went professional. Eoin, number four in the order, has gone on to be respected as one of the finest No. 9s in the game.

* * *

You HAVE to love Diarmuid's description of how he was first informed of Connacht's interest in him in the mid 1990s. He was a student at the University of Limerick at the time when a phone call came to his home and was taken by his mother Geraldine. On the line was George Hook, who was Connacht coach at the time and knew Diarmuid from his time at Clongowes Wood College. Diarmuid had been a member of the team that won the Leinster Schools Senior Cup in 1988 when George was a member of the coaching staff.

'George told Mum that there was a contract going at Connacht and asked if she could contact me and give me the news,' Diarmuid recalls. 'Now, there were no mobile phones and the only previous time she had been at UL was the day I first went there. So she drove out to the college and didn't know where to find me. She made her way to the canteen – and there she found me playing poker with the lads.'

Diarmuid escaped unscathed from that sticky meeting and made his way to Galway, where Hooky offered him a trial. Connacht played the Army and he scored a try having run half the length of the field. That earned him his spot in the squad and he was to make several appearances in the jersey. Like every rugby player born in Limerick, and although he enjoyed his days in Galway, Diarmuid would prefer to have spent his time in a Munster shirt. It might have happened, too. He did well in a Munster President's XV against an Irish XV and a few weeks later was offered a place. However, as he was abroad on holiday when the call came, he could not take up the opportunity and immediately seemed to fall off Munster's radar system. When he was subsequently passed over for the Leinster-based Brian McGoey with a whole host of No. 9s ruled out by injury, he lost interest himself in being a Munster player. All the better, then, when the call came from Connacht.

'If I have one regret concerning my rugby career it's that I didn't set my goals higher and that is even more the case now when I see what Eoin has done,' says Diarmuid. 'Like all the family, I am very proud of what he has achieved but certainly not surprised. The work he put into making the grade has been absolutely fantastic. When I got the call from Connacht and was picked on the bench for some form of an Irish trial, I was delighted. It was as if I had reached my goal. It was my claim to fame, if you like. But no matter what the weather and the circumstances, Eoin was always at me to go out and pass a rugby ball and we did so until it was getting to the stage that I told him he'd be better off going and working on his fitness because he could already pass the ball. Every scrum half worth his salt has to be able to do that.

'Then there's his attitude. He never gets depressed when he's not picked for a game. He will always do the best he can and look to the next match, and back in 2007 he had his just reward when he was selected for the World Cup and played against France and Argentina. From time to time, I see Dad disappointed that he's not on the team or whatever, but he knows that it will only make Eoin more determined and play better if he can at all. We know he's not a Brian O'Driscoll and he has played over 50 per cent of his rugby at this point. But he has achieved an awful lot and I know there's a lot more still to come.'

Nowadays, Diarmuid Reddan heads up Don Reddan Insurances in Limerick (although you suspect Dad hasn't completely passed over the reins) and is one of the top twenty bridge players in the country. Goes to show, doesn't it, that the poker game into which Geraldine walked all those years ago mightn't have done any harm after all!

* * *

ONE OF Alan's earliest memories is of his father heading off to San Francisco in 1979 on a tour with Old Crescent. He was told to draw out the shape of his foot on a sheet of paper so that Dad could bring home a present of the Adidas Rom runners that were all the rage at the time. Here in Ireland, shoes were size 5 or 6 or 7 whereas over there they were 42s or 43s or whatever. So he reckoned the only way they could get the right size was drawing the shape on a sheet of paper – and he got it right, too, with a beautiful blue pair of runners!

Alan was an outstanding player in his younger days as a centre, so proficient indeed that many years later Hugh Farrelly of the *Irish Independent* included him in his top Irish

Schools XV team consisting of players who never made the jump to senior international status. He was paid the following tribute: 'Reddan was part of the famous Crescent team along with Paul Wallace and Shane Leahy that destroyed all opposition on the way to the Munster Schools' Senior Cup title. A classy centre, he served Lansdowne and Galwegians well in the AIL and was part of Warren Gatland's renowned Connacht in the late 1990s. He was picked for Ireland A but that was as high Reddan went.'

Although he moved to Dublin at the age of twenty-two, Alan was still of interest to Munster and spent twelve months travelling up and down before Connacht came knocking on the door. He was working in the bank at the time but was given two years' leave of absence to see how things worked out.

'It was the first year of professionalism and Junior Charlie, Mark McConnell and Graham Heaslip and myself were given contracts,' Alan recalls. 'Warren Gatland came in as coach but there was a difference about who was going to coach us between himself and Eddie O'Sullivan, and Gatland didn't coach us at all in the end. I suppose you could call it the amateurish era and the professional era crossing over, and we certainly never got to play the number of matches they have these days. There were only the inter-pros and no such thing as the Celtic League or European Cup, and you were generally done and dusted with provincial games by Christmas. This meant the coaches were left wondering what they would do with us, so it was important to try to get into the A squad and the Irish squads. I played club rugby with

Lansdowne in Dublin and Galwegians in Galway. I made a decision when I was twenty-six and faced with the scenario in Connacht where the coach said one week he wanted me and told me the next he didn't want me. So my stand on that was that I didn't want a contract, I was going back to work because I didn't believe the five games a year I was getting and the pecking order I was in was going to allow me the opportunity to achieve what I wanted. I felt that the cost to the rest of my life in continuing this way would have been too great. Rugby was very much semi-pro/pro, and you were not earning large sums. So I decided to go back to work and it was the right thing to do. In the end, I played in every Irish team, bar the full team and later enjoyed many hugely enjoyable and successful times with Lansdowne and Clontarf.'

* * *

Eoin Reddan enjoyed a distinguished Schools' career at Crescent and played for two years afterwards with Old Crescent before deciding to go down the professional route. It was 2004 and not for the first time, a Reddan was heading west!

'Connacht were very good to me,' he stresses. 'Gerry Kelly had coached me when I was selected for Irish Schools and there would have been a few scrum halves ahead of me in that age group who would have been up for potential contracts but Gerry and Steph Nel turned to me. They knew from Diarmuid and Alan that I would work hard and would fit in. If I hadn't had that chance, I don't think I would have gone anywhere. Connacht was brilliant for me. I was competing at scrum half with a guy called Jimmy Ferris. He was very good to me, a good bit older, but very helpful all the time and I have been lucky in that respect throughout my career. I ended up playing quite a number of games that season and the following year Jimmy had to retire because of injury and I ended up playing a lot more.

'At the end of that season, I had the opportunity to go to London, but chose Munster because I was from Munster and always wanted to play for Munster. At the time it might not have been the best call because they had a lot of scrum halves – but my heart won. I wanted to go there, to play there, surrounded by the friends I grew up with. It was what everybody wanted and I went for it. I felt I couldn't have lived with myself if I hadn't gone for it, maybe I would always be asking myself, what if? I played a little, but we went through a bit of a hard patch, we didn't win that many games that season and lost a bit of form and confidence. The first season I played quite a lot of games up to Christmas, but in my last year I only started twice. There are times in your career that you look back and think you can put the blame on someone else but there are times when you think, to be fair, I probably didn't treat not being picked with the same amount of experience that I'd be able to deal with it now. There is no point in blaming anyone else because you never get anything out of it. Whatever an impartial third party person might think, I would have to look at it and ask how I could have done things better. And I'd definitely have to answer that I could have done better when I was in Munster. Peter Stringer was playing very well and the team was winning, so you couldn't expect them to chop and change someone for the sake of it. I had no argument with that. I had a meeting in 2005 with Garrett Fitzgerald and was told I had no contract but literally within three hours, I took a phone call from Warren Gatland asking me to come and play for Wasps. I had been in touch with Wasps the previous year and told them why I was staying in Munster and didn't play one off against the other. I was straight up with Gatland and told him it wasn't the right thing for me. So the next year he was quite keen to see what I was at. During the phone call, I said, "Absolutely yes, I'll come." Wasps is a club that wants people who want to be there, that's as important to them as getting a good player; players who aren't too concerned about how much they were earning or other external factors. At the time, I couldn't wait to get there and they were delighted, and that helped when I arrived. Warren and Shaun Edwards signed me but Warren had gone to Wales by the time I arrived and Ian McGeechan was head coach.

'For me at the time, it was a totally different environment. With the salary cap in the UK, if they spend, say, £5,000 on you, they have to now invest time to make that £5,000 work for them so they spend a lot of time making you a better player. They don't have the kind of money that we have in Ireland. Everyone who went to Wasps was worked on seriously to turn that guy into a big player and there was never a stage where they would let a guy fall by the wayside because that would be considered a waste of money. That kind of environment helped me. Matt Dawson [England

and Lions scrum half] was there and obviously at the top of his game and he was very helpful and he is someone I have massive respect for. But I worked hard as well.

'The first trophies I ever won were the English Powergen Cup in 2006, the Heineken Cup in 2007 and the Guinness English Premiership in 2008. Those were great years for me and the club. We beat Llanelli in the final of the Powergen and it was important for the club to have some silverware in the trophy cabinet. For me, it was the first time I had ever won anything and it was great to be part of it. There is considerable pressure when you arrive at Wasps to add something tangible … if you join a club that has won ten trophies in ten years and the year you arrive they win nothing, that's not exactly reflecting well on you. So there is pressure to put your name to something and be able to say I helped with this success.

'I started that final against Llanelli and the same year, 2006, I got my first Irish cap as a sub against France. I came on on the wing. They were running out because of injuries and David Humphreys was told to warm up and he laughed and said, "I'm not going on, put him on." It was a case of give him his first cap. I didn't wait a half second. This was one of the nicest things anyone has ever done for me.

'The Heineken Cup came our way in 2007. I scored twice against Leinster in the quarter-final at Adams Park. We had a seriously good team … guys like Dallaglio, Joe Worsley, Simon Shaw, Phil Vickery, Raphael Ibanez, Fraser Waters, Josh Lewsey, Alex King … it was a massive team to be part of and a great time to be involved. We beat Leinster in the quarters, Northampton in the semis and Leicester in the final.

'Was it one of the biggest things Wasps ever won? Well, they won eighteen trophies in eighteen years and did the double two years before. I still remember thinking, yeah, we are getting better but the pressure was still there. Leinster is a bit like that now. But Wasps don't have an indigenous support like Leinster or Munster. I literally walked home alone the night we won the Heineken Cup. There's no one stopping you in the street saying well done ... you arrive at training the following week and it's a case of someone saying you had better win it again.

'During the 2011 Six Nations, Leinster had 17,000 at the RDS game when none of the internationals were available, whereas Wasps would be lucky to have 10,000 to watch a full team. How did they survive financially? Well, they didn't in a way, it's a flawed model, even though they are still a major force in the English Premiership. They didn't have the support and the ground sorted. The more trophies they won, the more the value of the players went up and up and up. Other clubs were coming in saying, "We'll take him, we'll take him", Wasps couldn't compete. The last trophy they won, I was playing that day, I'd say twelve players were gone in the next two years. Can you imagine Munster and Leinster having twelve of the 1st XV gone in that space of time?'

If Eoin Reddan really enjoyed his time at Wasps, it is clear that the feeling was mutual. Ian McGeechan, their Director of Rugby for much of the time Eoin spent at Adams Park and renowned for his achievements as coach of the British and Irish Lions, observed in his autobiography, *Lion Man*, that 'another good example of an outsider becoming a true

Wasp was Eoin Reddan whom we signed as a young scrum half from Ireland and who advanced so emphatically with us that he became one of our key players. It was obvious that if Eoin wanted to play for Ireland, he was going to have to go back home, so he signed for Leinster. Essentially, he didn't want to go, he was brilliant for us in the way he played and the way he understood the game. He was another who really bought into the Wasps thing. In the dressing-room after the final game, he was in tears as he said his goodbyes.'

* * *

WITH EOIN as a front line candidate for Ireland's No. 9 jersey in 2006, it was inevitable that the IRFU would want him home sooner rather than later. Given that he had just helped Wasps to win the Guinness Premiership and so round off a remarkable hat-trick of trophies in successive seasons, and having another year on his contract, Eoin was not in any great hurry. But, of course, there were obvious advantages to such a move.

'Naturally, I wanted to play for Ireland and I realised my best chance of doing that was to come home and play every week in front of the selectors.' Once the news broke that Eoin was on his way back, speculation inevitably arose as to whether the choice would be his native Munster or their great rivals, Leinster. A delicate decision needed to be made. Brother Alan has lived in Dublin for some time and, as a Munster exile, had a more than normal interest in the deliberations.

'I'll give you an example of where it gets really strange,'

he states. 'Do you remember Wasps beating Munster at Lansdowne Road and we were all screaming for Munster. Two years later, Eoin was playing for Wasps and we were all shouting for Wasps. And then Wasps play Leinster and we are shouting for Wasps because he is playing for Wasps. And then he moves to Leinster and now we are shouting for Leinster. Having made that step mentally, that rugby is a professional game, and that your family are going to support you no matter who you're playing for, the whole point about it being a wrench is pushed to one side because you do a lot of things to get to where you want to be.

'I didn't find it difficult that Eoin would be playing for Leinster, and sometimes against Munster. Not in the slightest. I find it baffling when friends of mine question why I would support Leinster when they are playing against Munster. But I would support Leinster because my brother is playing for Leinster. That's how I'm made, whereas friends of mine have huge issues. Remember when Leinster won the Heineken Cup in Edinburgh … friends of mine went there and wore the red jersey to the match and other friends went there as Leinster supporters and took off the red jersey and put on the blue jersey. And some of those in the red jersey started giving out to the guys in the blue jerseys.'

Eoin reckons that playing for Wasps in between his stint at Munster and moving to Leinster helped to defuse any aggro that might have hung in the air ('Wasps gave me my break and I'll always have a massive amount of feelings for them and hope for them to do well'). 'That gap in between did break it down a bit. As Alan says, friends and family were always very supportive no matter what I did. It would be great for me to give you a line saying that Munster had their chance with me and to hell with that. But when I look back at that Munster thing, I look back at it from an individual point of view. I don't look back and blame anyone else. I look at it and see what I could have done better, so it had nothing to do with that. So I'm there at Wasps and I'm after missing out on a Grand Slam with Ireland and I want to get back on the Irish team and it's a big challenge considering that the squad has gone on to win a Grand Slam and I'm delighted for all my friends who have done that. So how do I get back on this team?

'Well, Michael Cheika came to London to see me and to be honest, he absolutely blew me away. I was very impressed with the man both in terms of his rugby knowledge and desire to win. Now, I'm sure he is the kind of guy who might put the odd nose out of joint here and there, but there is nothing wrong with that when that guy is on your team or leading you – you need that. Leinster was a better move for me because there was a better chance of playing all the time. They needed me more than Munster. Can you imagine the IRFU allowing me to go to Munster with Tomás [O'Leary] and Peter already there and Leinster only having Chris Whitaker? It didn't seem a realistic option. And the other important thing is that I was still in contract when I left Wasps. When Wasps and Leinster start talking, you cannot go to your club and go, "I want you to talk to five different clubs about where I might go." It had to be a fairly simple process of a club I knew that was interested in me and my club had to be interested in talking to them. Because of that, I couldn't have Wasps going off and talking to Leinster and Munster and weighing one against the other. It was the best option for me at the time.'

Accordingly, Eoin made the wise and practicable decision to go to Leinster and both club and player have every reason to be happy about that. By the end of the 2011 Six Nations, he had extended his caps tally to twenty-nine, scored a first international try in a testing game against Scotland at Murrayfield and starred in the thrashing of Grand Slam seekers England in the final match of the series. After that he was off in search of further Heineken Cup glory with the Boys in Blue. A single point defeat by Munster in the Magners League at Thomond Park stalled their progress only minimally, but might have provided him with a few salutary moments at the ground he knew so well from his earliest days. No problem there, though, he insists.

'When I'm in Thomond Park, I don't get any bitterness from anyone, ever. I don't get any before the game, during the game, after the game. Munster fans know their rugby and they knew at the time that Munster had two Irish scrum halves both playing for Ireland and Leinster had an Aussie scrum half. There was never going to be anything else happening and everyone was aware of that. When I'm warming up at Thomond Park, I have a great chat with fans with little or no slagging. I'm from Limerick, it's my home, and that will never change, so it doesn't matter who I'm playing for.

'Decisions are what you make, it's about what you do when you get there having made those decisions. I've made the most of the opportunities I've had, a point well made by our victory in the Heineken Cup. The way we came back in the second half of the final against Northampton was amazing and a memory that will never die. I don't think too far ahead. Leinster is a very good place to be, very good off the pitch. We have massive crowds all the time, they really are pushing off the pitch and as a player, that's great. You can see everyone worrying about their little bit and everyone going forward together because of it. You worry about your own skills and bits for the weekend. Joe Schmidt is an excellent coach, he knows a lot about rugby and managing a squad. He is always on the money and right when he tells you something. He is extremely experienced in coaching, has coached some very good players and we are getting the benefit of that.

'Yeah, the life of a professional rugby player is great. As I say, I've been lucky; Connacht was up and coming, then Munster, Wasps and Leinster have all been Heineken Cup winners, now hopefully there's a World Cup to come, so I've been surrounded by good coaches. I don't see it as hard work. I enjoy pre-season every year. The hardest part is not being picked and if you are not playing, you have to deal with that in the right way. In a sick way, I seem to like that part of it.'

* * *

IRELAND'S POOR start to the 2007 World Cup opened the door for Eoin to display his qualities on the biggest stage of all. Prior to that, he was playing second fiddle to Peter Stringer. The prospects for the team were hardly the brightest when Eoin lined out at the Stade de France on that September evening with Ireland having scraped wins over Namibia and Georgia and needing big performances against France and Argentina to reach the knock-out stages. Had the damage already been done?

'I don't think so ... it would be a cop-out for me to look back and say, sure, I came in when the damage was done,' he asserts. 'If we had won that game [against France], we were back in the hunt; I was playing and it was full game on ... We played well that day, although we gave away too many penalties and stuff, but it's too easy to look back and say it was too late.

'That was the beginning of a decent run in the Irish jersey. I've never been able to really hold down the position but that is not a reflection on me, it's more a reflection on the people I'm competing with and that's a good thing. I enjoy that part of the game. While it can be mentally draining, you enjoy the thrill of that and knowing you have been in a battle with someone and come out on top or whatever. I would have a massive respect for anyone I've ever competed with.

'There are so many things that can go right and wrong for you in rugby. You can only worry about what you're doing yourself – like what happened to Cian and his knee, nothing like that happened to me. I consider myself lucky, I wouldn't look at it as a negative that I have not held down a place on the team. I'm up against good guys all the time; the Ireland team by its nature doesn't win all of its games all of the time. We have to work hard to win trophies and stuff like that so I feel it's a good personal challenge when you're not picked and you're in a fight with someone to see how you come out of it. It makes you a better player, helps you to face every day with its ups and downs and I enjoy it. Obviously, I want to play every day but …'

* * *

DON REDDAN will always be grateful to his sons for the manner in which they rallied around for the many years of their mother Geraldine's illness before her passing in 2010. Blessed with a quiet but delightful sense of humour, Ger fully supported the men in her life while trying – usually successfully! – to keep rugby in perspective.

'The family were so supportive of each other and Mum was such a wonderful person, it was almost amazing the way we reacted to what was going on,' Eoin explains. 'It could have been horrible were it not for Mum and Dad and the way they approached everything. It pulled us together and you draw strength from that.' Alan feels that 'it makes you realise what's important and how much you can do for your family and how much people can do for you if you let them in.' Eoin adds, 'Mum might be lying in bed barely able to move her hand but she could still do an unbelievable amount for everyone just by her nature and the way she would smile at you and the form she'd be in. She was still giving, still teaching people; no matter what happens to you, no matter what goes wrong, there are ways you can stay upbeat, be positive and get on with it. She was great from that point of view. In one way, it's hard when someone so close to you gets sick, but in another way it was an unbelievable experience seeing Dad and his devotion to her. It was huge. He had a bad fall a few years ago in Kilkee, but he bounced back hard and you hope a bit of that is in you. I'd have learned so much about Mum and Dad individually and their relationship in the last ten years or so when she was sick. He would have gone on caring for Mum for a hundred years.'

Obviously, Geraldine Reddan got a great kick out of her sons' achievements on and off the sporting arenas. Alan recounts earlier dinner table conversations as they were growing up and how they'd be discussing matches and who won this match and so on and she would remind them: '"Right, we're going to talk about school now for a while, we can't focus on rugby all the time." She was a teacher and would keep it real at all times and always be very strong.'

Given her background, Geraldine Reddan was gratified to know before her passing away that Eoin had not just established himself as one of his country's finest rugby players but had also taken her words about education very much to heart. He had completed a course in Business Studies at UL before becoming a full-time professional and has been studying for a Masters in Financial Management, even when fully committed to the cause of Ireland and Leinster on the rugby field.

JOHN AND BARRY O'DRISCOLL

John O'Driscoll was the best player I ever saw at the club.

London Irish coach Pat Parfrey

MUNSTER RUGBY fans are not prone to dishing out accolades without good reason. So when John O'Driscoll discovered that he had been included in the Munsterfans forum 'Greatest Irish team of all time' he was entitled to at least a quiet smile of satisfaction. The Manchester-based dermatologist is far too unassuming to place a whole lot of emphasis on the selection, but he wouldn't be human if he wasn't pleased to figure in a side that contained numerous legends of the game in this country including a second cousin and some great friends and contemporaries. Just look at the chosen team: Tom Kiernan, Denis Hickie, Brian O'Driscoll, Mike Gibson, Simon Geoghegan, Ollie Campbell, Colin Patterson, Nick Popplewell, Keith Wood, Ray McLoughlin, Paul O'Connell, Willie John McBride, John O'Driscoll, Fergus Slattery and Jamie Heaslip.

Very few contributors to the fans' website found reason to quibble. Some wondered about the absence of Jack Kyle and whether Willie John McBride would be able to cut it in today's professional game. But John O'Driscoll? Not a murmur of complaint, its own indication of the massive respect in which he has been held as an outstanding back-row forward since twice touring with the Lions and playing a major part in Ireland's Triple Crown triumph in 1982. John earned twenty-six Irish caps in a career that stretched from 1978 to 1984 and in that time he also played in six Tests for the Lions on the tours of South Africa in 1980 and New Zealand three years later. Nowadays, he is the Exiles representative on the IRFU committee, demonstrating an ongoing commitment to the game in this country. This should come as no surprise, given that his brother Barry was the first chairman of the Exiles sub-committee on the Union. Barry, a general practitioner, also based in Manchester, played four times for Ireland in 1971.

* * *

THE RISE of the O'Driscoll brothers to the top of the rugby tree began in the unlikely surrounds of Leap, County Cork, and Balbriggan, County Dublin. Leap is to be found between Skibbereen and Rosscarbery in one of the most beautiful parts of West Cork and that is where Florence O'Driscoll grew up. John smiles at his dad's unusual Christian name, musing that 'it's well-known in West Cork but there aren't too many Florences in Dublin and by the time he got over to England, there were no male Florences at all. I think the name was the bane of his life and I don't know why he didn't change it by deed poll because everyone assumed it was going to be a woman when they were meeting Dad. My mum was a MacAuley from Balbriggan. She was one of a family of thirteen.

'There were six of us and the other five were born in Dublin, but I am a long way after them. Barry is the next to me and he is twelve years older. My oldest sister is twenty-two years older so there is quite a stretch. I suppose I must have been an after-thought! Actually, my eldest brother, Billy, was born in Singapore because my father was a medic in the colonial service. He trained at UCD and later became a GP in Manchester. Dad was one of three boys. One was a GP in Manchester and he died of TB in the late 1940s and his family are all around the Skerries area. Then there was Liam who was Frank's father and so Brian's grandfather. They were all doctors and there was also a sister who was a nun and she only died a few years ago.'

The eldest of the O'Driscoll males, Billy, began his secondary education at Douai (public school) and played a bit of rugby as a scrum half, but Barry and John both went to Stonyhurst. However, they already had a fair share of rugby knowledge before ever darkening the gates of the famed Jesuit academy.

'From a very early age, my father loved rugby,' John explains. 'He played at UCD. He'd have been born in 1905 and there wouldn't have been a lot of jobs for Irish doctors around his time and that's why he joined the colonial service and went off to Singapore. From the age of five to fourteen, I spent every Saturday watching rugby and for many years watching Barry at Stonyhurst and after that at Manchester University and Manchester RFC. We also tried to travel and watch him in final trials. It's what my father loved to do and I used to tag along with him.

'I also watched Barry play with Connacht, which must seem like a strange alliance given that the family connection was Munster and Leinster. Connacht got to know Barry through Dr Joe Costelloe, a man who very sadly died of lung cancer even though he never smoked and never drank. Joe was a great bloke. He was at Liverpool at one stage and got to know Barry. He was playing for Manchester and Lancashire so that's how Barry got involved. I played for Connacht because Barry played for Connacht and it was fantastic. There was some vague connection through the grandparents and I loved my time there.

'When I started playing for Connacht in the mid 1970s, we didn't win many matches, we didn't win any actually for quite a few years, but we were rarely badly beaten. We gave almost every side a hard time. At the end of the day, they would have just a little too much class for us. However, there was always a wonderful atmosphere. There was a great determination going into every match and all the coaches, all the alickadoos, they were enthusiastic. There were never any recriminations, nobody ever said, we don't want people coming over from London and we are losing, what are we doing? It couldn't happen today when it's all based on success. Connacht knew they were doing their best and it paid dividends towards the end of my career when we began to win a few matches while still always giving teams a hard time. We had a nuggety pack and determined backs ... we might have lacked something against the others, Keith

Crossan might run in a couple of tries because he was too fast for us out wide, but we were never destroyed. There were great characters there as well and I never regretted playing for Connacht.

'I went to medical school in London at the age of eighteen and it was natural to go down to London Irish. I never thought of myself as anything other than Irish. You have to understand what Manchester was like. Manchester and Liverpool are very Irish cities. Almost everyone I met when I was young were Irish doctors or of Irish extraction. If you went to a Catholic school in Manchester, most of the students were Irish. So I was always brought up feeling Irish. We went to West Cork every summer for three weeks and I would also go over to Liam's, my father's brother, in Clontarf, so I spent a lot of my time in Ireland and was brought up in an Irish atmosphere.

'My mother had a broad Irish accent all through her life, even though she lived for fifty years in England. My father, of course, always said that to acquire an accent you had to listen but she was talking all the time!

'So it never occurred to me that I was anything other than Irish. And all I ever wanted to do from the age of nine or ten was to play rugby for Ireland. That was my ambition in life. When I joined London Irish, Mick Molloy was there and of course he was also playing for Connacht and was very influential. A great friend and a great guy. He got me involved with Connacht and that was hugely significant for me. I got a final Irish trial in 1977 and made the side in 1978. Before the final trial that year, I had not played rugby for eight weeks beforehand. I had a fractured cheek bone and didn't play the inter-pros either, but Connacht were very supportive of me, even though I hadn't played for them that year, especially Tony Browne, one of their many outstanding officials and later President of the IRFU, and they pushed me for the trial. Because it was a facial injury, I was still able to train very hard. I got a special mask made to cover the area and the trial was one of those days when the ball bounces for you. I was lucky and I got in. But then I was concussed in my first match against Scotland and was replaced by a great player, Stewart McKinney, who scored a try just as I was going off!

'I didn't get back in again until the tour of Australia in 1979 and stayed in after that. It was a great time to be playing Irish rugby. I cannot imagine anything more fun than playing with that Irish side and those individuals, guys like Ollie [Campbell], Tony [Ward], Willie [Duggan], Slatts [Fergus Slattery], Donal Lenihan and all those people. I played most of my back row rugby with Willie and Slatts. But there was great character in the team, everyone worked very hard on the pitch and had great fun off it.

'We did really well in Australia in 1979, because they were on top of their game at the time and had hammered Wales, and we were not given much chance. But we beat them in both Tests. That was a great tour which many people will remember for the Tony Ward-Ollie Campbell controversy. But it was a happy one as well, with great players – Rodney O'Donnell, Mike Gibson, Ollie, Colin Patterson, Phil Orr, Willie, Slatts, Johnny Moloney, normally a scrum half playing both matches on the wing ... and so on ... we beat them 27–12 in Brisbane and 9–3 in Sydney.

'We came back and had a reasonable season in 1980 and I sort of slipped into the Lions trip to South Africa. I played all the Tests and that was another very enjoyable and happy tour. Billy Beaumont was a very good captain. Noisy [Noel] Murphy was coach, Syd Millar was manager and the three of them were very good. The 1983 tour to New Zealand was different ... in 1980, all the way through we felt we were unfortunate not to be winning the Test series. We won all the provincial matches and it was good to win the last Test with a team that included other Irish internationals Ollie Campbell, Johnny Robbie and Colm Tucker. And I also had the distinction of scoring an important try that day.

'Ciaran Fitzgerald was captain in 1983 and he came in for some very unfair criticism from sections of the British media. It was like there was a campaign against him. The media out there were not balanced. It wasn't that Ciaran had got there under false credentials, having captained a Triple Crown-winning side the previous year. I wouldn't say it was an unhappy tour, but it was different from 1980. It didn't go well for us in the Test matches. I will not say we were unlucky because that would be wrong. New Zealand were the better side.

'I had heard about cliques on previous Lions tours but on neither of those tours was that the case. The countries got on well with each other. But if you're not winning, it piles on the pressure. It does make a difference. But both tours were a wonderful experience. I loved both – and the Irish tours as well. On all of them there were great blokes, great individuals

– you didn't have to worry about work, all you were doing was playing rugby and having a bit of fun. It was all you had to think about, so I loved touring. You were away a long time but it's a long life …

'Colm Tucker was on the 1980 Lions tour and played in two of the Test matches. I really enjoyed playing with him. He was a very good player and a great bloke. He loved that tour. We were both No. 6s and so we played left and right at scrum time.'

By the very nature of things, great players and even better friends go their different ways as time goes by. Sadly, they rarely meet up again except for funerals and the like. Very, very sadly Moss Keane finally succumbed to the cancer that had ravaged his massive frame for several years in October 2010. John O'Driscoll was one of the many household names of Irish rugby present at the obsequies in Portarlington, where he met up once again with his old mates. It was a sad occasion, of course, but Moss would have been proud at how his old comrades remembered him while once again meeting and recounting old tales and events. It's what makes rugby football such a unique sport.

* * *

SANDWICHED BETWEEN the two Lions tours was Ireland's first Triple Crown triumph in forty-four years in 1982. As if to demonstrate how correct John O'Driscoll was in lauding the teams and players of that era, they played some great rugby while at the same time invariably performing with considerable wisdom, as befitted a team coached by Tom Kiernan.

'That team had been around together for three or four years and it was good to win something to remember it by,' says John. 'Everything just came together. We had lost all four games in the Five Nations in 1981 with the same team. Tommy Kiernan was our coach and to his eternal credit, and with the help of selectors like Brian O'Brien, P.J. Dwyer and Dion Glass, he kept us together even though people were saying that this team was finished. That was vital, because I think all the players realised this was the right side.

'In the first match we beat England at Twickenham, the day of Locky's [Gerry McLoughlin] try when he managed to score in spite of eight of us holding on to him and pulling him back! We beat Wales in Dublin and then Scotland. It was very pleasant for that group of players who had come all the way through to win something. The final match against Scotland was not spectacular, but if ever there was one we wanted to win, that was it. Ollie kicked his goals as he generally did and the country rejoiced and obviously it was a major highlight of my career.'

There was a gap of a month between the game against Scotland and the Grand Slam decider against France in Paris. By then, the euphoria that had overtaken the country seemed to have subsumed Ciaran Fitzgerald's team. Willie Duggan's withdrawal a day before the game didn't help, but the country as a whole and maybe team members as well felt deep down that the job had already been done. In those days the Triple Crown probably outweighed the Grand Slam in significance.

John O'Driscoll did all he could to combine a budding medical career with the inevitable demands imposed on an international rugby player. He represented Lancashire and Surrey in the English County Championship and had the distinction of lining out with the Barbarians. However, he realised that between London Irish and Connacht and his commitment to the Irish team, he had to restrict the amount of time he devoted to the game. Not that this troubled him unduly.

'London Irish was a great rugby and social club in those days. They ran an enormous number of sides at every level. We had some good teams and got to the John Player Cup [English Championship] final in 1980 but lost to Leicester. Mick Smith from Ennis scored the game's only try for us. His father was a world champion cross-country runner and as Mick was a big, thickset guy, I could never figure that out. But we were not robbed, Leicester were too strong for us. It was a big deal for London Irish because we had done well to reach the final. We were coached by Pat Parfrey, now a doctor in Canada, and he still brings teams from there to this side of the world.'

* * *

As WE have seen, Barry O'Driscoll was twelve years ahead of John in age and it was he who set the trend of family members attending Stonyhurst. He was a versatile rugby player who played primarily at fullback but also slotted in frequently at centre. He had the misfortune to be around at the same time as the great Tom Kiernan and as a result was confined to four appearances in the green jersey. When the Corkman suffered a broken leg in the drawn game against France at Lansdowne

Road in 1971, Barry came in as his replacement and landed two penalties to augment a try by Ulsterman Eddie Grant. The selectors were happy with what they saw and retained Barry for the next game against England, again at Lansdowne Road. It was one of those days when the visiting fullback Bob Hiller, not for the only time by any means, broke Irish hearts by knocking over three penalties to contribute all of his side's nine points. As John points out, 'Bob Hiller was the scourge of Irish teams. He used to love to be derided by Irishmen. He's quite a nice fellow, very laid back. He was big and chunky and he had this torpedo kick … in those days, people didn't kick goals like that, not like nowadays when they all do it. He was a metronome before they had metronomes. And that's one of the big differences between the game then and now.'

Although wings Eddie Grant, again, and Alan Duggan ran in Irish tries, they were worth only six points at the time and so it was an English victory by 9–6. Grant scored yet another try in the 17–5 defeat of Scotland at Murrayfield with stand-in captain Mike Gibson also contributing handsomely. There was no escape, though, when a crack Welsh team that included the likes of J.P.R. Williams, Barry John, Gareth Edwards and Mervyn Davies beat the Irish decisively at the Cardiff Arms Park by 23–9.

Tom Kiernan was back to full fitness for the following season and Barry had to be content with those four caps. But he continued to give great service to Connacht and to his club, Manchester, and on retirement became heavily involved with the Irish Exiles. The Exiles, ironically enough the brainchild of Tom Kiernan, is a group of rugby enthusiasts largely based in England which was set up to recruit Irish-qualified players in Great Britain and France and also to support Irish players who had moved to these countries. Barry was chairman of the Exiles, which was to become a sub-committee of the IRFU, when their team first competed in the inter-provincial championship and also during a period when they provided several distinguished players to the Irish cause, including Simon Geoghegan and Rob Saunders.

'Barry was an immense influence on me basically,' says John. 'I used to watch him play at school when I was still a toddler. In the afternoons, he would be out practising his goal kicking and he needed someone to kick the ball back to him. So that is where I got my training in catching and kicking. He was very determined about his rugby, not a very big guy, smaller than me, kind of nuggety if you like. Of course, he was around at the same time as Tommy Kiernan and so had to wait quite a while before getting a cap. Every year, my father and I would watch the final trial and I was desperately keen that he would get a cap. It was from watching Barry that I got the appetite for rugby. Irish rugby was the main thing in our house, it always had been and I had no doubt what I wanted to do. Watching Barry play was what you did on a Saturday.'

John thinks long and hard when asked whether he'd like to play in this day and age before musing: 'I don't know but I think I would. I would have to play rugby. I wouldn't enjoy too much rugby and am glad I played at my time. Some people still seem to have long careers. Brian O'Driscoll is the classic example.

'I wouldn't say it's a better game today, I would say it's different. I wouldn't have played rugby at any other time. I think I was blessed to play it when I did. I say that purely from the point of view of the teams I played in, the individuals I played alongside, like Slattery, Duggan, Moss Keane; it was just a wonderful time to play rugby and I wouldn't want to have played it before then or later.

'Professional rugby is different. But if you want to play it, I think Ireland is the place to do so. One of the things that is quite difficult is the number of games they play nowadays, games of high intensity. Now I played a lot of rugby, but a lot of it was not of high intensity. That came in your internationals, your inter-pro matches and a few club matches but there were an awful lot of club matches that were not high intensity. If you're playing in Ireland, where it's all tied into the IRFU, the players are quite well looked after. In other countries, you have different agendas between the international team and your club and I believe some of the players in the English Premiership end up playing too many matches. In my day, if I couldn't play, I didn't play and that was it and there were no recriminations. I knew there was a certain amount of rugby that was key and I could concentrate on that. I did not want to play thirty-five or forty high intensity games per season, whether I was paid for it or not, or I was doing anything else or not. That wouldn't have suited me. And that is why Ireland must be one of the best places to play professional rugby – and also because the provinces do well in the Heineken Cup and the Celtic League and so on.'

Nowadays, John concentrates his efforts on the Exiles

set-up, a role that Barry undertook in the early days. He is more heavily involved in the medical side of rugby and has worked with the International Board in that area. Gary O'Driscoll, doctor to the Arsenal Football Club, a role he fulfilled earlier with the Irish rugby team, is Barry's son and all are concerned with the physical demands imposed by the professional game. Because England and France on this side of the world and the major southern hemisphere countries on the other have much larger playing numbers from which to draw, there appears to be an ever-increasing view that Irish rugby should consider following in Jack Charlton's footsteps with the Irish football team back in the 1990s and take on board players who have only the slightest connection with this country. This is not how John O'Driscoll and his colleagues on the IRFU would describe his *raison d'être*, but certainly they are all keeping a very watchful eye out for young players with close Irish links.

'When I coached the Exiles we actually played in the inter-provincial championship and provided quite a few players to Ireland, but that was never going to continue when professional rugby came in,' says John. 'Now, it's under-18s, 19s, 20s. We have a very strong network in Britain. The nature of rugby is that for the inter-provincial sides you need a certain number of new players every year and there are so many people in Britain of Irish origin that we've got to look at that. Next year, we will be playing in the under-18 and 19 inter-pro championship, we are very active and I think that's important. We have a professional recruitment officer, Mark Blair. We are playing more and more matches away from London, some in the Midlands, and also have training camps. We have to give those with a strong Irish background the opportunity to be seen and hopefully it will create more provincial and international players. I watch a fair few matches and people report back. We have a spotter's network, if you like, and we're building that up further.'

You can take the O'Driscolls out of Ireland but you certainly cannot take Ireland out of the O'Driscolls!

ULTAN AND DONNCHA O'CALLAGHAN

Body on fire, head in the fridge, that was O'Callaghan.

Lawrence Dallaglio describes Donncha O'Callaghan's mindset in the 2011 Ireland–England game

The O'Callaghans of Bishopstown, Cork, have established a well-deserved reputation as one of the finest rugby families in the land – and one of the most entertaining! Donncha, holder of seventy-two Irish caps at the end of the 2011 RBS Six Nations Championship along with two Heineken Cup medals, is the best known, but that doesn't mean he has things all his own way where his mum, Marie, brothers Eddie, Ultan and Emmett, and sister Eimear are concerned.

They are all hugely proud of this massive (6 ft 6 inch, 17½ stone) hulk of a man. It is just that they and everyone who knows Donncha need to be wary where this practical joker and prankster are concerned. Only too well aware of this, early in 2010 his Munster and Ireland team-mate and close friend Paul O'Connell decided to get his retaliation in first. Invited to appear on the *Late Late Show*, O'Connell informed the nation with as straight a face as he could manage: 'I got around 500 points in the Leaving Cert – that would be about 410 points more than Donncha O'Callaghan.' And he went on: 'He had a great tan [on his wedding day a few days before Christmas] considering he hadn't been away. You see, he uses sunbeds.'

Paulie, however, was making himself a hostage to fortune. Donncha was waiting in the long grass and when he got his chance a few months later, he told Ryan Tubridy and the country at large that 'it took eighty-five minutes to do Paul O'Connell's make-up when he was on the *Late Late*'. And there was more. After the births within a few months of each other in 2010 of Sophie O'Callaghan and Paddy O'Connell, Donncha revealed just what Paul thought of his new arrival: 'Paddy O'Connell can drink more milk than any other child, Paddy's leg length is off the chart, Paddy is actually very advanced. Typical, Paul has to make everything competitive.'

When two of Ireland's most celebrated sportsmen are able to go on the *Late Late Show* and slag each other off like this, you can only imagine what they're like when they get together with the rest of their team-mates. Nobody, no matter how famous, escapes and it is often a test of a man's mettle whether he can take this kind of stuff and give it back in good measure. Although New Zealand's Doug Howlett was already a superstar when he arrived in Munster, he quickly learned that reputations meant nothing in that particular milieu. It was the way in which he fed into what could be loosely called 'a system' that enabled him to become a huge success on and off the pitch.

* * *

DONNCHA O'CALLAGHAN and his three brothers were fortunate enough to grow up in an area of Cork that had Highfield Rugby Club just over the wall on one side of the house and Bishopstown GAA club a few hundred yards up the road. The boys recall a time when there was hardly any television and it was a case of making their own fun, whether it was playing games or doing the things that all kids do. The older ones looked after the younger siblings and that is one reason why Ultan and Donncha, between whom there is an eight-year gap, always had a special bond.

'We'd get up on a Saturday morning, have breakfast, make our way up to Bishopstown GAA club for ten o'clock training until a quarter past eleven, then hop over the ditch to Highfield for rugby training around half-eleven and after that it was on to Wilton or Glasheen or wherever for soccer,' Ultan explains. 'I was never any good at the soccer, so I was always put in goal, but Eddie and Emmett were handy and Donncha and Eimear came floating along with us. Sunday was then spent going to watch whatever game that was on around the city.

'We went to school at Cólaiste an Spriod Naomh where we were given a great love of sport through the teachers. One of the biggest influences on us was Don Lynch, a nephew of Jack Lynch. He was a great GAA man and he always had you trying your hardest on and off the pitch, in your school work and having respect for your parents and that kind of thing.

'Eddie and I went on to Bishopstown Community School and around this time our father passed away. He was forty years of age, he had a massive heart attack, and Mum was left to raise five young kids on a widow's pension at the age of thirty-six. Donncha and I share the same birthday, he was five and I was thirteen when Dad died.

'But, you know, it brought us together very tightly as a family. Eddie and I left school early at Inter Cert and went into an apprenticeship in the plastering business. It was very different then, it was all about getting out and providing, but there was also plenty of time for leisure and sport and that is where we got our release.

'It was tough at home, you can't go easily from having your dad and then being without him. It meant that we valued everything we had in each other, in health, and lived in the present. A sense of humour was a big part of it, learning to look and laugh at each other, and find the funny side to things. At school, at home, I found we had good people around us – the extended family, the neighbours, all were outstanding to Mum and us as a young family. The positive role models were people in Bishopstown GAA club and Highfield Rugby Club, people like Pat McDonnell, Don Lynch, Ted Stack at Highfield, huge men who taught us the value of sport and how you live your life: you play hard, you play with respect, you play with honesty, you give your all but it's your discipline, your respect for one another and for the referee that carries you through.

'There were times at home when we lost the run of ourselves. Mum would sit down with us and the threat always was, I'll tell Ted Stack or I'll tell Pat McDonnell, and you won't be allowed to play rugby or football or soccer. We enjoyed each other's company and of course the younger ones were pawned off as we used to call it on the rest of us – Eddie would be stuck with Eimear and I'd be stuck with Donncha. I would have to get him dressed and get him up to the GAA club or to Highfield and he was with me from eight years of age.'

As Ultan reached his late teens, he was making a serious mark on the rugby pitch. At seventeen, he partnered Eddie Halvey, who later played for Ireland, in the Munster Youths second-row, and played senior at Highfield with Shay Fahy at No. 8 and George O'Sullivan at out-half – with Donncha as the sand boy!

'Donncha looks back on those days as his apprenticeship,' says Ultan. 'He was watching it all, especially the rugby, he was a big young fella, he was coming on with the sand, he was in the dressing-room and at training sessions and a lot of that washed off on him.

'Then the AIL came along at a time when I was also playing for Ireland 21s, was captain of Munster 20s and I had this aspiration to play at the highest possible level. Highfield lost out to Young Munster in a play-off to get into the AIL in 1989; Miko [Benson] had a drop kick for them late on that sailed over like a wet duck. That left Highfield confined to the old Munster Senior League.

'With the arrival of the AIL, I was being approached by other clubs. Ray Coughlan, a Highfield man, was outstanding. He told me that to be a good player you have to be around good players and as much as it upset all of us, the right thing to do was to move and spread your wings and not be the big fish in a small pond. So I went down the road to Cork Con and never regretted a day of it. I spent the best sixteen years of my life down there. It was the early fuel of the AIL that turned us into the animal that we now see – the machine of Munster rugby. Donncha came with me, Emmett stayed with Highfield and we used to have great banter about it.

'My profile was out there and they were looking into the family to see who else was there. Emmett was happy where he was, Eddie was only a social player, but people like Garrett Fitzgerald and Matt Foley in Christians saw potential in Donncha, a lazy potential as Donncha calls it. He was the same height and size then as now with all the puppy fat on to that. When he was about fifteen and a half or sixteen, CBC approached Mum. I remember Matt chatting to her and putting the case – how they saw potential and they'd like him to realise that at Christians both on the academic side as well as pushing him on to Munster Schools and maybe Irish Schools as well.'

Donncha had just completed his Inter Cert at Bishopstown Community School and played Munster Youths out of Highfield. The wily Foley and Fitzgerald were shrewd in their judgement. Donncha O'Callaghan was on his way to greatness as a world-class second-row forward and one of the most charismatic characters in the game.

'Up to then, Donncha had huge potential but he wasn't fulfilling it,' Ultan recalls. 'Garrett Fitzgerald, Pakie Derham and Donal Daly had big influences on him. He told me that he wanted to play for Munster Schools and have a pop at the Irish team but that he needed me to help him with a strength and weights programme and nutrition. He knew he had to start getting fitter and stronger. I told him there was no easy way and he fell in with me. I was working off Dave Mahedy's Munster training programme and he joined me in the gym, in the running programmes and the nutrition and transformed himself. When he went into pre-season training, he was a fit, lean machine and he has gone at every session ever since in the same way. I often said to him, "Donncha, we may not be the most skilful, we may not be the most graceful on the pitch, but when it comes to rugby, it's about graft and putting your body on the line and not shying away. If you can let your work rate and your honesty come through, selectors and coaches will always see it. You need your ball players, your x-factor, but without the work horses, that x-factor can't be realised." We saw those virtues in Donncha in the Ireland-England game this year when he put in more tackles than any other player on the field.

'Donncha had two and a half years at Christians and he blew the roof off the place. He became a Munster and an Irish schoolboy and Irish under-19 and won a World Cup [in 1998] with Declan Kidney, Brian O'Driscoll and Paddy Wallace. He went straight into Declan's Munster squad along with Micko, Paulie, Marcus, Jerry … there was a whole generation at the time. This would have been 1997, 1998, 1999, 2000, and he's travelling in the car with me and we're going to play inter-provincial games, he's on the training squad and playing AIL with Cork Con. Con would have been a place with that sense of expectation and drive and ambition. We had a golden spell when we were still playing with Munster and in the AIL you'd have 6,000 to 8,000 at a Shannon–Garryowen or Con–Cookies [Young Munster] game.

'So it was a great environment for Donncha to come into and while he had a reputation to live up to, it wasn't made easy for him in Con. Ken Murphy and Donal Sheehan were the second-rows that the coaches Pakie [Derham] and Brads [Michael Bradley] went with, and Donncha of course was growling about it and I was the captain ... we'd go down on a Tuesday and knock seven bells out of each other on the pitch and sit down and pick the team afterwards. I'd have to tell him on the way home that he wasn't in and he'd let rip and he'd let rip again when we got home. Mum would be like, "Would you ever stop, the two of you." That would go on for all of that night and the next day you would have all picture, no sound, and then Thursday he would go and pull the head off Ken and Donal at training.

'But it led to everything we achieved on the Saturday because we got so much value from him for the twenty, twenty-five minutes that he'd spend on the pitch. We won the AIL in 1999. I had been around from 1992/1993 and the quality of players at the time was huge. It's hard to describe it. You had Pat O'Hara, Paul Collins, Ger Earls, Ger Clohessy, Mick Copley, Shay Fahy, Len Dinneen, Ben Cronin, Barry Howell, Dave Corkery, Eddie Halvey ... it was hell for leather when we went to a Munster session – and whoever got in for the first game usually held the jersey. And then you were within touching distance of an Irish jersey. I played a few Heineken Cup games and in lots of Probables and Possibles trials but it never came my way. But it was a different set-up – you had selectors, and who you were and where you came from was very important ... that's why I wanted Donncha to pursue the Christians route and the traditional way of doing things and I think it served him well.

'I have so much respect for Declan Kidney. He came in as Munster coach and sat me down and said, "You're twenty-eight and have taken out a mortgage and I want to offer you a contract." And my exact words back were, "Thanks very much Declan, but I'm on the other side of it now, I have a good job, I'm engaged." You must remember none of us thought professional rugby would last beyond a couple of years. Anyone you went to, Tommy [Kiernan], Noisy [Murphy], they were, like, caution, caution, and that caution was right because we never envisaged the animal that it has become.

'I became a part-time player … I was getting up at 6 a.m. and training with the other part-timers, Seán McCahill, Kenny Murphy, Jason Holland, Terry Kingston, that transition group as we used to call it, until about half-seven, then we got into the work clothes and we'd meet again at half-five. We then went to club training – it was cuckoo stuff even if I have no regrets about it. Anthony Foley was the upcoming, younger model as an eight and we supported each other, but I never gave him anything easy so that he'd fight for it in training. He was always a natural, the bedrock that everything was built on. I contributed as much as I could on the training pitch when there were injuries and when fellas had doubts and that's what made Munster what it is.

'Donncha was watching all of this and the way I always channelled the hurt and the bitterness in a positive way. He thought I should have got more, but I told him that half-two on Saturday is all that matters. Great things were happening around that time, there was a great synergy in all the clubs. We were building the identity of Munster and what we built from 1996 up to 2000 was awesome as we went from being an amateur outfit almost to European Cup champions.

'It was then that we older fellas needed to step off the stage and leave the younger lads to take over. That's where the new energy came from, your Donnchas, Mickos, Pauls, Marcuses, Jerrys, Johns, Anthonys, your Nialls and Declans … there was never any bit of bitterness or upset or hurt. Killian Keane was another guy in the same situation and he and I got a call up to the Barbarians. We played the Combined Services and it was a nice one to get in on before you exited the stage.'

Ultan quit plastering to become a company representative, before taking a Rugby Development Officer position with the IRFU for South Munster. Promotion followed to Provincial Development Manager, and now he is head of the Munster rugby domestic department, responsible for everything outside of the professional game.

* * *

DONNCHA'S CAREER was really taking off in the early days of the new millennium at a time when the relationship between the brothers was becoming deeper and closer. 'He began confiding in me on some of the deeper issues within him,' says Ultan. 'He was pushing hard for the Munster senior jersey but Gaillimh [Mick Galwey] was there, John Langford, Micko, Paul; in other words, five quality guys going for two jerseys. He came on for a game against Castres and was pulled off very quickly. I remember talking afterwards to Niall [O'Donovan] and Anthony [Foley]. Anthony said he could have got hurt because he was a boy playing against men and that was not good for him. Someone was going to do him. He had the game but not the frame or the bulk ... he was a young twenty-one-year-old against a grizzly bear Castres pack.

'Donncha used that to fuel the bitterness and the hurt that made him think: "I will never again be in a position that I don't have the raw materials of the size and the strength." He just became bordering on obsessive and what you now see is the ultra pro ... absolutely meticulous. He went under Liam Hennessy's wing and blossomed into the size of animal that you see today.

'We went from being brothers to being more than that. You had to manage his level of expectation – he'd say, "Ultan, I know I'm improving, I know I'm putting in the work but do Declan and Eddie O'Sullivan see that?" You're trying to get him to channel that frustration to see if he can do better ... it ends up creating that drive that meant he wasn't happy just to be on the Munster and Ireland bench. His aspirations were always higher and it's still going on to this day. We still analyse the game, we talk about the emotional side of the thing, the game that goes on outside of the game, that you have the balance of life right, and it's got to the stage that younger people are coming to him. He takes his job – and that's what it is – very, very seriously.'

Because of so many stories about Donncha's pranks, such as the time he enticed a row of ducks into a Munster team room with unfortunate results (let's say, he spent much of the afternoon cleaning up after them), supposedly taking a lobster for a walk on a leash during one of his first overseas jaunts or allegedly pulling down Alistair Campbell's tracksuit bottoms during the 2005 Lions tour, there was a notion that he didn't take the game seriously enough. And when he proposed to continue playing on in a game in Cardiff in 2006 in a pair of red underpants, having lost his shorts, that view intensified still further. Donncha explains his standpoint: 'It was not a lark or anything like that, it was a bloody important point in a bloody important match. I feared the referee would play on without me. I remember Paulie once losing both front teeth and carrying on to the next line-out, so I thought if he can do it without teeth, I can do it without shorts. I'm embarrassed about it and wish it hadn't happened and hadn't been shown everywhere. It's not the image I want to project, not because I'm shy, but because I'm a serious professional. People will say that I mess around a bit, but when I get out on the pitch, I like to think I want it as much as Paulie.'

* * *

DONNCHA O'CALLAGHAN made his international debut against Wales in 2003 and apart from interruptions caused by injury, has been a regular ever since. He was an integral part of the Irish side that completed the Grand Slam for the first time in sixty-one years in Cardiff in 2009 and, of course, was central to Ireland's four Triple Crown successes in the same decade. He has two Heineken Cup winners' medals and toured with the Lions in New Zealand in 2005 and South Africa four years later. The enormous respect in which Donncha was held on the second of those tours was demonstrated by his appointment as captain of the side that defeated the Southern Kings.

'The team will be captained by a proud Munsterman, Donncha O'Callaghan, an experienced Lion and very popular Lions tourist,' said head Lions coach, Ian McGeechan, in announcing the decision. 'This will be his tenth Lions match including two Tests in New Zealand during the 2005 tour.'

Donncha was past his thirty-first birthday when his longevity in the game was further recognised by a new three-year contract that he signed with the IRFU in November 2010. At the time, he clearly showed where his loyalty and heart lay as he pointed out that 'as players, we are looked after so well by the national and provincial management teams and I feel incredibly privileged to be able to play the sport I love for Munster and Ireland. Munster is my home province and the decision to continue here was an easy one when you consider the standard of players in the squad and the incredible support I have received from the fans and my family.'

Tony McGahan, his 'boss' at Munster, put it in a nutshell when stating: 'This is a massive boost for Munster given the strong interest in Donncha from overseas clubs with far greater financial resources than Munster. It's a very encouraging sign for younger players to see a player of his calibre agreeing a new deal.' The 2011 Six Nations Championship proved a big disappointment for an Irish team clearly capable of landing a second Grand Slam in three years; instead they had to settle for mid-table. Early in the campaign, they conceded a very high ratio of penalties and Donncha was perceived as one of the culprits. Maybe, maybe not, but when it came to the crunch match, England's arrival at the Aviva Stadium in Lansdowne Road in search of a Grand Slam, Donncha and his team-mates were waiting and ready. As Ultan pointed out, he was immense that day, so much so that Lawrence Dallaglio, who knew what it was to be part of an English Grand Slam-winning side in the old stadium, put his performance something like this: 'We used to have a saying when I played, "body on fire, head in the fridge",' he wrote of the ideal mental attitude required of a top player on a big day. 'The difference in the mentality of both teams was perfectly demonstrated in the performance of Donncha O'Callaghan. He went in search of work, stood in the line of countless England ball carriers and knocked them each time. In the rucks, he was always making a nuisance of himself, driving through, slowing up the ball and unrelentingly disciplined. He has given silly penalties away but that wasn't going to happen here – body on fire, head in the fridge, that was O'Callaghan.'

* * *

PERHAPS AS A result of his father passing away when he was only five, Donncha has a very special relationship with his mother Marie, while Ultan also acknowledges that 'when you have three brothers and a sister and an extended family, the craic was always what lifted us. We were brought up in a house where there was always fun and we would be trying to put one over on each other. Donncha was always able to have a finger on the pulse of how things were, he could turn something serious into a laugh and that is a gift. In his twenties, he did find it a bit frustrating being described as a joker and I told him, "That's who you are and don't change while letting it be known that you train harder and prepare better than any other professional."

'Some of the top coaches in the world like Ian McGeechan and Graham Henry were blown away by the stuff that Donncha brought to fellow internationals. Martin Johnson also excelled in preparation and intensity, Muhammad Ali stuff, and they are people who know the game. You have to stay true to yourself and he has now got to the stage where he has the balance right. He goes on the *Late Late Show* and gets it just right. The most beautiful thing I could say about Donncha is that he's the same with the lads, with mom, with us, as he was with Ryan Tubridy that night and that is Donncha. Within the seriousness, he's having the craic. While on that show, he discussed all the fun things but he also discussed Haiti, UNICEF and got across what's dear to him.

'In every way, we are very proud of him. Success hasn't changed him, he will come to christenings, parties, Chuckies [a children's activity centre] … he's an outstanding, beautiful brother and a better friend. We speak our minds to each other but we have never fallen out. If our father had only lived to see him achieve so much … he has played for Munster, he has played for Ireland, he has played for the Lions, he has shaken hands with the Queen, he has met Nelson Mandela and all the top brass everywhere … and mom met Prince William during the Lions tour in New Zealand in 2005 and dined with him.'

Donncha and his girlfriend Jenny Harte (now his wife), stayed on in South Africa for a couple of weeks after the Lions tour in 2009. Brother Ultan and his wife Carol (they now have five children: Alice, Ted, Maisie, Miah and Archie) honeymooned there in 2000 and on their return discussed the many contrasting aspects of that wonderful country. What he witnessed and experienced was an inspiration for Donncha, who had read about the life and times of Nelson Mandela, and he and Jenny took the opportunity to examine and see South Africa for themselves. Having displayed his concern for those confined to life in the townships and for whom there seemed to be precious little future, he was approached by UNICEF to act as one of their ambassadors. He was more than happy to oblige and when invited to Haiti to meet the victims of the appalling January 2010 earthquake and help to rebuild their morale, he responded with typically wholehearted enthusiasm. What he encountered had much the same impact on him as South Africa. While it was a harrowing sight to say the least, there were also many encouraging signs, not least that the kids had sporting activities to occupy their minds. 'The chance that these children are getting to play sport and enjoy themselves is so important for their health and well-being,' said Donncha at the time. 'It gives them a chance to learn so many life lessons. In our midst could have been a future Olympic medallist or a Lionel Messi. You can tell that these kids love their sport and being in school, while also understanding their fears for the future. One of the most impressive places I visited was Notre Dame de l'Assomption School to take part in the special sports programme set up for the 6,000 children living in the nearby camp. My only regret is that we didn't have the capacity to provide this programme for every child.

'One of the saddest things is that they will probably never know the number of children killed in the earthquake. But what we do know, and an issue UNICEF is working to address every day, is that there are 800,000 children living in tents in Port au Prince and 330,000 similarly affected outside the capital. Meeting families living in these unthinkable conditions is so difficult. They bear their fate with such dignity and fortitude. They are truly remarkable.'

While in Haiti, Donncha stayed in Camp Charlie with most of the UNICEF staff. He had previously camped as an eleven-year-old, but this time had to squeeze his towering frame into a 2 by 2 metre tent for the week's visit. He was happy to do so, recounting how 'sitting at dinner and watching staff from all over the world chat, each and every one committed to building the best possible future for Haiti's children, is a powerful memory that I took away with me. It was truly humbling to speak with the children and certainly I was nowhere as focused as them at that age.'

Appropriately, he also tried out his fathering skills at the baby tent in the camp which was set up for mothers of newborn babies. Little did he know how useful they would become in a short but traumatic few days! 'When I arrived in New York on the way home, I noticed there were two missed calls from Jenny. Then there was a text telling me to call as quickly as possible with the classic advice of don't panic, but of course that's exactly what I did. It was some shock for she was five weeks early, but it was still game on and I was wondering how I could possibly get to Cork in time. The signs were positive when the pilot came on to say that the wind was at our backs and we'd be in fifteen minutes ahead of schedule and as it happened, Jenny had everything under control and I got there with two hours to spare.'

* * *

AND FITTINGLY, THE last word to Donners – on Paulie!

'He is just jealous – he has no hair, no tan, no teeth. Look at the two of us and it's clear who the better second-row is – better-looking I should say.'

RAY AND PHELIM McLOUGHLIN

Ray was incredible – a man of supreme rugby
knowledge.

Lions and Welsh flanker, John Taylor

BALLINASLOE ISN'T exactly a hotbed of rugby. True, the town's
rugby club combined with Athlone to form the Buccaneers in
the glory years of the All-Ireland League through the 1990s
and much of the new millennium, to test the very best that the
rest of the country could offer. However, it is for Gaelic games
and especially hurling that the town is best known in a sporting
context and yet, in brothers Ray and Phelim McLoughlin, it
boasts two of the most significant figures in Irish rugby.

Phelim has one international cap to his credit and also
distinguished himself in the Connacht jersey for many years
before helping to build the Exiles into a formidable force and
a valuable source of players to a succession of Irish teams.
Ray earned for himself a reputation as one of rugby's greatest
ever prop forwards and a deep and shrewd reader of the
game's many intricacies. Although he has now passed his
seventy-second birthday, he is as interested as ever in where
the modern game is going and especially how the area in

which he and Phelim specialised is threatening the game's very well-being – the set scrum.

'The thing I don't like about rugby today is that some of the laws are ridiculous,' Ray maintains. 'So many kickable penalties are awarded for subjective judgements … referees have to decide, is the prop straight or not, is he going in at an angle or not. I see referees waving about what props did when they cannot know who is doing what. I wouldn't know, so how the hell can they know? The fact that there are laws requiring subjective judgements by referees who have no chance of knowing … what would Alain Rolland know about a prop forward? He has never been there.

'But it's not their fault. It's the fault of the laws. They are forcing the referees to make subjective judgements. Points are being scored from subjective judgements and it's ridiculous. I think it was Jamie Heaslip who was penalised in a recent Ireland–France game for not rolling away. But he was pinned, he could not move. It's a farce that some matches are decided by penalties and it's really a penalty contest for much of the time.

'In the case of the scrum, there should be no kickable offence. If three scrums collapse and the referee cannot decide what's what, he should toss a coin and then give a kick to touch for whoever wins the toss. I mean that. What is better? Basically, what the toss of the coin would mean is that the referee cannot judge – at all – what's happening, so he tosses a coin. Whoever is infringing knows there is a 50–50 chance they are going to be penalised – but not by a kick at goal. It doesn't deserve getting three points.

'I will give you an example. One of the rules is that you must have a straight back at scrum time. There is no such thing as a straight back, especially if there is another guy trying to bend your neck in. A tighthead prop like John Hayes has no chance of straightening a scrum and not being turned-in. There's a natural turn-in force because of the alignment of the heads. The guy playing tighthead prop has two choices if you are being turned-in, and that is to push from your left or pull from your right. There is nothing to push off, there is no wall there. The way you pull is, you lock the scrum, you put your arm outside the loosehead and hold it there. But the referees interpret that as trying to bring the scrum down. It's absolutely ridiculous and all this stuff about crouch, pause, engage and so on is killing the game.

'The guys making these laws ... I don't know why the Syd Millars of this world don't get stuck into it. The guys making these laws don't know anything about the mechanics of the scrum. It's a game within a game, the whole refereeing stuff. I don't blame the referees, I blame the laws.'

This is no ordinary guy talking. Ray McLoughlin, Ireland captain and two times Lion and long regarded as one of the greatest practitioners of the front row art that rugby has ever known, is discussing the influence of the modern laws and their interpretation by referees who have never packed down in a scrum in their lives. The idea of not awarding shots at goal for alleged scrummaging infringements will strike a chord with the majority of rugby fans, although tossing a coin to settle several of the issues involved will assuredly meet with a mixed reaction. However, when it's a man of Ray McLoughlin's stature expressing these views, the International Rugby Board simply has to sit up and take notice. He has always been recognised as a very wise philosopher on the game of rugby and few have earned a greater level of respect over the years. Those eminent historians of Irish rugby, Ned Van Esbeck and Sean Diffley, were just two of his many admirers. Ned wrote that 'McLoughlin's approach would be totally in accord with the game as it's played today and perhaps his greatest accomplishment is that he helped to prepare the way for many of the traumatic changes that followed in the wake of his leadership.' Sean was similarly effusive as he contended that Ray 'succeeded brilliantly in leaving behind a blueprint that succeeding captains would ignore at their peril ... he was the individual who changed the direction of the Irish game and set it, at international level, on the right path'. John Reason, a British rugby writer not exactly remembered for a love of all things Irish, was a huge fan of Ray McLoughlin, and in his fine book, *The Victorious Lions*, published after the 1971 tour of New Zealand, observed: 'McLoughlin not only had great strength but also great scrummaging technique and intelligence to go with it. Indeed, his intelligence quota had earned him such a reputation as a brain among the Lions that he was known to them as Sir John Wilder after the tycoon in the television series called *The Power Game*. He was almost never called Ray – either Sir John or Wilder. He was a combative man, too, and liked nothing better than to meet people who thought they could beat him at the art of propping.'

* * *

IT WOULD BE fair to state that Raymond John McLoughlin did not quite envisage earning such a reputation as he grew up in the GAA stronghold that was his native Ballinasloe. He and brothers Phelim and Colm loved sport from an early age, encouraged by their father who was a social welfare officer, but as Ray tells it, 'He also did about four part-time jobs to keep us going.' There are also two girls in the family, Muire and Enda, who now live respectively in Galway and Kinvara. Colm, who has resided for many years in Dubai, is today closely identified with the Dubai international tennis tournament that the Duty Free shop sponsors every year.

The McLoughlins dabbled in sport from an early age and especially hurling and football, winning minor championship medals and earning trials for the county. Once they moved on to Garbally College and took up rugby, that became the immediate priority. Ray's rugby career began in the early 1950s in the backs before he moved to the back row and he played on Connacht Schools' teams that beat Leinster and Munster.

Phelim McLoughlin is also one of the best-known and respected rugby personalities in Ireland even though he has not lived in this country for many years. He wasn't all that active on the rugby front in his earlier days in Ballinasloe but, on going to university in Newcastle, showed distinct promise as a tough scrummaging prop and quickly settled down there, playing for the Northern club and Northumberland. His native province was also well aware of his prowess and he made his first appearance in the Connacht jersey in 1969. As always, it was a bit of a struggle for the western province and after one particularly salutary lesson at Ravenhill at the hands of Ulster, a local writer noted that Connacht players 'were drawn from London, Newcastle, Manchester and Dublin with a little sprinkling of home-based lads'.

Undaunted, Phelim continued to catch the eye until the Irish selectors gave him the call for the game against Australia at Lansdowne Road in January 1976. Ollie Campbell and John Robbie were other new caps that day, but Australia won 20–10 and Phelim was never picked again. However, his love of the game was palpable as he soldiered on well into his thirties and later worked tirelessly on behalf of Irishmen playing in the UK. He was involved from the outset in the formation of the Irish Exiles in 1989 and Phelim and his allies were successful to the extent that the Exiles actually fielded a fine side in the inter-provincial championship for a few years from 1992. This in turn led to the selection for Ireland over the years of people of the calibre of Jim Staples, Simon Geoghegan, Rob Saunders and Gary Halpin, while eleven Exiles have been capped since 1989. And when it came to speaking up for his native province, Phelim is believed to have been the only non-Connacht member of the IRFU committee to support their cause when their very future was just about safeguarded at a meeting in 2003. He served as the Exiles' representative on the IRFU committee for ten years, a task now performed by John O'Driscoll, a man also featured in these pages.

* * *

THE GOOD days were few and far between but the pride in the Connacht jersey never waned. The McLoughlin brothers did their fair share and Ray's career spanned seventeen years, beginning in 1958. In 1966, he was a member of a side that included eight internationals (Johnny Dooley, Dickie Roche, Mick Molloy, P.J. Dwyer, Mick Leahy, Éamonn Maguire and Locky Butler were the others), even though there was a widely held view that Connacht players were at a serious disadvantage because they did not have an Irish team selector.

'I don't think there was ever any actual bias,' says Ray. 'The selectors were just amateurs in those days. They got confidence in guys they saw a lot of. But they would never see the Connacht guys. The fact that I was playing in Dublin all the time with UCD, the Universities against Leinster and of course with Connacht in the inter-pros meant that coming from Connacht wasn't any disadvantage to me. Maybe it was different for the guys playing down in Galway because they wouldn't be seen as much.

'I was one of the nine new caps against England at Twickenham in 1962. We lost 16–0 and quite a few never got a second game. It wasn't a very auspicious debut to say the least. I remember how naïve we were. In those days the prop forwards could do what they liked. There were no referees stopping you from bringing the scrum down, you could bury a guy's nose in the mud all day and you wouldn't be pulled. I had a reputation as a tighthead prop for doing a fair bit of damage. Going into one match, Noel Murphy came up to me and said, "Now, Ray, none of that old stuff today, these guys are all very tough", so I went in almost intimidated from doing what I would normally do. Having lost the match but been given a second chance, I didn't listen to that kind of advice any more.

'We went out against England and shure, Jaysus, it was ten minutes before we adjusted to being in a match at all. It was at the extreme end of amateurism, if you like, although it's with great amusement I look back on all of that because things are so different now. We had absolutely no preparation before the matches. We would meet on the Friday at lunchtime in the Shelbourne Hotel. There would be a team meeting at 2 o'clock and the players would go in along with the five selectors and the three sub-selectors and they'd all give their view as to how the match would be played. So we had eight different views twenty-four hours before the match. We were supposed to be out in Belvedere at 3 o'clock, but by the time all the selectors had given their views which left everyone totally confused, it would be twenty-past three, and our captain Bill Mulcahy would say, "Lads, we better get out and do a bit of training." So we'd go out to Belvedere, run around the field a couple of times, have a couple of scrums and line-outs, get into the showers, soap ourselves down, sing *Ireland Boys Hurrah*, go back to the hotel, go to the pictures that night and wake up in the morning and meet drunken guys from the night before telling us how to play the match. There was no place for us to hide. There were fellas still there drinking from the night before, telling you how to play the match, and what an eejit you were and you shouldn't be on the team or whatever.

'The only chance we had of getting our heads together was the hour before the match. Even then you would be called out for a photograph. Now Bill Mulcahy was a good captain, but he had no chance with that and wouldn't be offensive to the selectors. When I was captain later, I threw them all out because I said I wouldn't take the job otherwise. It was ridiculous.

'I was appointed captain in 1965 and the first thing I insisted on was I didn't want any selectors or sub-selectors at the team meetings. Number two, there would be no pictures on the Friday night, we wanted a room in the Shelbourne to spend a few hours together trying to prepare for the matches. Number three, I wanted us out of the hotel on the Saturday morning. That was a total distraction. Instead, we went to the Royal Marine Hotel in Dun Laoghaire, no selectors or committee people on the bus and if there were, they could not speak. We would have our team meeting, we would walk the pier and the main thing was to get the guys thinking of what they were going to do. They call it visualisation these days. We went to the dressing-room an hour and a half before the kick-off and had the pictures straightaway.

'At the start, all of this caused consternation in the IRFU. Jack Coffey, a very nice man, was one of the selectors if not the chairman at the time, and he came to me and said, "Ray, we can't have this, it's all part of the international game, my dear boy." Now he was a really nice man so when he said that, he wasn't being condescending or anything. It was just his style. So, I said, "Jack, fair enough, get another captain." Charlie Harte, a Connachtman, was president of the IRFU at the time, and came to me to ask what this was all about. I told him, "It's very simple, I just won't be captain unless that's the way it is." He went back and, fair dues, normally the president had no control over the selectors but the bottom line was, they gave me all I wanted.

'As captain, I'd tell the players, there are ten line-out calls, six signals in the scrums, five things you can do here, four things you can do there. If you go out on the field and have a line-out fifteen yards from the line, you don't want to be running through all the options. If you go out without having practised that, you have to search for the options that relate to a line-out fifteen yards from the line. So my view was that you practised it in your head and figured out what is relevant there. And if you practised that, and if there was such a situation, only the relevant things came to mind – you didn't have forty-eight different things to sift through to discover what was relevant. I got guys to respect their own responsibilities, each one to visualise their options on the field, think of the things you should consider at that point and get to the stage that when it happened, it came automatically.

'During the team meetings we gave a lot of thought to defensive options, attacking options and so on. At the time, it was very easy to do because we had some very good players with lots of nous – like Tom Kiernan, Noel Murphy, Mick Doyle, Ronnie Lamont, Kevin Flynn, Mike Gibson, Roger Young. You could hardly get guys who were better switched on. Also, my view was don't try and force guys to do things they're not happy with. So we would talk through the kind of defensive set-up for this and that and what kind of attacking options we had. We would kick it around and eventually arrive at a consensus and we would call it something and go at that. It took a lot of time. We had signals for all of these things and went out in a position to call things that everybody recognised for what they were and to which everybody was tuned in to play whatever part they were called upon to play. So it was all very straightforward even though people called it revolutionary at the time. But it's only kid's stuff compared with today.'

Not everybody agreed with McLoughlin's way of doing things. However, among his many admirers was another legend of the Irish game, Willie John McBride, who in his autobiography wrote: 'He could have been a revolutionary and the game not alone in Ireland but in general terms owes a debt to Ray McLoughlin that will never be repaid. His contribution was inestimable, yet, like many another visionary, he paid the price of rejection at a time when he had so much to give as a captain and a leader. From the outset, he had his critics and they were not all administrators. There were players who found the task of total commitment beyond their mental and physical capacities. I don't argue that all McLoughlin's theories were correct but I am absolutely sure that the basic premise of his methods and approach were right. Time and events have proved him to have been correct in what matters most, the basic philosophy applicable to international rugby. He altered things beyond recall – that is his monument.'

* * *

RAY MCLOUGHLIN is not one of those who dwells in the past and believes rugby was a greater game in his time. Far from it, in fact. 'It's much better watching today,' he insists. 'From my time, I remember some good matches but also some awful matches as well. Take Ireland vs England, Lansdowne Road, 1963. Richard Sharp was playing out-half for England and the previous year he had run riot in my first cap at Twickenham, so my job was to collapse the scrum. I was given instructions – collapse the scrum. It was a mucky day and England hardly ever got the ball. It was a nil-all draw. We were rolling around in the mud all day, I kept burying my man in the scrum and that was my job done. Nowadays you wouldn't be allowed to do that. It was great fun for us but for the crowd it must have been awful.

'As I've said, there are things about the game today that I don't like, but it has moved on, it's different and it's professional. Some of the guys I played with claim it was much better the way it was but that's a load of crap. We had better times maybe. The Lions tours were unmatchable. There is nothing like them today. 'Twas terrific to play in our time, particularly at a high level, but it's terrific watching today so we have had the best of both worlds. I think Ireland has gone about the professional game really well.

'The future? All the other countries want to win and they have their coaching teams as well. The average win rate over the last ten years has been 47 per cent or something like that, and Ireland shouldn't expect more than 50–50 relative to England, France and those. So, leaving Italy out of it, if Ireland achieved 50 per cent, it's more than they should expect because they don't have the resources to match the others.

'Would I like to have been part of the professional era? Well, let's put it this way … I'm very happy at the way things went but if I was born in this era, I'm sure I'd like that as well. I wouldn't have any negativity about it. Guys compare our time with this. That's all codology. There are pluses and minuses in everything. Everything is different. I would relate to this era and have no problem about it. The big question for professional guys these days is that they haven't much time to do anything else. So, by the time they get to thirty-two or thirty-three, there is a big issue as to where they go. In a way, I would probably prefer our day in that sense. I did give it a lot of time, I used to train nearly every day, but you can do that and still have a job or go to university. The options were there to look at other things and have another life and they are not there that much any more. Still, people say today's players don't have much fun but that's also a load of rubbish.

'There is always a bit of a reaction to quick change in life. On the Lions tour in New Zealand in 1971, I was in charge of the forwards and we used to have guys up in the stand who weren't playing, with notebooks noting down all the line-outs, who won them and how many crooked-ins there were, all the statistics that were useful afterwards and they all thought I was a bit of a head banger. At least some of them did anyway and they used to joke about it. One who did not, though, was Carwyn James [the famous Welsh coach]. Nowadays, they do that except they do it on computers and videos and every time somebody scratches his arse they have it on the video. All we were doing was a real pedestrian layman's version of that. You can only move guys so fast through the gears.'

* * *

THERE WERE many high points in Ray's career but some low moments as well – most notably when he captained a side in 1965 that travelled to Cardiff with every high hope of a rare Triple Crown victory. It was not to be. Today, he argues that 'we really could have won that match. First of all, a try was scored in the first half which wasn't allowed. It definitely wasn't a forward pass. It was scored by myself from a pass by Willie John [McBride] and would have been my second in international rugby. The real problem was that there was double banking in the line-out. The Welsh literally fouled every line-out using the double banking as kind of a shield. The referee was a fellow called Brooks who stood out in the middle of the field and couldn't see any of it. We didn't have the best of line-out options anyway and when you are in the Cardiff Arms Park nobody can hear a word you are saying. You can only be heard by the guy next to you and so the only way you can communicate is by signals. The essence of losing the match was the line-outs … they had Keith Rowlands, Brian Price and Mervyn Davies and we really only had Willie John, and one guy just can't deal with three.'

Nevertheless, this was still a fine Irish side and in another short few weeks Ray was leading his country to its first ever victory over South Africa. A year later, Tom Kiernan replaced him as captain and there was a belief at the time that this cost him the leadership of the Lions tour of Australia in 1966. However, Ray was quick to shrug off the disappointment and he has the happiest memories of his two Lions tours, even if injury intervened on both occasions.

'In 1966 we were good enough to beat the All Blacks

in one or two of the Tests, but just didn't get it together,' he muses. 'We played it very loose in Australia and the philosophy when we got to New Zealand was to do the same thing. We were super fit but you had to get the ball. In those days, you could barge and bullock away in the line-outs and there were hardly any penalties. Anyway, we went about New Zealand in the wrong way.

'I was injured for a few matches because I pulled a hamstring – would you believe it – playing soccer! You see, I was being written up in the papers out there for being the hard man of the Lions pack so there was fierce slagging about this injury. A cartoon was published in the New Zealand papers that I still have somewhere. There I was in a hospital ward with my leg up and Des O'Brien [the Irish manager of the Lions] with the doctor and the chart. The caption quoted Des saying, "He injured it playing soccer!", with an exclamation mark and it showed me blushing!

'We were away for five months and I absolutely loved it even though we lost the Test matches. New Zealand is a fantastic place to tour. I loved the people. We went to an awful lot of places. You must remember that Lions tours then and now are two totally different things. Now it's three Test matches, a few others that don't count, and home. Back then, every game counted. As well as the Test matches there would be at least eight others which were a big challenge. The fervour of the people about rugby, the earthiness of all the guys you played against, the quaintness of the towns. I loved it.

'Our manager Des O'Brien was a really, really nice man.

He worked with Guinness and was connected with the head of Guinness in New Zealand, a guy called Martin. We were in Timaru and I just mentioned to Des that when I was a kid my mother used to give me Guinness with my porridge. They thought this was very quaint so anyway, I went down for breakfast the following morning and the waiter asked if I would like some porridge. He brought it along and then asked if I would like some Guinness with it and I said, no, not at all, I haven't done that for years. No, he said, go on and he handed me this bottle of Guinness. He told me to stand up so he could hand it to me. I didn't cop what was going on and the next thing, out from behind a curtain comes a guy with a camera and takes a picture. On the front of all the papers in New Zealand next day is this great big picture of a guy in a Lions blazer with a pint of Guinness in his hand. Well, I must have got a hundred letters from mothers all over New Zealand lambasting me for giving a bad example to their kids, who now all wanted Guinness in their porridge!

'The 1971 tour was also great but very different. We lost the first match against Queensland and everybody was shocked, but we didn't lose another after that, except for one of the Tests in New Zealand. I chipped my thumb in the Canterbury match and probably could have played with a plaster. But the doctor said no, if you don't get this set and treated properly you could have arthritis in ten years time, so I decided I wasn't going to risk that. I was in charge of the forwards up to then but I stayed on for another month.

'It was disappointing all right, but the way I look back at those things is like this. I had been expected to be captain in

1966 and people often asked me if I was very disappointed. I was at the time but not greatly so ... as I have said, I had a terrific tour. Looking back, things went pretty well and my life has been pretty good since then and I wouldn't want to take a chance of re-running it and things not working out as well. If I were captain of that 1966 tour, everything about my life afterwards would be different. Everything. I may have met a different woman, I might have got a different job. It could have been disastrous. So, really, I have no regrets about any individual situation, no negative views at all. Life's a mixture of pluses and minuses and you cannot expect to go through it without some minuses. The package of pluses and minuses I have is just fine and if I had to live it again, I might have a worse package.'

The 1971 Lions were the first to defeat New Zealand in a Test series. Ray McLoughlin and the Scot Sandy Carmichael were the front line props until they were both ruled out of the tour due to the injuries sustained in the Canterbury match. Ireland's Seán Lynch and another Scot, Ian 'Mighty Mouse' McLauchlan, replaced them for the Tests. But Ray's wisdom was still availed of by Carwyn James, whose compatriot, John Taylor, another shrewd observer of the rugby game, wrote on the Lions return: 'Ray was sorely missed. He was the wisehead, the intelligentsia of forward play. He and Carwyn would spend hours together, Carwyn trying to learn from Ray the intricacies of forward play. He was one of the best technicians the game has ever known.'

It was during the 1966 Lions tour that Ray McLoughlin learned how best to cope with the demands of the loosehead prop position. Oddly enough, the Lions found themselves short in that area and asked Ray to move across from the tight side. He didn't realise it then, but it was a development in his rugby career that was to have far-reaching and beneficial consequences and helped to prolong his career a lot longer than he could possibly have visualised. Interestingly, one of his successors in the No. 3 jersey, Peter Clohessy, also followed the same route with similarly successful results. And, coincidentally, Ray and Peter were later chosen on the *Irish Times* Irish team of all time several years later.

Following the Lions tour Ray explains, 'I was twenty-seven, had no job having been eight years at university. I was down in London about two hours from the London Irish training ground and had kind of had my fill of the game. For eight years, I had done nothing but play rugby for Connacht, UCD, Northumberland, Gosforth, British Universities, Blackrock, Ireland, the Lions. That was all very fine, but I felt I had better concentrate on doing a bit of work. I came over to Ireland to run a battery factory in Roscommon with 205 people in it and that was an experience I can tell you. I learned more in two years there than I could have learned in ten years at ICI [Imperial Chemical Industries]. I lived in Athlone and was working eighteen hours a day and was completely unfit. So I thought I should do something about it and went out to Athlone rugby grounds running around on non-training nights. But somebody saw me and they immediately picked me for Athlone at a time when I wasn't fit enough for an old woman's team. And as soon as Connacht saw me with Athlone, they put me on their team. And as soon as the Irish selectors saw me on the Connacht team, they put me in the final trial and I wasn't fit enough for that kind of stuff at all. They picked me as a reserve in 1970 and I was happy with that because you didn't have to tog out in those days and I enjoyed the trips. You were part of the B team training against the first team and during the year I discovered I was handling it quite well and it stirred my enthusiasm. So I started playing the following year and got fit and got a taste for it and played for another five years.'

In all, Ray McLoughlin won forty Irish caps, captained the team on seven occasions, played three Tests for the Lions on the 1966 tour of Australia and New Zealand and was deprived of further Lions Test honours because of the thumb injury picked up in the battle of Canterbury in 1971. And, of course, he was a member of the Barbarians team that beat the All Blacks in a famous game in Cardiff in 1973. Apart from being one of the deepest and most perceptive thinkers on the game, he was also ahead of his time where personal fitness was concerned.

'I packed down at just under sixteen stone and even though other guys were heavier than me, I did a lot of weights so I was very strong,' he says. 'I did athletics in Garbally where we had a very enlightened priest, Fr Ryall, and I was doing weights from the age of fifteen or sixteen and I did them non-stop in UCD with Brian O'Halloran for three or four nights every week, often because we had no money and nothing else to do. You can pack an awful lot of extra strength into the same body if you lift weights and I lifted very heavy weights.'

There you have the essence of the man, forever thinking

ahead, figuring out how he can improve whatever mission he undertakes and that of those nearest and dearest to him. Not surprisingly, he was hugely successful in the business world ... but that is a story for somebody else to tell!

ROBERT AND DAVID KEARNEY

Rob Kearney gave an immaculate performance – he
was massively reassuring.

Lions' manager Ian McGeechan after second Lions Test,
South Africa, 2009

THE BELIEF that all Leinster rugby players come from Dublin
has been exposed as an absolute illusion. As the Boys in Blue
marched imperiously to a couple of Heineken Cups in the
space of three years, as well as a Magners League victory,
people like Seán O'Brien from County Carlow, Leo Cullen
from Wicklow and Gordon D'Arcy from County Wexford
were establishing themselves as key members of the side,
while also accomplishing daring deeds in the cause of the
national XV.

And then there are the Kearneys from County Louth.
Rob, his country's fullback in the Six Nations Grand Slam
in 2009 and a star of the Lions tour in South Africa later
that year, spent much of 2011 coping with a bad knee injury
but was fit and poised to make an impact come the Rugby
World Cup in the fall of the year. Ireland could ill afford to
do without Rob, a footballer blessed with a siege gun for a

left boot, although far from one-footed, and also blessed with a shrewd and inventive footballing brain. His twenty-one year-old brother, David, is an international who has played either on the wing or at fullback at almost every level of the game except on the senior side with many shrewd judges convinced he will make the big breakthrough sooner rather than later. The third brother in the family is Richard, the eldest, who displayed great promise during his school days only to gradually drift away from rugby and take up what the others accept is 'a real job'.

The Kearneys come from the famed Cooley Peninsula, where from their earliest days the boys combined the more traditional Gaelic football with rugby. 'For the three of us growing up, to the age of thirteen, everything was about the Cooley Kickhams and we probably played considerably more Gaelic football than we did rugby,' says Rob. 'However, our dad, also David, was heavily involved with Dundalk Rugby Club and still is. He played for Dundalk and Leinster juniors. We started off with mini-rugby under-7 but it was erratic – it was Gaelic three times a week, rugby only once or so. The great thing about the two seasons was that they rarely clashed. When rugby ended in April, the Gaelic season would be just kicking off and championship time with Louth was starting. From that perspective, we were twelve-month athletes around the clock, six for rugby and Gaelic for the other six. When you're a kid of that age, it's brilliant, the more sport you play the better.

'I had three minor seasons with Louth. We had one brilliant team – we were knocked out by Dublin in a semi-final in a replay that we should have won. That was to be our year to have a go at the thing, but the Dubs beat us and went on to win the All-Ireland. A lot of that side are now on their senior team. In the first game, I remember Mark Vaughan scored a point off a free with the last kick to bring us to the replay. We were unlucky that day. It was our big chance. By then, though, I had followed Richard to Clongowes and rugby was taking over.'

According to David, for him 'it was probably different. I had two older brothers and remember them going to Clongowes, Richard especially. So I loved going to the rugby matches that Rob and Richard played. When we went to Clongowes, rugby became the number one sport although at the same time we'd be heavily involved in Gaelic when on our breaks and played a few games for Cooley Kickhams. I played under-16s for Louth but when I reached 18s level, I was playing a lot of Leinster Schools' rugby and Leinster 19s rugby and didn't play Gaelic for Louth. We'd be going over to England and playing against English academies and I played Leinster Schools as well in fifth year so in the summertime as well you'd be doing rugby sessions every two weeks or so.'

For Rob, 'Clongowes was the start of playing serious rugby although before that we were always very much a rugby orientated family. It's when things started to kick off. The college was in the family system because my grandfather, my dad and my older brother had all gone there. There were six years of boarding and I loved it, we had so much fun and made some really brilliant, close friends. If I had the opportunity, I would do the same with my own kids. I really enjoyed it. As a school, Clongowes will maintain that rugby is not the centrepiece, and giving you a broader education and a greater understanding of life is probably their mission statement, although rugby of course is a sport that has dominated throughout.

'Ironically, the story of our Leinster Schools' Cup campaigns is as follows: three Kearneys, three finals – against Terenure, Blackrock and St Michaels – all lost. Richard's team 100% should have won; my year, we were beaten by the better team; David's team were 50–50. Richard was a centre in fifth year, in sixth year they shoved him into the back of the scrum and he played openside. Today, he has a real job and is busy so it's mainly boxing and a bit of gym fitness stuff for him – but he wouldn't box either of us, though!

'After Clongowes, it was UCD for me. With the nature of the Leinster system, it doesn't matter what college you go to. It's more important to get into the academy system which both of us did. And me more so than Dave, I was quite lucky with the speed at which I was propelled in. Michael Cheika took me in in his first year and I would have made my debut for Leinster when I was nineteen so it all happened very quickly. I had played Leinster Schools and Ireland Schools, but you never expect anything in case it doesn't happen. If you like, Cheika and myself made our Magners League debut on the same day. It's hard to describe how things progressed from there as it continued to happen very quickly for me. Three months after that, I was called into the Ireland autumn international squad and so before I knew where I was, I was in the thick of things. I wasn't, of course, playing international rugby, but when you are in the squad you get a huge feel for things.

'It was a brilliant time because there were guys like Brian O'Driscoll involved. It was a little overwhelming at the start, but you soon get over that and get to grips with it. You realised very quickly that you are competing with these guys for places so you have to stop idolising them like you once did. They would be encouraging you all right, but there would also be a little touch of them being wary of this young fellow trying to come through. It's a selfish world at the best of times and it took a few years before I developed any relationship with some of the older guys. You have to earn your crust a little bit, which I was made to do. It's a good attitude, it toughens you up and teaches you to appreciate the atmosphere and surroundings of your new job and your new role.'

According to Dave, 'When I came out of school, I did a year in the sub-academy, then a year in the academy, then a Development contract and now a full contract. I played Ireland Schools, under-20s for two years and made my Leinster debut at the age of nineteen against the Dragons. Rob was playing, just coming back after the mumps, so it was a really young team. It was Rob's first game back from illness and his first game was the only time we played together.'

Dave then went off to the under-20s World Cup in Japan and did well in several games for an Ireland side that acquitted itself commendably without seriously challenging for top honours. 'I had a couple of games at the start of the 2009/2010 season but tore my quadriceps so I was out for about five months, January to the end of the season,' he recalls. 'I came back at the start of this season, and had a couple of games that I was delighted to get. Being on a full contract gives you a little bit of security but when it comes to an end, you have to weigh up your options and see what you want to do from there. I see myself very much as a rugby player. It's my passion and what I hope to do for several more years. I know it's not going to be easy, it's one of the problems with being in a club like Leinster with so many talented backs. As Rob was saying, at the end of the day, they are your competition and as much as you idolised them as a young fellow, you are still looking to get their place and their jersey. I like to play fullback and wing. I played fullback for the Wolfhounds a few months ago and enjoyed that.'

Rob wonders if 'the day of the fullback being the last line of defence is gone? I'm not too sure. It is and it isn't. I think people are under-estimating the change-over from wing to fullback. I would certainly think that they are two very different positions. A fullback can play wing quite easily but it's much harder for a wing to play fullback. I would see the skill sets in the two positions as very different – people think they are all back three positions so it's all the same, but it's not. I've played both positions for Ireland and made my debut on the wing against Argentina before the last World Cup when all the front line players were rested.

'You never forget any international game but the first is always one that stands out more than any other. That was the breakthrough, although then there was the World Cup and unfortunately I wasn't selected for any of that. However, since then, barring the injury that kept me out of the entire 2011

Six Nations, I have played every game since the World Cup. I was establishing myself as Ireland's fullback from Girvan [Dempsey] and Geordan [Murphy]. I first had to knock Girvan off his perch at Leinster. I remember my fourth game for Ireland. Girvan was named at fullback against Wales, Geordan and myself were on the wings. Girvan was injured so Geordan went fullback on the Wednesday. Then Geordan was injured on the Friday so I went fullback the day before the game. I loved it and got on very well and I suppose from then on fullback was my favoured position. Michael Bradley on the summer tour of Australia and New Zealand played me there ahead of both Girvan and Geordan. Eddie [O'Sullivan] finished after the English game in the Six Nations and Declan was announced as coach but he didn't take over until after the summer tour.'

* * *

Nothing pleases the Kearney siblings more than the passion that their parents have for rugby and their interest in following the boys no matter where they might be playing.

'David Kearney senior loves it,' says Rob. 'Himself and my mother Siobhán live for the rugby at the weekends although she's not so good, the old nerves do for her like any mother. She is only normal there and I suppose having two of us to worry about, she has even more sleepless nights. In fairness, though, they go to all the matches. They'll travel to all the away Heineken Cup and international games, the Magners League they don't do as much, but they're the only ones they'll miss.'

David says, 'I get a great kick out of it as well. And watching Rob playing for Ireland spurs me on that extra bit. It's what I want. Maybe I'm only one or two injuries away from a place in the Leinster back line. Obviously, the Six Nations is a good time for getting matches when the internationals are away.' Quite clearly, Rob is a great support in every respect and he points out that 'Dave's like all the young lads, he has gotten some exposure and game time and been able to prove what he can do. You have so many quality outside backs vying for three positions that game time becomes more and more limited. He has done really well this season, he has taken his chances and is one of Leinster's top try scorers from a limited number of matches.'

Rob Kearney probably has the best part of a decade still to play in the highest echelons of the game but readily agrees that there may not be anything to match the Grand Slam triumph of 2009 and a Lions tour – even if it was a year that brought a very unlikely illness setback.

'It was unbelievable, it just seemed as if the Six Nations went as perfectly as possible and nothing could get any better,' he says. 'It actually started off ropy enough. I played on the wing in the autumn series and was playing fullbackish for Leinster. It became clear that should be where I play, but Declan used Girvan, Geordan and Keith Earls, all three in the fullback role. After that, I finally secured my place at fullback ahead of Girvan for Leinster and had a good December and January.'

It was a well-kept secret for quite a while, but Ireland being Ireland (and good journalists being good journalists!), news of the famous Irish squad get together in Enfield finally made the headlines. And central to the entire cause célèbre was one of the younger members, a certain Rob Kearney. When the subject is broached, he smiles quietly and groans, 'Here we go again.' But when pressed to explain what prompted him to speak out, he doesn't demur. 'I suppose it was a rush of blood to the head and it sort of got out of hand a little bit,' he explains. 'The message that got out was that I was criticising the Munster players for bluntly not showing as much heart in the green jersey as they did in the red jersey, which isn't true and that's not what happened at all. It was more – and it still is there and I'd like to think that Leinster are getting that same ethos as well – that when you looked down at Thomond Park, there was something special about the place – and there is. Teams found it really difficult to come there and play. Munster teams always played with an incredible passion and togetherness and I had that in my school team. I always felt it was solely down to togetherness within a team, a strong bond and camaraderie within the changing-room and that the Irish team lacked that a little bit. It was more just looking on and saying, how is Munster able to create this culture and ethos down in Thomond Park and why isn't it happening for Ireland? It was a statement of that, rather than pointing a finger saying that you do it there but you don't do it here for Ireland. I think the nature of my message was misinterpreted a little bit.

'As I was speaking, I was thinking, what am I saying? I have never been so scared in my life. Unbelievably so. No, I wasn't trying to bite my tongue. We were in little groups, there were only seven of us in the room, and I didn't expect it to be reeled out again in the big meeting. There was silence and Marcus Horan stood up and said, well, there is an elephant in the room and someone needs to be accountable for that. There was silence again and I was just thinking, there's no way I can stay quiet, I need to back it up, and I got up and said pretty much what I said to you. And as it happened, there were no repercussions, none at all. It was really good. All the Munster lads came up to me and some said, it needed to be said and you're dead right, and judging by that I got a little more respect from them by voicing my opinion as I did.

'Enfield was a big moment because we won the Grand Slam but had we got the Wooden Spoon, I could have been the villain of the whole thing for stirring up this whole bag of rubbish.'

Perhaps, but not likely. The response of Donncha O'Callaghan, as Munster as they come, said it all: 'For a young player like Rob coming into the squad to say what he said was, well, he just went through the roof in my estimation. I would do anything for him now. He was saying that sometimes he looks at Munster and wonders if these guys get to the same levels when they are playing with him. He asked questions of some of us in the room. I thought, fair play to him. It was a crucial moment for the team. Marcus and Rob could have sat in the room and shut their mouths but they didn't. They showed a lot of balls.'

Before Ireland got on with the business of the 2009 Six Nations, Leinster needed a few good results to propel them into the knock-out stages of the Heineken Cup. They were still flying, to some extent anyway, on Munster's coat tails, but desperately anxious to rectify the situation.

'The big game that year was Edinburgh away,' Rob believes. 'It was a banana skin for us. Two seasons before that, we were knocked out of the Magners and the Heineken at Murrayfield against average Edinburgh sides. We fronted up this time. There was a change in Leinster that day, that soft underbelly was starting to leave us.'

With Leinster safely through and Munster also waiting in the wings, Irish rugby was on a serious high going into the Six Nations. It was Declan Kidney's first year in charge and he was seen as the man with the Midas touch after all his achievements with Munster. For some of the older players like John Hayes, Brian O'Driscoll and Ronan O'Gara, it represented perhaps their final chance of leaving a lasting mark on the international game in this country.

'We played France first in Croke Park and I was lucky to be playing that day. I tripped over Alan Gaffney at training in Limerick on the Tuesday. My ankle was massive, I was on crutches on Wednesday and Thursday; two days before the game, my ankle was black. I was drugged up on a load of painkillers and I don't know how I got through the game. But I did so safely and it was a great day beating France in Croke Park, three tries, Jamie, Brian and Gordon on his comeback, and after that it was on to Rome. I got clotheslined [high tackled] in the first minute and Andrea Masi got a twelve-week ban for it. That's my memory of that game. We won and played quite well and there was a week's break and then we had England at home.

'It was tough. Any time you play England in Croke Park, it's a massive occasion, maybe not as big as the one two years before, when it was the main event, but an historic occasion all the same. It was another dogfight that we won 16–14. I was so nervous. I was a spectator in 2007 and I think there was a view throughout the country that England were not a great side and that we would beat them easily enough. But that wasn't the case and for me it turned out to be the toughest game of the lot.'

It was on the eve of this match that skipper O'Driscoll delivered the line that left all of us present absolutely baffled and indeed most of us are still not quite sure what he meant. Derek Foley of the *Star* asked Brian about Martin Johnson's influence as England coach and he replied: 'Knowledge is knowing that a tomato is a fruit, wisdom is knowing not to put it in a fruit salad.' With that kind of *je ne sais quoi* spirit in the squad, it was hardly surprising that still greater things lay in the offing!

'We went on to give probably our poorest display of the competition at Murrayfield in Scotland because I think in the back of everyone's head there was a potential Grand Slam final a week later,' Rob accepts. 'Even though you say we are focused on this game, it's sometimes difficult not to look a week in advance. We were lucky to win that day and now found ourselves fighting for a Triple Crown and Grand Slam.

'It was a massive week. The whole country was rugby, rugby, rugby, Grand Slam, Grand Slam, Grand Slam. Crazy. It seems such a long time ago, but it's only two years

… Cardiff was electric and the Millennium is one of my favourite stadiums. Warren [Gatland, Welsh coach and formerly of Galwegians, Connacht and Ireland] was stirring it, as he always does, so no surprise there. But you would be amazed at how little attention players pay to that, especially with Warren as he always has something to say before any big game so you take it for granted from him. It was a huge occasion, we won it through the ups and downs of the game. The night before I injured my back and woke up the next day and it was in spasm. If it was any other game, I would have been off after ten minutes, but because it was for the Grand Slam it was very difficult to pull yourself. My memory is of being in pain throughout. So I came off after sixty-five minutes; I had to go and could hardly budge and should probably have gone sooner. I had to be literally helped off the physio table at half time. You sort of keep it quiet a little bit, you are in the corner and no one is looking, but into the second half it became clear that I just wasn't operating. When you have someone like Geordan to come on, it was a case of take me off and put him on.

'Now I was watching. The whole thing goes in slow motion when it's into the last few minutes. Rog got his drop goal, Stephen lined up his penalty and I really thought he was going to get it.' The rest, as they say, is history and Rob Kearney and his mates had finally bridged a sixty-one year gap since Ireland previously completed the Grand Slam. And a huge perk of the occasion for all concerned was that among those in the crowd was the legendary Jack Kyle, the inspiration behind the previous clean sweep back in 1948.

Ironically, David was not there to enjoy the occasion: 'I was on the under-20 side against Wales the night before. If I really wanted to, I probably could have stayed, but everyone was heading home so I wanted to stick with the lads. Mum, Dad and Richard were there, but our younger sister, Sarah, stayed away. She's twenty and sick of rugby at this stage … it's all that's ever on TV, it's all that's ever spoken about at home and so being an only girl, she has a lot to put up with.'

* * *

THE HOMECOMING CELEBRATIONS for the Grand Slam, including Tommy Bowe's 'rendering' of *The Black Velvet Band*, captivated the nation on the following day and for the next week as well. But Leinster – and Rob Kearney – had other things on their minds.

'We were away to Harlequins in the Heineken Cup in the Stoop, a game infamous for "bloodgate", but also a defining one for Leinster rugby,' he asserts with every good reason. 'We changed our ethos and culture a little bit that day. It was a massive defensive display. We won it solely on our defence. We were completely unaware of what was going on with Harlequins and the blood issue. It was shocking but that sort of thing happens loads. After the Harlequins game, I sat down and wasn't feeling great. I called Arthur Tanner [the Leinster doctor] over and said I'm a bit sore around here [indicating his throat]. Arthur looked around the area and the outcome was that I was out of action for two months with the mumps. I was in the Blackrock Clinic for ten days on a drip and missed the semi-final against Munster and only got back a week before the final and was on the bench, No. 22. So the end of the campaign was a bit of a dampener. I came on for nine minutes and got three touches and was in pretty bad form afterwards, even though we had won. Why? Probably because I only got the nine minutes. It's difficult when you are used to playing week in, week out. Dave got the mumps the summer before when he was in Wales for the under-20 World Cup. You swell up, cannot eat, cannot drink. I was very ill.

'I remember getting a call from the Lions doctor and there was doubt about whether I would tour with the Lions or not. So my world for those few months was turned upside down a little bit, but thankfully I recovered. I was lucky I had a nice Lions tour to South Africa to look forward to. I probably owed my Lions selection to the Six Nations and having Wasps in our Heineken group. I had two pretty good games against them in front of Ian McGeechan, Warren Gatland, Shaun Edwards and so on.

'I was watching the team announcement on television like everyone else – except I was in the Blackrock Clinic and so ill at the time and so zombied that it wasn't something I could get excited about. I was fully knackered. The perception was that I was No. 2 to Lee Byrne for the tour, but in my mind it was 50–50. Before the last two warm-up games, Rob Howley called the two of us and told us you're 50–50 at the moment and it all depends on how it goes in the next two matches. I thought I played well but he got the nod anyway. Then he came off after thirty-six minutes and there I was all of a sudden playing for the Lions Test team. It was the biggest moment in my career, bigger even than my debut for Ireland, because the Lions were something that I always loved and saw as the pinnacle of my sport. You can't get any higher and there's such a magical feeling to that whole idea of the British and Irish Lions that it was really, really special.

'I played quite well and on the following Tuesday I was named at fullback for the second Test with Lee Byrne on the bench. That was nice for me given that the two of us had been battling away and then on the Thursday he hurt his thumb and his tour was over. Losing that match 25–28 was absolutely gutting. I got the try – Stephen Jones passed to me, I could have passed to Tommy [Bowe], he was there watching and I was waiting to give it, to pass and pass, but François Steyn was hanging off me and just kept pushing on to Tommy and so I went for it and made it. That was the toughest sporting loss I ever had. We won the third Test but it was sort of a dead duck by then.

'I loved that tour. A Lions tour is something you cannot put into words, you cannot describe it unless you have been on it. From the first day, it was brilliant craic. Meeting all these lads who rip each other for the whole season before that and all of a sudden you find yourself on the same team. We got on well together and it's what you play rugby for, it's the pinnacle and always your goal and to be finally there was sweet. My mum stayed at home because Sarah was doing her Leaving Cert and David junior was off ripping it up for the under-20s in Japan and playing very well. So Dad was caught between the two sons – where do I go – but because the Lions are the Lions, there was only one winner so he and

Richard came out for the Tests. It's brilliant for the parents to be so involved. They love it and are best friends with all the other parents now, they go to a game and have a bit of craic.'

* * *

THE 2010/11 season came as a very sobering experience for Rob Kearney. While training in the build-up to the South African game in November, he injured the cartilage behind the patella in his left knee. Misdiagnosis didn't help and he played three matches with the problem knowing that something serious was wrong. He was operated on and informed that he was out for the remainder of the season, but with every likelihood of having fully recovered in good time to begin his preparations for the Rugby World Cup in New Zealand in the autumn.

He could have beaten the six month 'sentence' but has learned the value of patience, explaining: 'Maybe I was in a place in my career where I was starting to take playing week in, week out, for granted. The break has been good for me because my hunger levels are probably better than ever. Your whole world is going a million miles an hour so it's only when you're injured that your life goes on pause.' And yet he dismissed the idea that the No. 15 jersey was more likely to be his because of the movement in the position during his absence: 'It's not my place to say that. I knew there would be quality players to step up and they have made no secret of the fact that they always wanted to play fullback. I was the same. That's only normal.'

At twenty-five and with that mighty left boot and tons of

Top: Richard, David and Paul Wallace, who enjoy a unique record of achievement in rugby history. © INPHO/Billy Stickland

Above: Richard and Henry Wallace line out for the first ever Irish Colleges' side. *Courtesy of the Wallace family*

Right: Paul wishes David luck before one of his first matches for Ireland. *Courtesy of the Wallace family*

Above: Dick Spring, 2nd from left, introducing his brother Donal and nephew Graham, right, to their professional partner, David Feherty, at the Murphy's Pro-Am at Druids Glen.
© SPORTSFILE

Right: Donal Spring in action for Ireland.
Courtesy of the Limerick Leader

Below: Don Reddan, left, with his sons Eoin, Diarmuid, Alan and Cian. *Courtesy of the Reddan family*

Denis, left, and John Fogarty enjoy a joke.
Courtesy of Denis Fogarty

Ultan, left, and Donncha
O'Callaghan celebrate a
Cork Constitution All-
Ireland League victory.
*Courtesy of Ultan
O'Callaghan*

A Connacht team including Phelim McLoughlin, standing 4th from left, and Ray McLoughlin, extreme right, front row. *Courtesy of Ralph O'Gorman*

Peter Clohessy, left, clubmate John 'Paco' Fitzgerald, right, with Keith Wood, centre, completing a pretty formidable Irish front row. *Courtesy of the Limerick Leader*

Ger Clohessy, 2nd from left, captain of the Young Munster team that won the 1993 All-Ireland League, aboard an open-top bus with his mother Meg, wife Maeve and father Noel. *Courtesy of the Limerick Leader*

The Kiernans were a versatile family. Tom, standing 2nd from right, and Jim, seated, centre, before a big cricket match at the Mardyke, Cork. *Courtesy of Cork Cricket Club*

John O'Driscoll in action for Ireland against England. *Courtesy of the Limerick Leader*

The Ireland team that beat Scotland in 1968 with Tommy Doyle, standing, extreme right, Mick Doyle seated, 3rd from left, and captained by Tom Kiernan.
Courtesy of Tommy Doyle

The Humphreys brothers: David, background, and Ian launching another thundering left-footed kick. © Dickson Digital

Guy and Simon Easterby in September 2001.
© INPHO/Andrew Paton

Ireland players, from left, Ronan O'Gara, Gordon D'Arcy, Rob Kearney, David
Kearney, Shane Jennings and Paddy Wallace during squad training.
© Stephen McCarthy / SPORTSFILE

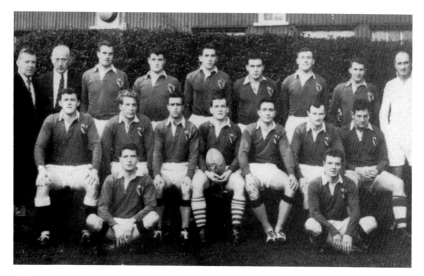

A Connacht team in the 1960s with Danno Heaslip, on the ground, right, and Ray McLoughlin, seated, extreme right. *Courtesy of Ralph O'Gorman*

Ireland's Simon Best, left, Andrew Trimble, centre, and Rory Best, right, with the RBS Triple Crown trophy in 2006 after beating England at Twickenham.
© Brendan Moran / SPORTSFILE

natural ability in every facet of the game, the future can only hold good for Rob Kearney. And much the same also applies to kid brother Dave!

JIM AND TOM KIERNAN

Some of the matches we saw in our day, they were
more like a funeral than a rugby match.

Jim Kiernan

CAPTAIN OF Ireland, captain of the Lions, prolific points scorer,
proud possessor of fifty-four Irish caps and seven Munster
Senior Cup medals, IRFU president ... these are only some
of the honours that have come Tom Kiernan's way since he
first kicked a rugby ball in the Mardyke in Cork as a child
of little more than five or six years. But the family honours
aren't confined to Tom alone ... his older brother, Jim, was
also a rugby player of the highest calibre, picking up three
Munster Cup medals in his own right, representing Munster
on numerous occasions and later having the great distinction
of watching his son, Michael, drop the goal that clinched the
1985 Triple Crown for Ireland as well as following in the
footsteps of Uncle Tom by touring with the Lions.

Nor does the Kiernan dynasty stop there. Jim and Tom
are also closely related to the Murphy clan – their mother
was a Murphy. She was a first cousin of Noel F. Murphy, who
played for Ireland, as did his son, Noel junior, and grandson

Kenny, three different generations of Irish international rugby players, Lions tourists and a coach and two presidents of the IRFU. And lest we forget, Jim's brothers-in-law Gerald Reidy and Mick Lane were both capped by Ireland and Gerald was elected president of the Union as well! As rugby pedigrees go, it would be difficult to find any better.

* * *

THE KIERNAN family grew up on Cork's Western Road, in the 1940–50s, literally within a few seconds walk of the famed Mardyke grounds, home of countless memorable Munster Cup matches and several famous encounters with major overseas touring teams. Not only that, but Presentation Brothers College (or PBC or even more simply, Pres) was 300 yards away. An early introduction to sport became inevitable and not only did Jim go on to display undisputed class as a footballer of the highest quality, but he also performed so well on the cricket pitch that he was picked by Ireland, an honour that also fell to his close neighbour, Noel Cantwell, the renowned Ireland, West Ham United and Manchester United footballer.

A love of rugby and Cork Constitution coursed through the Kiernan veins. Typical of arguably the most meticulously run club in the country, Con were ahead of their time in that they catered for what in more recent times has become known as 'mini rugby' long before it became fashionable. A well-known photograph of the 'Connettes' taken in the 1940s featured a number of famous players, including Marney Cunningham, Tom Kiernan and Noel Murphy, second cousins who were to go on to achieve legendary status in the game. Also in the photo are Jim Kiernan and a certain Edmund van Esbeck, who later enjoyed an unparalleled reputation as one of rugby's finest scribes and wrote the definitive history of the IRFU, the Constitution club and several others.

Jim's first school was Sullivan's Quay and he recalls, 'They didn't have any sport there. I made my confirmation in fifth class in Pres, my first year there, and we were already into rugby through the Connettes. Mr McGrath would pick two teams, one in Pres jerseys and the other in Christians jerseys, and everybody else went up in the stand to watch. This was the culmination of weekly or fortnightly get-togethers, but this was the match and it was huge.

'We won the Schools Junior Cup in 1946 with a team captained by Jerry Daly, a brother of Dan, that also included Charlie Hennessy and Austin Bradley [Michael's father] and most of the same guys were on the side that won the Senior Cup two years later. Anthony McHale was captain and Liam Mackessy, Vince Giltinane and Pat Cunningham [a brother of Marney, a great wing forward who won seven caps in 1955–56 and gave it all up to join the priesthood, and Jos, a fine hooker for Cork Con and Munster] once again were very important members of the side. What I remember best about it is that it was the first time that Pres and Christians met in the final and one incident stands out for me. I fielded a ball about ten yards from our line in the corner and instead of putting it back into touch, I passed it to McHale, who had a huge boot and could kick the ball half the length of the field. But Jimmy Keane of Christians came through and missed an intercept by a fraction of an inch. I hate to think of what would have happened had he held it.'

Tom went to Pres from the start. 'It was my only school. In the junior or primary school, there was a competition within the school for the Kiely Cup in fourth, fifth and sixth year; you would be, what, eleven, twelve, thirteen. We were the only class to win it in fifth year with Jerry Walsh as captain. Sixth year used to always win it because of the age difference. Then we went into secondary and in the junior cup year we beat Glenstal in the final in Limerick. I was scrum half and Jerry Walsh again captained our side. Jerry was captain once more when we beat Crescent in the senior final at Thomond Park in 1957. I was in the centre with him and it wasn't until my second year in UCC that I became a fullback. Dessie Scannell, a fine tennis player, broke a leg and I was moved there for the Colours match.'

Although Jim and Tom are separated in age by some eight years, there were similarities between them from the outset. They both won Munster Senior and Junior Cup medals at Pres where rugby was, and remains, a serious part of the curriculum. Ronan O'Gara and Peter Stringer of the modern generation are just some of those who attended the college and learned the game there. Ireland coach Declan Kidney is another – and he was also a member of the teaching staff.

* * *

BY A striking coincidence, another outstanding Cork rugby player, Ray Hennessy, played a major role in the developing careers of both Jim and Tom Kiernan. Even though Jim captained the Constitution side that won the Munster Cup in 1957, he did so from the centre position, with Hennessy in Jim's favoured position of fullback. Four months later, Jim had joined Dolphin as did Derry O'Shaughnessy, another member of that Constitution side. 'We trained them,' quipped Tom and Jim could only laugh before explaining what happened from his perspective: 'Basically, I was twenty-seven or twenty-eight and Ray Hennessy was only coming out of school. I had an uncle who was actually my godfather as well, Timmy Murphy, known as Pebbles, and he was a selector at Con. He put me in the centre. I reckoned that if I continued in the centre, I would only play for another year or two, whereas if I was at fullback, I could play for another three or four. So I asked myself, well, what would I prefer to do and I said I'd prefer to play for three or four more years. So I went to Dolphin and played fullback. Our sister, Anne, had married Gerald Reidy of Dolphin and Mick Lane was another brother-in-law and he was also Dolphin, but it was my own call. I said to that particular uncle and godfather of mine, look I want to play fullback and if you are not going to pick me there, I will go and join another club. He said, you can if you like so, and I did. The people I got on with understood. Trevor Murphy left Con to join Garryowen as a gesture of support and he was as much into Con as any of us. I played on for at least four more years with Dolphin [captaining the team in 1961–2] and eventually became club president. I also became a Munster and Ireland selector and was on the "Big Five" when we won the Triple Crown in 1985.'

* * *

Tom Kiernan's international career was launched in 1960. He went on to wear the green jersey on fifty-four occasions, captain his country twenty-four times, make two Lions tours, captaining the tourists in 1968, and hold almost every conceivable administrative position in the game. And yet, it's conceivable that were it not for Ray Hennessy's withdrawal from the 1960 final Irish trial, he might never have reached such exalted heights in the game.

'When Jim went to Dolphin, Ray Hennessy played with Con and Munster at fullback and got three final trials,' Tom explains. 'I was centre for Munster and fullback for the Irish Universities and played well in a match in Dublin and was picked at fullback on the Possibles for the final trial. What happens? Hennessy is told by his friends, "You've only to turn up and you'll walk on the team." But you know the way it was in those days, they'd say to him, you're on, what do you want to play for? So Ray cried off. That's how the story goes anyway. I moved over and if I back heeled the ball, 'twould have gone over the bar. I got the place and Ray never got a cap afterwards. Ray's wife's sister Frankie [O'Gorman] was and is my wife's best friend and he was always a great friend of mine and still is.'

Tommy Kiernan's selection ahead of Ray Hennessy at the start of the 1960 campaign heralded the arrival on the scene of one of Ireland's greatest ever fullbacks. His international career spanned fourteen years and contained many high points and a few that might have knocked the stuffing out of a lesser man. Significant among the latter was the day in Cardiff in 1965 when Ireland travelled to the old Arms

Park (now majestically transformed into the Millennium Stadium) in search of what would have been a famous Triple Crown victory. It remains an occasion etched into the memories of those of us present that day and the thousands watching on their black and white television sets. Both countries were blessed with magnificent rugby players ... Ray McLoughlin was the much-respected captain of Ireland and was surrounded by men of the calibre of Tom Kiernan, Jerry Walsh, Kevin Flynn, Mike Gibson at out-half, Willie John McBride and Noel Murphy. It would have taken a major effort for the Irish to defeat Wales in their own backyard and with so much at stake, but there was still great confidence that it could happen. The Welsh prevailed by 14–8, with their captain Clive Rowlands almost kicking the cover off the ball in a tactical performance well suited to the laws of the time.

Tom, who had originally held the captaincy in 1963 before being succeeded by Bill Mulcahy and Ray McLoughlin, took over the captaincy from McLoughlin after three poor results in 1966 and his elevation coincided with a 9–6 win over Wales at Lansdowne Road that avenged the previous year's defeat and deprived the Welsh of an eleventh successive Triple Crown (he was superseded as captain by Noel Murphy in 1967, took it up again the following year and retained it until the end of his international career in 1973). He skippered the national side on another twenty-three occasions, an outstanding record of achievement especially given the limited number of matches played at the time. There was not the distinction of winning a Triple Crown in this period, although needless to say, there were several fine results. One such came in January 1969, when Ireland beat France for the first time in eleven years by 17–9 at Lansdowne Road. Munster team-mates Johnny Moroney and Barry McGann were the stars of the occasion, with the former personally contributing a then record total of fourteen points. That game was notable for a 'record' of a different nature – Mick Hipwell replaced the injured Noel Murphy, the first time Ireland had made a substitution in the course of a game.

Ireland–Wales games in the 1960s were rarely without incident; in 1969, the 24–11 loss in Cardiff remains more memorable for the punch by Brian Price that levelled Noel Murphy in full view of the referee, Mr McMahon of Scotland, and also the young Prince of Wales. Rugby didn't do sendings off or, perish the thought, red cards at the time and Price escaped the ultimate sanction which his actions probably merited. Equally, though, Tom Kiernan and his men had no complaint about the final score line. Wales were good, very good, and so there was general amazement when Ireland ran up fourteen points without reply at Lansdowne Road in 1970 when the Welsh were widely regarded as 'a team of all the talents' and came confidently in search of yet another Triple Crown. Tommy and his Cork Con club mate Barry McGann were key men on that occasion, although the picture of Alan Duggan diving to score the only try is a classic of the genre. If that was a deeply satisfying day for the captain and other gifted stalwarts of the side like Mike Gibson (now in the centre to make way for McGann at number 10), Syd Millar, Willie John McBride, Fergus Slattery and Ken Goodall, there were two more in the fateful year of 1972. Tom brought his team to the old Colombes Stadium seeking their first win in twenty years in the French capital. It truly was a combination of the old and the new – on the one hand Kiernan, Gibson, McLoughlin and McBride, on the other newcomers in Tom Grace, Johnny Moloney and Stewart McKinney among others. The value of a try had been increased that season from three points to four, but as it transpired this made no material difference as the Irish turned in an inspired performance. Ray McLoughlin carried half of France over the line for a great forwards try, debutant Moloney got another and, as usual, Tom Kiernan kicked the rest of the points.

If anything, there was even better to come a few weeks later at Twickenham. Ireland trailed 12–7 with five minutes to go before McGann dropped a peach of a goal and then deep into stoppage time, Moloney and McGann put Kevin Flynn in position to sell the most outrageous dummy ever seen before touching triumphantly down behind the posts. Tom added the points, and Ireland won by 16–12 and were well set for both the Triple Crown and Championship. And that is when the bottom suddenly fell out of Ireland's rugby world. The Troubles in the north were under way and the weak-livered officials of the Scottish and Welsh Unions were known to have misgivings about travelling to Dublin. An Irish delegation led by President Dom Dineen and including Judge Charles Conroy, Harry McKibbin, Ronnie Dawson and Sinclair Irwin, travelled to Edinburgh to try and reassure the Scots that they had nothing to worry about. To no avail. Scotland the Brave would not travel and neither, as it transpired, would the Welsh leave the land of their fathers.

Ireland's gilt-edged chance of a coveted Grand Slam had been dashed and their captain and his players were left to rue this for the rest of their lives. England, though, came the following year, and emotional tears flowed freely down the faces of all Irishmen and women at Lansdowne Road that memorable afternoon as the so-called 'auld enemy' trotted out to a deafening roar and a five-minute reception from a Lansdowne Road crowd that registered its gratitude in such a moving way that the image of the country at a very dark time came across worldwide in a very favourable manner. In the circumstances England had little chance of averting an Irish victory by eighteen points to nine. For once, the Irish captain, Tom Kiernan, was trumped by his counterpart at that evening's official dinner when John Pullin remarked that 'we may not be much good but at least we turn up'. Tom went on to mark his fifty-fourth and last match for his country and his twenty-fourth as captain with a try against Scotland at Murrayfield in 1973.

* * *

TOM WOULD have hoped for a better return from his second Lions tour of South Africa in 1968. Rugby in the northern hemisphere at the time was buzzing, not least because of the calibre of a magnificent Welsh side, and sure enough the likes of Gareth Edwards, Barry John, J.P.R. Williams and Mervyn Davies were there to lend their special talents to the cause. For Tom Kiernan to be chosen as captain, with so much other talent available to the Lions committee, speaks volumes for the respect in which he was regarded by the game's leaders. The wisdom of their appointment quickly became apparent and hopes of a first series victory over the Springboks were high after the first Test was won by twenty-five points to twenty. It certainly was not the captain's fault that two of the next three games were lost and one drawn, but it would be another six years before the Lions lowered the Boks' colours on home territory. However, in between those two Lions tours, Tom had the satisfaction of leading Ireland to victory over South Africa at Lansdowne Road. And it was a late Kiernan penalty that forged a famous breakthrough 9–6 victory.

Tom also played three matches for Munster against major overseas opposition. The first was against the hugely successful All Blacks at Thomond Park in December 1963 when a side many stones lighter than the opposition and vastly less experienced came within inches of a remarkable victory. The Kiwis scraped home by 6–3, but notice had been served, in itself giving due credence to Tom's oft-repeated comment that beating New Zealand 'had to happen some day'. And, of course, it did under his command fifteen years later!

Before that, however, he was to derive deep satisfaction from leading Munster to an 11–8 win over the Australians at Musgrave Park in 1967. Jerry Walsh, Tom's great friend from his earliest days, was there to lend his renowned crash tackling to the mix and up front were his redoubtable Constitution club mates Noel Murphy and Liam Coughlan, the unrelated O'Callaghans, Phil and Mick, at prop, and another great Con man, Jerry Murray, in the second-row. Johnny Moroney scored Munster's try, Tom kicked eight points, the Wallabies replying with a try by Cardy, a penalty by Brass and a conversion by Ryan. And so Munster led 11–8 as the game entered its final minute. And it is here that Tom takes up the story: 'It was the first time an Irish province had beaten a touring team so it was a famous occasion. We were three points ahead with time almost up when Australia got a penalty in front of the Dolphin pavilion about thirty yards out and near the touchline. Instead of going for goal, they went for the win and kicked a stormer up in the air. Paddy McGrath was on the wing and he knocked it on so there was a scrum under our posts. Up they came and the scrum formed. Noisy [Noel Murphy] asked the ref how long there was to go and he said, well, it's time up. So I said, blow the f***ing whistle then and he did so. The ref was Ray Gilliland from the north and the Australians got up from the scrum and were not a bit happy. Would you blame them?! That happened, no doubt about it, no exaggeration.'

Oddly enough, Tom was never an Irish selector, even when he was national coach in 1980/81 and again in 1982/83, and it was only when he managed and coached teams on tours 'down under' that he had a say in team selection. 'I was given full voice. Paddy Madigan was chairman and they were good years, especially when we won the Triple Crown for the first time after thirty-four years in 1982,' he says. 'But the match against Scotland the day we won the Crown was awful. Our matches against Scotland tend to be dour. They deprived us of the Triple Crown last year [2010] when we should have won it, this year we won the match when we could easily have lost it.

'Winning the Triple Crown after that length of time was a great relief and took the monkey off our backs. But they were funny times. In my first year we didn't win a game, the second year we had a Triple Crown and then finished top in the third followed by another disaster the following year, Willie John's [McBride], which was a whitewash and he left. The fifth year, Mick Doyle was coach and they won the Triple Crown and the following year he was coach again and they were white-washed.'

The Kiernan connection to the 1985 Triple Crown side was further enhanced by the fact that Jim was a selector and his son Michael dropped the winning goal in the decisive final match against England. It was a very proud moment for the whole family although, like all dads in those kinds of circumstances, Jim worried what would have been said had the kick not gone over the bar, musing that 'nine times out of ten, you'd slice it wide or miskick it'. Tom quickly dismissed those fears, declaring, 'Personally I think the decision was right because I don't think they had any chance of scoring out wide.'

Looking back at this remove, Jim insists he wouldn't have been too anxious about Michael's performance: 'I was used to him playing, to uncles playing, Tom playing … by getting uptight you weren't going to contribute anything. I don't think I ever got that uptight about a match. From experience, you realise that he could also make an awful balls of it so you wouldn't play it up too much. And Michael didn't win the Triple Crown for Ireland … there were eighty other minutes of play, a large proportion of which he made no contribution to … the team played well and deserved to win.'

Uncle Tom says, 'If Michael had missed that drop goal, I wouldn't have thought he was the worst player in the world or any better than he was five minutes beforehand because he got it.'

* * *

A PICTURE of Tom Kiernan on bended knee and in suit and tie on the sideline as his Munster team put the All Blacks to the sword at Thomond Park in 1978 remains one of the most iconic images of that unforgettable occasion. There were no glass panelled, centrally heated boxes high in the stands back in those days, no laptops, no earpieces, no extra coaches to concentrate on this, that and the other. Tom Kiernan masterminded the entire operation himself and no one could have done it better. He explains how it all came to pass.

'We went on a trip to London at the beginning of the season where we played Middlesex and an Exiles side. During the two days before the games, we trained at St Paul's School, Hammersmith, and there we set a standard of fitness for the team as a whole, with special targets for the backs and forwards, the backs concentrating on sharpness and the forwards concentrating on endurance. After that we met on three Wednesdays in Fermoy and on the Sunday and Monday prior to the match in St Munchin's College, Limerick.'

At this point I deign to interrupt Tom's flow of thought to point out that the squad fared anything but well in those two games in London and indeed took something of a hammering from Middlesex. Remedial action needed to be taken in a few positions and this had the desired result.

And while the sessions in Fermoy have also become a part of legend and were frequently referred to in John Breen's great play *Alone We Stand* in somewhat jocose fashion, they did instil the kind of spirit and commitment that was to prove so vital on the big day. I remember well the highly respected New Zealand journalist, Terry McLean (who was to be posthumously inducted into the International Rugby Hall of Fame with Tom Kiernan in 2007) being much taken with what he saw in the sessions at St Munchin's. 'There's much more to Kiernan's team than what people are seeing,' he predicted with remarkable prescience.

And as Tom continues, it appears that McLean wasn't the only one who felt a shock might be on the cards: 'At the latter session, it was obvious to most onlookers that the Munster team was fitter and sharper than was the case in many years and that we would give the All Blacks a tough game. I was always of the belief that we had the skills. We planned on the use of two-man line-outs using Donal Spring and Moss Keane, but weren't given much opportunity to use this tactic because they had the vast majority of throw-ins from touch and anyway we were in our own half for most of the match and one doesn't risk short line-outs in those circumstances.

'It should also be acknowledged that Munster had its share of luck. And the fact that we scored first meant they had to come back at us. I was particularly pleased at the way Munster took their chances which was an affirmation of the sharpness the team had attained in its pre-match training. Another pleasing aspect was the controlled discipline of the side.'

A day after the match, All Blacks coach Jack Gleeson

couldn't conceal his frustration at the way his team's best efforts to get back into the game were foiled and thwarted by the superb opposition defence and unfortunately referred to it as 'kamikaze'. This didn't at all sit well with his Munster counterpart. 'One of the New Zealand officials explained his team's defeat by alleging kamikaze tactics on our parts. I'm not entirely sure what that means, but tackling is as integral a part of rugby as is a majestic centre three-quarter break and score under the posts. The perfect timing and execution of a tackle gives me as much pleasure to watch as any other element of rugby. There were two noteworthy tackles during the match by Seamus Dennison. He was injured in the first and I thought he might have to come off. But he repeated the tackle some minutes later.'

The match might have taken place all of thirty-three years ago, but for those of us fortunate enough to have been present, it is as easy to remember almost every incident of the game as if it had taken place only the other day. Tom recalls the brilliantly taken first-half try thus: 'It came from a great piece of anticipation by Bowen, who in the first place had to run around his man to get to Ward's kick ahead. He then beat two men and when finally tackled, managed to keep his balance and deliver the ball to Cantillon who went on to score. All of this was evidence of sharpness on Bowen's part. Then there was Ward's second drop goal. A scrum had been spoiled and the ball came back on the Munster side under some pressure. In that semi-crisis, Tucker got a fine pass out to Ward who dropped a great goal in the circumstances – again a manifestation of sharpness.'

On the following day, Jack Gleeson gave Press Association rugby correspondent Terry Cooper the infamous 'kamikaze' interview, but it cut little ice with Terry McLean who asked in his excellent book on the tour: 'What was Kiernan to do – play as New Zealand wanted the match to be played, all open and free, with fine running from first to last? Or play to his strength, which principally was the absolute bravery of his men? Tommy Kiernan was not born yesterday. He knew what he wanted and got it. He played to the strength of his team and upon the suspected weaknesses of the All Blacks.'

Munster 12 (Chris Cantillon try, Tony Ward 2 drop goals, one conversion), New Zealand 0. Graham Mourie's All Blacks won every other match on the 1978 tour of Europe.

* * *

'Rugby today is a hundred times more aggressive from when I played,' says Jim. 'It requires ultimate fitness and so it's a different game really. Our idea was to win the ball and get it out to the wing. Now, you rarely ever see it go from scrum half to wing without some move. It's all about phases nowadays. It certainly is a huge improvement from the spectators' point of view … some of the matches we saw in our day, they were more like a funeral than a rugby match. It has speeded up and become a lot more aggressive.'

According to Tom, 'Kicking to touch was the big thing. I mean, Dan Daly kicked every ball he ever got in his life.' Jim points out that the philosophy was 'to keep it in the opposition 25 and something is bound to happen, you'll get a couple of penalties or a drop goal, and that maximised kicking to the corners.'

Both men are agreed that while putting the ball into the set scrums has 'become something of a farce', the line-out has changed radically, with Tom maintaining that this area of the game 'has improved about thirty per cent in the last eighteen months'. Referring to a Munster–Leinster game a few days before our chat, Tom pointed out that 'Munster had nine penalty kicks at goal and missed one and Leinster had six while the set scrum has become something of a joke. Whatever the fellows are doing and whatever the cause of it … a minute and a half, two minutes for a lot of the scrummages, so if you have twelve scrums and fifteen kickable penalties, just think of the amount of playing time you lose … I don't know, maybe the referees have something to say about it.

'And then there is this touch, pause, whatever they say going down, why don't they let the bloody fellows go down like they went down forever. There might be a medical reason for it, I don't know … I think the game is bloody good most of the time but there are these infuriating things they'll have to get around … sixteen kicks at goal on a good night with perfect conditions seems to be wrong – and the set scrummage, they're the two things I don't like. And then there's the rucks, you might know when you're at the bottom of a ruck whether you can get away from it or not, but you see fellows pinned down and I don't know how they're expected to roll away. Some might feign it but there are a lot of guys of every size who just cannot get out and they are penalised. Referees should be able to see whether fellows can get out but there are so many frees given for it that I just don't know.'

Jim was also taken aback at a television commentator who inferred that 'the game would improve if you took the wing-forwards out and reduced it to thirteen-a-side. Basically what you are doing is going down another step towards rugby league. I think it was a disgraceful thing to say. Do people want to watch rugby league? If they do, let them go and watch it.'

Tom suggested that 'there should be other mechanisms for sorting it out and I don't think going the rugby league road will do any good. Rugby league, after all, is about phases and you don't even have to challenge for it. Now, you might say to me, you don't have to challenge in the set scrums either because you never hear of a ball being won against the head today.'

As for his outstanding rugby memories, Jim thought long and hard before answering: 'Winning the cup with College [UCC] the first year out of school was a highlight, another would be Michael's drop goal and again Tom being appointed captain of the Lions. But I don't think I ever got over-exuberant about the game, but took it for what it is. The bad can happen as well as the good.' Which I suppose could be a reference in itself as to how Tom's captaincy of the 1968 Lions worked out. It was always going to be a daunting task with several of the players who had been members of the side in New Zealand two years previously captained by the Scot Mike Campbell-Lamerton having bad memories of that trip. Creating a better atmosphere and spirit was a big part of Tom's job but he, manager David Brooks and coach

Ronnie Dawson, coped splendidly, even if the Test series was lost 2–1 with one draw.

'Off the pitch, these tourists were the happiest bunch one could have met, even though some of their high-spirited moments prompted criticism in South African newspapers,' wrote the *Examiner*'s Barry Coughlan in his book *The Irish Lions*. 'From the viewpoint of losing the Test series, they failed in their mission but managed to return to these shores having won fifteen of their sixteen provincial matches. The Springboks won the first Test 25–20 when Tom Kiernan kicked five penalties and converted a try by Willie John McBride. The potential in the side was evident when the second ended in a 6–6 draw and so the third proved crucial. The Lions went down 11–6 but had enough chances to win. As is so often the case at the end of a long and arduous tour, the fourth Test was lost 19–6.

'Kiernan, who had not particularly enjoyed himself six years before, emerged as one of the greatest fullbacks of all time. Everything he did smacked of a great player. The Irishman was a popular choice for the captaincy. Ireland had enjoyed an excellent championship and he had been earmarked from the very beginning. Kiernan regretted that the team were unable to do better but conceded, "We had a good but not a great team. South Africa were just too strong for us, although I felt we might have had more success if we had avoided all those injuries."'

Tom's quick wit was evident from the time the Lions arrived in South Africa. Asked if they had learned some Afrikaans in preparation for the visit and understood the language, he told a reporter, 'Of course I do – provided it's spoken through Irish.' Tom became the sixth Irishman to captain the Lions having been, if you like, an underling in 1962 when the fine Scottish wing Arthur Smith was at the helm. He was one of six Irishmen in that squad and vied with England's John Willcox for the fullback position. An ankle injury cost him his place in the first two Tests although Willcox also proved himself an outstanding No. 15 and it was not his fault that they were a Test down with one to play. Tom got his chance in the third match and the other Irish in the side were McBride, Syd Millar and Bill Mulcahy. It was 3–3 with time nearly up when they tried to run the ball from their own line, a Richard Sharp pass went astray and the Springbok out-half Keith Oxlee grabbed a try that he converted himself.

Lions' captains and teams have become accustomed to disappointments over the years. Hard luck stories abound and Tom Kiernan's squad didn't always enjoy the rub of the green. But he was a great tourist and a great leader of men as his many outstanding achievements on and off the rugby field graphically demonstrate.

* * *

JIM AND Tom are clearly very close, but there is no way they are going to give each other a swelled head. When I suggested to Tom that Jim was a class footballer, the response was that 'he had that reputation anyway'. Jim's retort was to the effect that 'Tom was born lucky'. Maybe so, but apart from his achievements with Munster and Ireland, it is worthy of note that Tom won seven Munster Cups, one with UCC and six with Cork Constitution, and was on the College (4) and Cork Con (9) teams that captured the old Munster Senior League in thirteen consecutive seasons. And finally, given all the notice that the number of 'caps' players win these days with the provinces, very few if any could claim to have represented the province for sixteen straight years!

All in all, though, you are left to wonder where the game in this country would be were it not for the Kiernan-Murphy dynasty.

JOHN AND DENIS
FOGARTY

Munster and Leinster ... It's not that they hate each
other, they just hate to lose to each other.

John Fogarty

THE DATE 2 May 2009 will forever be etched in the minds
of Irish rugby followers. It was balmy that evening but Croke
Park, the home of Gaelic games in Ireland, was absolutely
heaving and buzzing with unsuppressed excitement as
Leinster and Munster prepared to do battle in the semi-final
of the Heineken Cup.

For the previous month, it wasn't just sporting Ireland
that couldn't wait for the day to come round. The rivalry
between the provinces extended back over a century and had
always been intense. But even that increased a thousandfold
when Munster clobbered Leinster by thirty points to six in
the 2006 Heineken Cup semi-final in front of a full house
at Lansdowne Road. That score line was bad enough for the
supporters of the losing side, but the fact that 75 per cent of
the fans in a stadium situated in the game's heartland in the
capital were bedecked in the red of Munster was a source of
deep embarrassment to Leinster supporters. They vowed they

would never lose on the terraces and stands again, whatever about on the field of play, and when the scene was re-enacted, albeit north of the Liffey, three years later, the Boys in Blue matched, if not quite outnumbered, the Red Army. As for the happenings on the Croke Park pitch itself, it was hardly a contest as Leinster exacted massive revenge, winning against the odds by twenty-five points to six.

There were innumerable fascinating little cameos that day and one of the most intriguing was that brothers would literally come face to face for a fifteen-minute period in the second half. Tipperary natives John (Leinster) and Denis (Munster) Fogarty were the respective replacement hookers and as the game entered its climactic closing moments, both were introduced to the fray.

As John remembers it, 'Denis and I had been chatting about the game even before the quarter-finals – if we win our next match and you win yours, we're going to meet in the semi-finals and that will be some game. And then we were on the phone thinking, bloody hell, we could be going head-to-head at Croke Park, which for everybody Irish is the place to play. We would have been brought there from an early age being from Tipp, and I remember back then walking on the pitch and thinking, this is the biggest place in the world.

'Denis and I talked and hoped that we would both get on and have a crack at each other. We discussed it in an excited way and as the day grew closer, it somehow became bigger than either of us had imagined. The atmosphere going into the game was unbelievable. I never thought it was going to be that big. People kept ringing me and were beginning to wreck my head a bit. Really, you don't want to hear too much about it. As it turned out, though, it was the biggest game I have ever been involved in. It really was a big week. It was a hugely emotional week, playing against a family member … weird, surreal, there was even an element of sadness.

'But there was not a sense of regret playing against my native place. I had been let go by Munster and was annoyed when they kept a Dublin guy, James Blaney. They had turned their backs on me and that was how I would have stupidly felt back then. I was sad to leave Munster and also a little bitter, although I completely changed as a player and took my job a lot more seriously after that. And when I moved to Leinster, I became a part of the scene very quickly. On my way there, I was thinking that not so very many years before, I used to hate Leinster. I used to look at them as those f*****s up the road. I never thought I'd end up there of all places; the dream would have been to play for my home province from day one to day end. But I was genuinely excited at going up there after five years at Connacht and Munster not wanting me in any shape or form. And then there was the privilege of playing with so many great players. I loved it and was excited to be there.

'They turned out to be the best three years of my career. My attitude changed from when I was a young fella. For me, rugby comes down to the jersey you wear and the fellas you're playing with, what you go through with them and that's why I quickly became involved with Leinster because they were a genuinely good bunch of fellas. They were working their backsides off to get rid of this tag they had around their necks and the attitude other people had towards them – the ladyboys stuff and all that and it was very harsh and very personal. It was taking away from their integrity as people. And, I can tell you, it was an effective tool in winning the Heineken Cup.

'As the game loomed, I didn't think too much about being from Munster. I was playing with a great group of fellas. There was great camaraderie. The impression I once had of Leinster was the wrong one. I just wanted to be part of a team that was going to beat Munster on a big stage because I suppose I wanted to get my own little bit of revenge. This was a team that didn't want me, okay the bitterness was gone a long time, but I still wanted to play against my own team and win. I had a point to make and it was a small point and only for myself, and I don't think anyone else would have given a damn, but I really wanted to beat them.

'Taking on the kid brother was really weird. I wanted him to do well and was thinking to myself, "Come on Denis" or whatever, and then straightaway I snapped back to "I'll break your bloody neck". I suppose there's a part of the older brother that will always mind the younger brother, but there's no need to mind Denis, I can tell you.

'I was on the pitch before him and didn't know the Munster change was coming. It was before a scrum and the next thing he was coming on and there was a little lump in my throat for about .4 of a second at the thought of the two of us being on the pitch at the same time, because it was what we had chatted about for weeks previously. I was absolutely definitely chuffed that Denis was on the pitch and we were playing in front of more than 82,000 people in one of the biggest games in the country's history. I think I gave him a smile and a wink.

'Munster and Leinster is the biggest rivalry in Irish rugby without a doubt. It's not that they hate each other, they just hate to lose to each other. They're the biggest games and you want to beat them so much but when your brother is playing, you want him to do well, to go well but you also want him to lose. As I say, it's surreal and I really don't know how to put the feelings, the emotions, into words. The Leinster–Munster thing … well, there's not one Leinster player who will say, "I hate a certain Munster guy", that he's a bad guy, except that on the pitch on the day of a match they are all bad guys. They are all trying to beat you, but you cannot let that happen.

'Leinster weren't supposed to win that game, but there was no gloating at the finish, no jumping around in the dressing-room. I made a beeline for Denis and don't remember exactly what I said except, "Are you all right?" and he said he was okay and I probably gave him a hug. If Denis wasn't my brother, I would still be very close to him because of the kind of fella he is. With Munster, you know you are going to get done the next time or the time after that. Other teams can gloat, but Munster and Leinster are not teams for that kind of stuff.

'I am hugely proud to have been part of that match and it meant a huge amount to the people at home. Cashel is a small enough town and it had three players in the game. Obviously it didn't go great from their point of view, but it was a huge occasion and it was huge for both sides of our family, the O'Connor side and the Fogarty side. They were extremely proud. Very emotional.'

Denis remembers, 'It was a huge day. John and I had been chatting about it all for weeks and there was huge excitement for our family, even though we were both subs and so there was no guarantee that either of us would be directly involved. There was obviously the possibility that we could meet at some stage of the game. The whole family and the cousins came up to enjoy it all and watch and wait for the moment when the two of us clashed.

'John got on before me and I think I got on for the last ten minutes. I had a few scrums with him which was great even if it was a little crazy. Going out in front of a record crowd of 82,000 was driving me mad enough without going out against yer man, but meeting him was always at the back of my mind although you're sitting on the bench and thinking about the game and the end result. I didn't know for sure that I would be coming on. I would never say it was a lost cause, but it was nearly dead when I got the nod. Of course we weren't going to lie down and I wasn't going to lie down.

'Going into our first scrum, he winked at me. So I just kind of grinned back and that was that and we went bursting at it. We have now played against each other a few times. At the very start of the 2009/10 season, we both started up in Donnybrook and he won that one as well, so he's had a few over on me. But we beat them at Thomond Park later that season and I scored a try and he was gutted. I didn't give him too much stick because there are always games coming up and you don't want to blow your trumpet too loudly. He leads 3–1 and now that he has retired, I cannot get my own back, and he reminds me of that, too.

'Sure, there is a touch of Munster in him deep down. He is from Tipp and Munster and it was the first provincial team he played with, but I must say he really enjoyed his time up in Leinster. I think he left here with a bit of bitterness, and he's kind of a bitter person when it comes to his rugby, even though there will always be a bit of red in him. And he got to pull on the green jersey, it was a great thing for him after an up and down career. I was delighted to see him get the cap and felt it was well deserved. My aim is to emulate him and it's what I'm working towards.'

* * *

JOHN FOGARTY WAS obliged to retire from rugby in the autumn of 2010 after a series of knocks to the head left him with frequent bouts of concussion, leading to headaches and sleeplessness. It had been a colourful career that was launched from an early age at Cashel RFC and Rockwell College, where he progressed to such an extent that he represented Ireland Schools and followed with appearances at under-21, Students and Development levels and captained Ireland A in three of his twelve matches at that level. However, it wasn't until he had played for Munster, Connacht and Leinster that he finally attained the greatest accolade of all, an Irish cap as a replacement against New Zealand on the summer tour of 2010.

Not long afterwards, it was all over for John, his premature retirement coming as a severe blow to himself and his family as they looked back upon a career that was blighted to some degree by downright bad luck where injury was concerned. A classic example came on the eve of the 2004 Heineken Cup final in Cardiff when he was to sit on the Munster bench for the game against Leicester Tigers. However, on the eve of the match he injured his shoulder while simulating a WWF bout (World Wrestling Federation, or in his brother's words, 'doing the eejit') with Donncha O'Callaghan in their hotel bedroom. James Blaney took over the role and came in for the final fifteen minutes.

After Munster ended his contract, John went on to spend five years at Connacht. He loved his time there and they loved him back in return. In all, he played 107 games in the Magners League and Amlin Cup for the western province before moving on to Leinster and playing a significant role in that 2009 Heineken Cup triumph. Nothing could keep John Fogarty down and again he repeated the mantra that 'I love rugby because it's all I ever wanted to do'. His sense of humour and quick wit endeared him to everybody and he would not allow his head to drop, even when coming out the wrong side of a bizarre situation in the build-up to the Ireland–Australia game at Croke Park in 2009. First choice Jerry Flannery was a doubtful starter and coach Declan Kidney informed John that he would start the game if Fla didn't make it. Equally, however, he would not be involved at all if Jerry proved his fitness, as the promising young Connacht No. 2, Seán Cronin, would sit on the bench to gain experience.

'I was on the Croke Park pitch for the warm-up when told that Jerry had come through a fitness test,' John recalls. 'And I was in the showers when the anthems were playing.'

It was in November 2010 that John Fogarty finally acknowledged that the game was up where his professional rugby career was concerned. He owed it to his wife Sinead and little daughter Katie-May, not to mention himself, to retire from an activity that had given him endless hours of happiness and satisfaction, an Irish cap and a Heineken European Cup medal, and yet one that might well cost him his life if he didn't desist forthwith. In a moving and thought-provoking chat with Brendan Fanning of the *Sunday Independent,* he explained how things had slowly but inexorably come to an end.

'I admitted to myself after the Toulouse game last year [2009] that there was something seriously wrong. There had been one scrum where I passed out. I don't remember what I was doing. It sounds terrible: blood out of my nose and a bit of a shake. The medics ask their questions and medically I must have been sound enough because I could remember the date and the day and all that stuff. It didn't knock me out.

'I used to tell Sinead as little as possible. She knew I got a bang that day in Toulouse but didn't know that I passed out. She could see what had happened to my moods which caused arguments. From then on, I had to be more honest with her but she was already pretty worried. And my mother was the same: "Will you just finish this game! Feck rugby, give it up."'

Well, he did – but only after touring with Ireland in New Zealand and getting that elusive first cap. However, it was during a holiday in Portugal on his return that the headaches returned and again Sinead tried to preach some common sense. 'You've been capped, you have a Heineken Cup medal, you've had a great career and played more Magners League matches than any other Irish player, would you not consider wrapping it up?' she pleaded. John saw reason in what Sinead was saying, but he still clung to hope, pointing out, 'I had signed a two year contract and they wouldn't have given it to me if I'd looked like a player who was finished. I wanted to go out as a twelve-year veteran turning thirty-five, I wanted to win a competition with Leinster as a starting player, not coming off the bench.'

But it was not to be. After yet another bang on the head in a game against Treviso in September 2010, a chat with Leinster doctor Arthur Tanner convinced him that the time had come to face up to his responsibilities. 'It came from him. I was leaving for the bus and was still a bit zonked and he came over and told me, "Johnny, you need to start thinking about this." I was like a bit of a zombie. I started to get panicky. I was very sensitive to noise and light.'

John did the cognitive tests and told himself everything was just fine. But Arthur Tanner wasn't the only doctor advising him to quit and eventually he saw the light, even if he did warn with that lovely way of his: 'I'm not going away. Rugby is still my life. I have an enormous passion for it. I have done some coaching and am keen to do a lot more. I have a ton of experience to share.'

* * *

IT SHOULD be borne in mind that rugby teams, even in this professional age, are full of pranksters and practical jokers. In this respect, the Fogartys are (in)famous. But it didn't affect their widespread popularity and when the news broke that John was retiring, his one-time Connacht team-mate and former international flanker Johnny O'Connor was moved to comment: 'If he wanted, he definitely has a career ahead of him as a stand-up comedian. He is a great lad, a really sound man and one of the funniest guys I have ever come across. He's the joker in the pack and always a good person to be around.'

Denis would not take issue with that description of his brother, although he insists that 'he is good at the comedy and the ball-hopping, but he's not as good as me'. Expanding on this delightfully happy and optimistic outlook on life, Denis hands most of the credit to his late father. 'We got it from Dad. He was very funny, always messing, joking, arsing around, taking the piss. We got these traits from him. So many funny things happened and one thing that John and I do remember was working with Dad a good few years ago in the garage. The newspapers arrived one day and in one of them was a magazine with a glossy picture of the new €50 note that was just about to be launched. Dad cut it out carefully so that it definitely looked like the real thing and went out to the forecourt and put it under a stone so that the €50 part was clearly visible. It really looked genuine. We went back in and watched the reaction of the people walking by. You wouldn't believe the number of people who were falling for it. It was all these kinds of little tricks that he used to play on other fellas, he'd rope us up and tell us, watch this, watch that … there are a few things I'm better at than John and getting up to a little bit of mischief is one of them.' John argues that point fairly vehemently, but was genuinely touched by the concern Denis showed for him when he was left with little option but to call an end to his rugby career.

'John's Masters in Sports Business in UCD is keeping him ticking over because he took it fairly hard initially when he was told that he should retire from rugby,' says Denis. 'He couldn't get his head around it. He said to me, "I have so much to offer physically … I'm very strong, very fit and not ready to finish just yet." He was close to being heartbroken at having his career taken away like that. I suppose it's easier when you look down the line and know when you are going to retire. He had just signed a new two-year contract.

'I had a few weeks off at the time so we went together to New York with his wife and my girlfriend Sarah for four or five days. We got away from rugby and just enjoyed ourselves. It gave him the chance to let go of it all, get out of there and get his head around what he had to do when he got back. So now he's doing his Masters in UCD and Ronnie McCormack is with him, as he also had to retire because of a neck injury and it's good for John having someone that's in the same line of work doing the same course. By the way, Sarah is from Crosshaven – I had to come down to Cork to find a woman. I was gutted.'

All said, of course, with that familiar infectious laugh! Which duly reminded Denis once again of his dad, to whom he pays a glowing tribute for the success he and John have enjoyed in the sporting arena.

'What drove us on was our father and our father's father. They loved rugby. My dad died suddenly three years ago and that hit both of us pretty hard. He just didn't wake up one morning. He was only fifty-six and it came as a great shock. It was one of the toughest things I ever had to deal with and it took me a very long time to get my head around it. I'll never get over losing someone so close to me, but it's a driving force now because he loved the two of us playing the game and he was such an inspiration for us to reach our goals.'

In fact, his father's influence led to youngsters born and reared in a hurling environment taking up and prospering at rugby. 'We were born just outside Cashel in what was a hurling environment,' Denis explains. 'We had a little bit of rugby through my dad, also Denis, who played with Cashel and when the parents moved to Cork for ten years, he played for Dolphin. We came back and went into Cashel to play under-age as my mother's side of the family – May – also had a bit of rugby. Obviously, though, hurling was also huge in Tipp and we played hurling and football with the local club, Rosegreen, just down the road from us and where Ballydoyle is now, Aidan O'Brien and all that.

'And that's where we went to primary school. There are four of us: Damien, John, my sister Niamh and myself. Damien was more into hurling but he also played a bit of rugby with Cashel and Thurles. John and I stuck to the rugby and they were great times. Damien and John would have been knocking lumps out of each other. There was always a bit of rivalry between them and then as I grew older, they decided to pick on me. But it was all in good faith, I got my hidings and just got on with it. I tried to get my own back but didn't get too far, although I had Mammy on my side.

'My dad owned a few Esso garages, he was a businessman, and we were shipped into nearby Rockwell as day boys one by one – and Niamh, too, when it became a mixed school.

We were already into rugby and once you got into second or third year and Junior Cup time, you weren't allowed to play more than one sport. Once you chose rugby, that was it really. John set the bar. He went on an Irish Schools tour to Australia in 1996 which they went through unbeaten, and after that he was off to college and I was into first year just after he left. I'd have been looking at the pictures on the walls in Rockwell of John in his Irish jersey and while I didn't think too much of it in the first few years, when it came to playing on the junior and senior teams, I would think, "Jeez, I wouldn't mind that."

'It was something I wanted and I worked hard for it. It was not easy because I didn't make the senior cup team in fifth year, but after that I broke in and first it was Munster and then Ireland Schools. It was funny, really. Because John played hooker, I wanted to play there as well. We'd be very close as brothers, very good friends, so it was a thing that I looked up to him and felt, if he could do it, I could also do it and hopefully I could do it better. As I grew older, I wanted to be better than that fecker.

'Why were we so close and still are? It was always that way. He nearly babied me when I got into Rockwell. He would say, "If anyone upsets you in that school, you tell me and I'll sort them out." He kind of left a thing behind him as he was leaving as if to say, "My brother is coming in next year and ye better look after him." I also had cousins in almost every year and he told them as well that they had better look after this fellow. We have grown closer and closer over the years. It's crazy, we are on the phone so much every day.

I couldn't put my finger on what made us so close. Maybe it was sharing what we called the end bedroom together. Jeez, it was freezing. It was an old garage converted into a bedroom and there was no insulation ... we used to be literally frozen down there, you could see the smoke coming out of us.

'Of course, we had to go our separate ways ... he went to college in Waterford and I went through Rockwell. I went on an under-19s World Cup to Italy and then to Cork Con because John was also playing with them while he was with Munster. I lived with him for about three years. I started all of the games in the under-21s World Cup in Scotland. We played and beat Tonga, Argentina, France and Australia in the semi-final. Jamie Heaslip, Tomás O'Leary and Tommy Bowe were on that side. John and my mum came over to watch but my dad was too nervous and only managed one match. He couldn't hack watching us but as it happened, we were outclassed in the final – New Zealand were very strong.

'John had just left to go to Connacht and Jerry [Flannery] came down here [to Munster] and James Blaney and Frankie [Sheahan] were also here and I was given a Development contract. I seemed to be picking up all sorts of little niggling injuries in my knee and shoulder, but was still fit enough to sit on the bench in the 2006 Heineken Cup final, unlike John two years earlier when he was messing on the bed with Donncha O'Callaghan and busted his shoulder.'

Yet another shoulder injury, the plague of so many rugby players, considerably reduced Denis Fogarty's appearances in the 2010/11 season and because of John's problems and premature retirement, it weighed heavily on his mind. The big brother was monitoring the situation carefully as Denis admitted. 'John would be worried if I didn't say anything, if I was not telling him stuff. When we are on the pitch and get bangs on the head, and the medics are coming on, the last thing you want is to go off and so you say, "I'm fine, there's nothing wrong with me." Yes, I have done that and I would do it again, the last thing I want to do is go off this pitch, especially in a red jersey, even though I know that sounds stupid.

'John tells me, "Make them aware if you do get a knock", because he knows how it is and what I and a lot of rugby players have done in the past. Let them know, because when you're concussed on the pitch and you say you're fine and can play on, it's not marked down as a concussion. If you're out like a light for a few seconds, you know you have been concussed. You're all over the place for a minute or two and you can still get on with it. You would have a headache that night and get up the next day and you might be a bit groggy but after a few days you're fine.

'John went through an awful time, he got constant headaches, he almost collapsed one day playing with his kid, but again it was the same thing … he just went, "I'll be all right, I'll be all right", until the day they collared him in Treviso after another bad knock. He had chronic headaches all the time and they said, that's it John, it's all over.'

Denis almost felt as badly about the situation as John – just another indication of just how close these guys have always been. Furthermore, and as if to underline just how difficult it is to batten down a place on a side of Munster's pedigree these days, Denis was battling not just with the often-injured Jerry Flanagan for the number two jersey, but also with Damien Varley and Mike Sherry towards the end of the 2010/11 campaign. As you would expect of such a wholehearted and committed individual, however, he regards this as just another challenge in the course of a career he is convinced will lead to the first of several Irish caps sooner rather than later.

MICK AND TOM DOYLE

I bet you're only suffering Guinness withdrawal pangs.

C.J. Haughey, in a get-well message to Irish coach Mick Doyle
after he took ill during the inaugural Rugby World Cup in New
Zealand in 1987

FOR MICK Doyle, the traffic was not moving quickly enough at Quinns Corner on the Ballygawley Road, Dungannon, on that fateful morning back in May 2004. So he decided to perform a quick u-turn to avoid the congestion only to run his Volvo S4 straight into the path of a Leyland Daf articulated lorry. The inevitable collision caused Doyle's immediate death and an outpouring of deep grief through the island of Ireland and many other parts of the world. One obituary described Mick as 'a fine example of the quintessentially hard, passionate and uncompromising flankers who have served Irish rugby so well down the years. Robust, committed and brave, he played at a time when the national team was undergoing something of a resurgence in the late 1960s, though Doyle will be best remembered for coaching Ireland to a rare Triple Crown and Five Nations Championship in 1985.'

Ian Martindale, his solicitor at the inquest in January

2006, was equally on the mark when he told Dungannon Coroner's Court that 'Michael Gerard Doyle/Mick Doyle/Doyler was one of the most charismatic figures in Irish rugby and indeed Irish sport'. Rev. David Frazier added that he was 'a great giant of a man, a lovable character, a man who meant so much to so many. He was a quiet, believing Christian without wearing it on his sleeve.' On the same day, IRFU president, John Quilligan, also struck the right note when describing Mick as 'a larger than life personality'.

Mick's passing at the age of sixty-three came as a great shock to those nearest and dearest to him: his first wife Lynne and second wife Mandy, his four children, Andrew, Sharon, Amanda and Emma, and his brother Tommy. Mick and Tommy had shared many great days and times together, not just in their birthplace, Castleisland, north Kerry, but also in some of rugby's most famous arenas. They were the wing-forwards in the Irish team that in 1968 drew with England at Twickenham and beat Scotland and Wales at Lansdowne Road. And so it was with a heavy heart that Tom spoke these eloquent words at Mick's interdenominational funeral service: 'Mick had a style, a passion and a belief that we all knew. He always lived life the same way, he did it because he loved it. He enriched everyone that he met. He has left a wonderful legacy, two wonderful wives and two wonderful families.'

* * *

LIFE FOR Mick and Tom Doyle began in the village of Currow and town of Castleisland in north Kerry. As happens in that part of the country, they were kicking footballs, both round and oval, from their earliest days, encouraged by their dad, Michael J.P. Doyle, a significant character in his own right who imbued much of his own zest for life and love of sport in his two boys. Doyle senior was a man of many parts and after he had revelled in the achievements of his two boys both on and off the sporting field and proved himself a shrewd and hard-working businessman, he emigrated to Morocco, which he loved to such an extent that he claimed it was 'the nearest thing I've found to Ballyheigue'.

Mick Doyle was born in October 1941 and Tom followed four years later. However, because his mother was not well after his birth, Mick lived the first twelve years or so of his life with his grandparents in Currow, whereas when Tom came along, he was reared by his parents in Castleisland until it was time to go to national school. However, from Tom's earliest memories, he and Mick were always extremely close. As with all youngsters growing up in Kerry, a football of some shape was invariably nearby and that in itself developed a healthy rivalry.

'My grandmother was a national teacher in Currow and it was from her that Mick got his real education,' said Tommy. 'You were surrounded from a very young age by personalities who always showed style and ability. I played with young fellas when I was six, seven and eight who could make a ball dance … you'd have had four of the likes of Colm Tucker in every town in Kerry. They learned from each other, and the rest of us, who might not have been so talented, had to learn pretty quickly if we wanted to compete with them. The school was known as Rannalough and a lot of fellas went out there from Castleisland to get a good education including Moss Keane, Mick Galwey and Kerry footballer Mick Fleming who was in my class. When I came of age to play for Currow, the first match was in Currans where Con Houlihan used to teach. I arrived with the boots, shorts and socks over the handlebars of the bicycle only to discover that Currow didn't need me but that Currans were short. So I got on their team and true to form, Currans won and I was never again asked to come on as a sub for Currow. I guaranteed my place by playing against them.

'Mick would have benefited in the same way I did, in that you would have had great footballers in every village team. They were all bigger and looked great … every fullback seemed to have to play with a cap in those days, it was a tradition of the time although many used them to keep the sun out of their eyes … you looked to these fellas in the belief that you could be as good as them at some stage of your life. Mick went to Newbridge College at a time when he was known to us all as Micheál, but came back as Mick. He won a minor championship in Kildare with Sarsfields in the same year that he won a minor title in Kerry with [Castleisland] Desmonds. But he also loved the rugby from the start and played inter-pro for Leinster that year as well.

'He got a Kerry football trial but was marking a very good player and wasn't picked. The consequence of that is that when I was picked by Kerry and won an All-Ireland medal, Mick declared that medal was his and even printed it in the paper in his own inimitable style that he had an All-Ireland medal. He had one all right – but he forgot to mention that it was mine! I followed Mick in the Gaelic and obviously in everything he did, and I had to do it as well, like brothers do. There were only the two of us and we would have been very competitive. There was nothing he could do that I thought I couldn't do better and vice versa.'

As if to make the point, Tom also played with Sarsfields in Newbridge and for the Leinster schoolboys on the rugby field. That year, too, he had an outstanding game for Desmonds at Fitzgerald Stadium and came to the notice of the Kerry minor selectors. After Kerry won the Munster title, they held a trial and Tom did well enough to be picked as a sub for the semi-final.

'I had only two matches with Kerry at midfield,' he recalls. 'I was brought on as a sub in the semi-final and was picked for the final. The famous Paddy Bawn Brosnan knew I was a rugby player and told me I was marking a very good player called Connaughton from Roscommon. He advised me that every time we went up for a ball, I should give him a dig of my elbow. Now, I was very good at fielding and could keep running all day and if only he had kept his mouth shut, I would have been fine. But I tried to do what I was told and was going for your man's head with my elbow and whether I was missing him or getting him I'm not sure, but I sure as hell still wasn't getting the ball. So I was taken off at half time, but we won the match and I got my All-Ireland medal.

'Moss Keane used to say the only difference between myself and Mick Galwey was that I played from the start in an All-Ireland final. Moss was always in envy of me for two things and I never realised it until later in life. In or around the year 2000, we were invited down to Currow for a celebration of our success – the late Mick and Moss, Mick Galwey and myself. We were standing outside the Community Hall in Currow where we were meeting all the locals when Moss says to me, "Tom, I'd have given anything for a ride on your racing bike." My father sold bikes among other things and Moss would see me cycling to school on a racing bike. So I said to him, "All you had to do was ask", but he was a shy kind of guy and said that he couldn't do that. About four or five years later, I found out he had one other ambition – "Tom," he said, "I'd have killed for your All-Ireland medal." He was very self-effacing, a lovely, lovely man.'

The admiration was mutual. In his autobiography, the sadly late but legendary Moss wrote of the Doyles: 'Poor Doyler – I retired the year he took over as Ireland's coach. I did him a big favour – I stayed retired. Doyler would have started me in his first season and maybe I could have hung on to win a second Triple Crown but I doubt it. Doyler's teams played rugby in his own image. They were fast, intelligent and imaginative. He had that Kerry thing about playing the game, not just to win, but also to honour the glory of sport itself. We grew very close as the years went on. It was good to be back in Currow, a village with more rugby internationals than pubs. Mick Doyle and his brother Tommy, Mick Galwey and myself all pulled on the green jersey. Only three of us wore the green-and-gold of Kerry, though. Doyler missed out on that one, something I never tired of reminding him. And Tommy Doyle, the man who was not a Lion, gained ample compensation. He won an All-Ireland minor medal for Kerry in 1962.'

While a love of Gaelic football is an intrinsic part of every Kerry man and woman, the Doyle brothers concentrated largely on rugby after Newbridge. Mick played for teams all over Ireland (Garryowen, UCD, Cork Constitution, Black-rock College) and for Cambridge University and Edinburgh Wanderers in the UK as he went through college to graduate as a veterinary surgeon. He was not the biggest of men for a back row forward and frequently played in the centre and out-half where his innate footballing skills enabled him to hold his own. But it was as an openside wing-forward that he was to make his name, both as an inter-provincial player with Munster and especially Leinster, and on the international stage with Ireland and the 1968 Lions, with whom he played in one Test match. Mick made his first appearance for his country against France on 23 January 1965 and immediately stamped his mark on the scene, scoring his side's only try in a 3–3 draw.

To register his side's only points on his debut against the formidable French was obviously a feather in Mick Doyle's cap. As it happened, he was to play twenty consecutive games in the green jersey and remarkably he was never dropped, even though at the time the country was blessed with some wonderful back row forwards. The Doyle-Lamont-Murphy axis was as good as any in the world game and probably got even stronger when Ken Goodall came on the scene to displace his Ulster colleague, Ronnie Lamont. With Tom Kiernan and Mike Gibson equally celebrated in the fullback and out-half positions and Ray McLoughlin outstanding in a formidable scrummaging unit, that Irish team achieved many excellent results without ever being fortunate enough to claim a Triple Crown or Championship. They defeated Australia at home and away in 1967 and 1968 and by this stage the other member of the Doyle family was also making his mark.

* * *

TOMMY DOYLE was well aware when he arrived at Newbridge that he had a lot to live up to, as he explained: 'Mick was very good at school. My first year at Newbridge was his last, just as it had been in Currow, and he was the senior boy, cock-o'-the-walk, and my memory is very vivid of him having the privilege of leading us all out from Mass or devotions or whatever … he'd walk up the aisle, genuflect at the front of the altar and out the side door and we'd all follow. But if you ever saw a swagger, this fella had a swagger you would die for! I definitely believe he developed his personality at Newbridge because everyone loved him and that was the way until the day he died. Just like Mick, I played for Leinster Schools in my last year and remember winning all my matches.

'The three of the great loves of his life were that UCD team, the Leinster team that he trained to numerous victories, and the Irish team at the height of their success – and very probably, secretly, the All-Ireland medal that he never won but claimed he did.

'I spent a few wonderful years at UCC in the 1960s and played in great teams with Jerry Walsh, Paddy McGrath,

Mick and Billy O'Mahony, Ollie Waldron and the like. Jerry Walsh was a fantastic rugby player, he was renowned for his bone-crushing tackles in the centre of the field, and was a very hard trainer. There was a cinder track down in the Mardyke next to the river and after a training session, Jerry used to bring myself, Billy O'Mahony and Len Harty down there. His system was to have us standing on a line, running maybe fifteen, twenty yards. You had to anticipate when the guy was going to call, you couldn't run before that, but you had to be quick off the mark to try to beat him. The secret was to try to beat the fella on his own call because he knew when he was going to shout. I owe Jerry Walsh a huge debt of gratitude for training me in how to get off the mark quickly as I wouldn't have been one of the fastest of men until I started training with Jerry.

'We were a fairly destructive bunch in UCC at the time. I remember going into Liam Mackessy's "Vineyard" for a pint one night and he greeted me with, "Jaysus, Doyle, the way you and O'Mahony play rugby, ye should be arrested." Anyway, the last year I was in UCC, my girlfriend at the time, now my wife, Elaine [Meegan, a north of Ireland girl whose father was the county vet in Cork], was playing hockey with the college. She used to ride horses and she brought me down to the famous Splaine family and they put me on every nag you could find and I was jumping fences, ditches, gates, everything, with the result that when I went up to Dublin the following year, I had strength in my legs that I never had before.'

Speed and an under-appreciated physical presence were two of his strong points, but Tom's inclusion in the Irish team for his three caps in 1968 was ironic, in that injury had prevented him playing for Leinster that season. However, as Paul MacWeeney described it in the Wanderers club history: 'Doyle surprised them all by gaining a place on the Irish XV against England, Scotland and Wales, sharing the flank forward duties with his elder brother, Mick, a unique distinction for members of the same family. Although unusually light at 12 st 2 lbs, Tommy had compensatory qualities in the shape of great pace, a strong tackle, good hands and a keen footballing brain. Joining Wanderers from UCC, he was a great asset to the club.'

Tommy was never on the losing side as Ireland drew 9–9 with England at Twickenham, defeated Scotland 14–6 and Wales 9–6 at Lansdowne Road. While the clear-cut win over Scotland was nothing exceptional, many will easily remember incidents in the other two matches. Bob Hiller, a fullback of no more than average ability, always seemed to grow wings on lining out against Ireland, and his last-minute equaliser that year wasn't the only time he tormented the men in green. And then there were the dramatic developments that unfolded in the final game of the campaign against Wales. Ned Van Esbeck's description of Gareth Edwards' 'drop goal' puts the central issue in the Welsh game in a slightly more genteel way than Tommy might after a pint or two! In his history of Irish rugby, Ned wrote about how a penalty by Kiernan and a drop goal by Gibson put Ireland 6–3 ahead well into the second half, before adding: 'Gareth Edwards, the Welsh scrum half, took a drop at goal that apparently went well wide of the left-hand upright. To the astonishment of the capacity crowd, the referee, Mr M.H. Titcomb of England, deemed the kick good. It was a decision that for a few moments threatened dire consequences in the form of an invasion of the pitch by a section of the crowd. But the incident ceased as quickly as it had begun and the game was restarted without undue delay. Ireland won when Mick Doyle got a try just before the end of the match. Justice was done.'

Tommy looks back on the experience with a gleam in that mischievous eye of his: 'Apart from the joy of it for yourself and your family, becoming an international meant you had the pleasure of meeting the greats of Irish rugby on a social and personal level. At the RIGS [Rugby International Golf Society] outings, you would meet the likes of Eugene Davy, Morgan Crowe, Jim McCarthy, Des O'Brien, Jackie Kyle. I played golf with Jackie and remember how my father at home in Castleisland had a couple of holy pictures on the wall of the Blessed Virgin and the Sacred Heart with lamps on them and in between a picture of Jackie without any lamp! I put that in the paper one time and later I was playing golf with Jackie up in the Grange and he told me, "Tommy, the greatest privilege of my life was to be quoted as sharing a place on the wall of the Doyle family between the Sacred Heart and the Blessed Virgin – but unfortunately there was no lamp."'

Tommy was not the biggest by any means and wasn't, by his own words, the fastest – but self-belief atoned for that in spades! 'As long as I played rugby, I never believed there was anyone in my position as good as me or better than me,' he declared. 'My father always told me, there's no point in being as good as the fella whose place you're trying to take. You have to be twice as good. Mick and I had an uncle, Bill Dennehy from Currow, my mother's brother. He went to Blackrock College and won a Leinster Schools medal, he joined Dolphin and won a Munster Cup medal. He also played on a famous Castleisland team with my father and won a Munster Junior cup medal that they shared with Waterpark. He had a huge bearing on Mick's progress. He was a very skilful footballer and while my father might not have been as skilful, he was very intelligent and they put a lot of thought into the game. And there was a man by the name of David Keane … they used to talk about rugby non-stop. Young players new to the game would be invited to the house for a bit of education on the game and I would be hiding behind the couch in my pyjamas listening to all of this. I heard about people like Cliff Morgan and Jack Kyle long before I understood who they were. The first time I got a rugby ball, I thought I was Jack Kyle because I knew he was special.'

By 1967, Tommy Doyle had moved to Dublin and joined Wanderers where Ronnie Dawson, who captained the Lions in 1959 in New Zealand, was the dominant figure. He was less than impressed on one of his earliest sightings of Tommy, whom he witnessed actually vomiting at one of his first training sessions. 'There was a look of disdain on his face,' Tommy recalls. However, relations between the pair changed very much for the better and Dawson had a positive influence on Tommy. He gave up the drink and trained harder than ever before, intent on winning a bet with two friends, Liam O'Connor and John Brown, that he would play for Ireland.

They were goading him about all the caps Mick was getting and going to get.

'Ronnie Dawson saw me training like mad and could see what I was trying to do but he told me, you won't get on the Leinster team and if you don't get on the Leinster team, you won't get on the Irish team. I'm sure Ronnie remembers my words. I said, "I don't care what team I get on, I'm going to play the rugby of my life and be as good as I can be and wherever that takes me, I'll be happy."

'We had a very good team in Wanderers at the time: Gerry Culliton, Kevin Flynn, Aubrey Bourke, Aubrey Shaw, Kevin McGowan, Ricky Muldowney, David Rowell and all those lads. I knew that I was making an impression and I was picked for Leinster but couldn't play because of injury and that's why I played for Ireland before I played for Leinster. You have to have the desire and enough ability to command a place. If you don't make it, there's always something missing.'

Injury, of course, can play its part, too, and Tommy recalls breaking a bone in his hand in 1967 before an Irish trial and in spite of intensive treatment, the medical opinion was that he would not be able to play. When he relayed the news to Dawson that he would have to miss the trial because of the hand injury, Ronnie told him: '"No problem." He cut out a bit of copper plate for my hand and he put orthopaedic felt on either side of it and wrapped it around my hand. I ran around all day with my hand in the air.'

He got away with that, but things didn't look great after the weighing and measuring operation that preceded all trials in those days. 'I was 12 stone 2 lbs, the lightest wing-forward ever, apart from the great Jim McCarthy, I suppose,' says Tommy. 'Derry Gleeson, a selector from UCC, on seeing the weights, commented in front of all the other selectors, "You're very light." Thinking quickly and for the benefit of the other selectors, "I am," I said, "but I'm as fast as shit." There was a lot of emotion in that statement I can tell you, from a Kerryman especially. I came off the pitch and Dawson told me I wouldn't get on for the first match. I was disgusted. I told him that I was after playing the game of my life, and he said, "I know, but you won't get on for the first match." Of course, he was right and they went to play France and were beaten.

'The selectors went into conclave and the question was, who is the fastest wing-forward in Ireland? Ewart Bell said it has to be Tommy Doyle. If Derry Gleeson hadn't said I was very light, I am not sure he would have known that I was as fast as I was! So I was picked to play against England. The excitement, of course, was massive, especially in Castleisland. On the morning of the match, I got a card at the hotel from a cousin, Mary O'Sullivan, with the message "Don't forget the Black and Tans". I am not a rebel, but if the Queen of England had arrived out on the pitch, I would have kicked her out of it. I wouldn't have meant any malice to her but … my boot was flying so high that the referee, who was a smallish man, tapped me on the shoulder after about ten minutes and told me, here, take it easy, you have a long way to go yet.

'Mick, of course, had loads of caps before this. We had the three games together. There was never a try scored against us and we were never beaten. Micheál Ó Muircheartaigh [of RTÉ fame] once said to me, "Tommy, you must be the only man in Ireland never to be beaten playing for Kerry and Ireland."

'We beat Scotland handily enough and then came up against the famous Gareth Edwards and Barry John when Wales came to Lansdowne Road. Dawson, my mentor, came up to me, telling me Barry John goes off this foot or that foot and all the talk was about the great Welsh half-backs and how they were going to torment the two Kerry brothers at wing-forward for Ireland. Well, it went all right for us. Having Mick there was brilliant, he knew all the ropes, and we had a great understanding.

'I remember sitting down with Barry John after that game in the old Hibernian hotel and his words still ring in my ear, "You little bugger, I didn't know which one of you was kicking me!" and I said that was the general idea, because if he went outside Mick would get him, and if he went inside I'd get him. The one thing I learned about Barry John was that you couldn't watch his hands. He was a genius with his hands.'

* * *

IT'S HARDLY surprising that nothing gave Mick Doyle greater pleasure than his achievements as a coach. It really began when he was handed the task at Leinster and he led them to five consecutive interprovincial titles from 1979 to 1983. Ireland had captured the Triple Crown in 1982 for the first time since 1949 under Tom Kiernan's coaching and when his tenure ended in 1983 Willie John McBride pipped Doyler for the top job. But Ireland suffered an ignominious whitewash and McBride, who was an inexperienced coach, was replaced in his turn by Doyle.

Players of the stature of Ollie Campbell, Moss Keane, Fergus Slattery, Willie Duggan and John O'Driscoll called it a day at the end of the 1984 season so the omens were not the brightest when Doyle took over the reins heading into the following year's campaign. But Mick was close to Mick Cuddy, the chairman of selectors, and he had *carte blanche* to run the team as he saw fit. He told his players to forget all about the country's traditional safety-first strategy and to instead get out there and 'give it a lash'.

Doyler pieced together a team ideally suited to help him realise his ambitions. Backs like Paul Dean at out-half, Brendan Mullin in the centre and Hugo MacNeill at fullback were more than prepared to run with the ball, and wings Trevor Ringland and Keith Crossan were masters of their particular art. They have never come much better than Michael Kiernan and Brendan Mullin in the centre, while Michael Bradley at scrum half worked off his No. 8 Brian Spillane and flankers Nigel Carr and Philip Matthews to perfection. Willie Anderson had been an outstanding No. 8 but Doyle identified him as the kind of player he wanted to plug a perceived gap in the second-row alongside Donal Lenihan, while he never had any doubt that skipper and hooker Ciaran Fitzgerald would get the required response from props Jim McCoy and Philip Orr.

In that year's Five Nations they defeated Scotland narrowly, drew with France, played out of their boots to beat Wales in Cardiff before edging out England with a late Michael Kiernan drop goal at Lansdowne Road. The eulogies rained down not only on Fitzgerald (leading an Irish team to glory for the second time in four years) and his players, but also on the coach. He had displayed remarkable foresight in not only relying on Kiernan, who hadn't been regarded as an expert in the discipline, as a place kicker, but also in opting for a running out-half like Dean, a youthful but relatively unproven back row, Anderson as a second-row, and McCoy to link with the more proven Orr and Fitzgerald in the front row. The outcome was nothing short of spectacular and Kiernan's drop goal in the dying minutes of the decisive clash with England is now a part of Irish rugby legend.

However, without the foresight of a son of Currow, County Kerry, it might never have come to pass. There was more to follow as he led Ireland to the first World Cup in New Zealand in 1987, although a heart attack – the first of two serious illnesses – that he suffered midway through the qualifying rounds didn't help. And when that phase of Mick's life was over, he turned to rugby punditry with remarkable facility. He was typically forthright and sometimes brutally honest in what he wrote in the *Sunday Independent* and said on RTÉ, and was not particularly popular in some quarters from time to time. It was Doyler's way, however, and when further bad luck in the way of a brain haemorrhage intervened, the sympathy was widespread and profound. And that in turn paled in comparison to the unqualified grief that poured forth after his tragic death.

* * *

'THE FUNNY thing is that we'd have been very similar even as our lives went two different ways,' Tommy muses today. 'When we rang each other, which we would do reasonably often, or met, we would talk for hours. We were very close. At the time he died, I was in the sand and gravel business and working on a contract down in Monasterevin and was driving around so much working with trucks that I had a thing in my head that I was going to be hit by a truck. So when I got the phone call that a truck had hit Mick, I thought, that truck was supposed to hit me. The police asked if I wanted to go up and meet the driver. I said no, tell him from me there is nothing we can do about it now. It was a dangerous area and Mick seems to have gone one way and tried to turn back but he couldn't see. To my knowledge, his peripheral vision was bad after the illness and he couldn't see. That is what I honestly believe happened. You only realise how close you are when somebody passes on. You can sail along when things are hunky dory but he was a big loss to his families and still is. And he left a great legacy to Irish rugby as well.'

Nowadays, regular games of golf over his home course at the Curragh and at Lahinch provide Tommy's main sporting interests, but when it comes to rugby and the direction the game is going in this country and further afield, there are few more passionate or knowledgeable observers of the scene.

DAVID AND IAN HUMPHREYS

In a way it would have been easier if I didn't respect
him so much.

*Ronan O'Gara discussing his rivalry with David Humphreys for
the out-half position on the Irish team*

GEORGE AND Deirdre Humphreys always loved sport, so
when their five children came along it was inevitable that
they would take to the playing fields in and around their
native Ballymena. They grew up in Broughshane in the 1980s
just outside the town that created two absolute legends of
rugby football in Willie John McBride and Syd Millar, but
David, the eldest and most celebrated of the quintet, admits
that as a youngster he much preferred soccer to rugby.

'As far back as I can remember, sport was always very
important to all of us,' says David. 'I will be honest, I grew
up wanting to be Kenny Dalglish playing for Liverpool and
didn't play rugby until I went to grammar school. Had I not
gone to grammar school, I probably would never have played
rugby but unfortunately I wasn't good enough at football and
that's the reason I ended up as a rugby player. And that is
why when people ask me about the highlight of my career, I

tell them it was playing at the old Wembley stadium. Having grown up watching FA Cup finals and dreaming of playing there, I got to play Wales for Ireland there and that was an unbelievable experience.'

The five Humphreys children all played sport. David recalls: 'We were very competitive; we played lots of tennis. We went on holidays to the south of France, and all we did was play tennis with a little bit of cricket. It was great. I have two sisters, Karen and Ruth, and two brothers, Marshall and Ian. Ruth played hockey for Irish Universities but Karen, who is about eighteen months below me, she played a hundred times for Ireland. We still laugh about this. She and I used to go off for international weekends. I would stay in the Berkeley Court, she would sleep on somebody's floor in the halls of residence at Trinity or somewhere. She was never too happy when I'd come back complaining about the food or something.'

* * *

KAREN HUMPHREYS is a dentist who had to try to combine amateur hockey with her career and by and large she succeeded marvellously well. A member of the Pegasus club, she made her Irish debut against Italy in Rome in 1993 on the way to playing in the following year's World Cup which took place in Dublin. She retired after the 2002 World Cup in Australia, having made one hundred international appearances, so between them David and Karen have the amazing total of 172 Irish caps to their credit!

Following in the footsteps of such an illustrious brother,

a man with seventy-two international caps, a European Cup and an MBE on his CV cannot have been easy for Ian. Perhaps Karen's achievements also added to the burden! Nor did it help that he was even known in some quarters as 'Baby Humph', but he is blessed with a good sense of humour and takes a slagging as well as the next guy. Down in Munster, they don't throw plaudits around like confetti, but when someone comes to the cauldron that is Thomond Park not once, but twice, and leaves a winner and a very worthy one as well, they are prepared to pay that person due credit.

Ian first showed the Red Army what he was capable of when lining out for Leicester Tigers in a Heineken Cup game in 2006. It was a wet, gloomy Limerick evening when the Tigers set out to accomplish something that no team before or since ever managed to do – beat Munster at Thomond Park in the Heineken Cup. They succeeded by a margin of 13–6 and until such time as that southern citadel – as it surely must do some day – falls once again, then Ian and his team-mates will be part of a little piece of rugby history. And as if that was not enough and having returned to his native heath at the end of his Tigers contract, Ian went back to Thomond on the last day of October in 2009 with Ulster and scored a superb try as once again the result fell decisively in his side's favour in a Magners League encounter.

Ian Humphreys was capped by Ireland at under-19, 21 and A levels. He skippered the Irish Rugby World Sevens in Hong Kong in 2005 having previously been voted player of the tournament in the European Sevens qualifier in Poland. But the biggest honour of all, a place on the full international side, continues to elude him and even though still only twenty-eight, he is inclined to believe that it probably will never happen for him after Ulster lost to Northampton in the quarter-finals of the Heineken Cup in 2011. He was not noted for his defensive qualities and inconsistency has also been a problem. However, those who had been impressed by his all-round composure, not least when kicking penalty goals with a thundering left foot, as best exemplified by the beauty he landed from well inside his own half to beat Biarritz in the 2011 Heineken Cup, felt this is something of a cop-out on the part of the selectors.

'Inconsistency and defence have been used against me by coaches but I think I have improved and been pretty good this season,' he claimed, with considerable justification. 'Also, my game management has come on a lot thanks to the help I've had from Brian McLaughlin, Ulster's head coach, and skills coach Neil Doak, and also our South African scrum half Ruan Pienaar. It was great to reach the quarter-final and while Northampton were probably the better side on the day, we weren't satisfied with that. People outside the squad were impressed that we got that far because it had been so long since we had done so, but our attitude is that we could have gone further. We want to be in the quarter-final of the Heineken and top four in the Magners every year. We're one of the teams who have tried to play a lot of rugby when others weren't prepared to do so and to play it with style.'

After the Northampton defeat and before a key Magners League clash with Leinster (which Leinster won 34–26), Ian accepted that his prospects of ever pulling on the green jersey are remote: 'I'm not really thinking about international rugby. I'm not saying I don't want to play but in my head I know it's not going to happen unless boys are injured. It's a little too late and the boys [Jonathan Sexton and Ronan O'Gara] have been playing well. It would be wrong to say I don't want to play for Ireland but I'm just happy to be playing for Ulster, doing well and enjoying my rugby. This is where I want to be. I left Leicester to come home and play first team rugby. I could easily have sat on the bench but I wanted to start in these competitions.'

* * *

GEORGE HUMPHREYS enjoyed nothing more than playing sport with his children as they grew up and were well on their way to becoming major personalities in their chosen activities. David recalls how his dad spent a lot of time in the back garden kicking a football and so on. 'There's no doubt that he instilled in us that interest in and passion for sport,' says David. 'We went to Ballymena Academy, and from the first day it was rugby or cross-country, no football. And if you saw the cross-country course at Ballymena, you wouldn't want to be running around it. So I tried the rugby, scored a few tries on the first day and thought, I enjoy this. We had a big group of boys there and it was great fun. As time went by, I never saw rugby as a career and played for seven years as an amateur, so I feel that I have had a foot in both camps. I wouldn't change anything, I absolutely loved my time at university playing rugby there and then fortunately having the opportunity to play professional sport.'

Interestingly, David qualified as a solicitor and worked for a while in a company with the legendary Mike Gibson before rugby took over. He has never gone back. The quizzical expression that crosses his face indicates that he is as surprised about that as anyone else. 'It's funny all right, in some ways I was very lucky,' he admits. 'The day rugby went professional, I had a decision to make. Some people said I was mad, but as against that people like Mike Gibson and people in his firm, said, "Look, you've qualified now, off you go. Go away and enjoy yourself." I thought I would be back in five years and that I had forty years to be a solicitor, a few years now will do you no harm. That was about 1996 and I am still not back. The last two years of my rugby career I had no intention of staying involved in professional sport, none whatsoever. So I spent eight hours a week in the office during the last two years of my professional career, work shadowing, getting work experience and getting myself ready for that transition back into what is a very different way of life. Right up until two months before I finished, that was what was happening. And then, right out of the blue, Ulster came and said, "We'd like you to stay involved." Whether it was a good decision or not, I said yes, I'm happy to do it and I very much enjoy what we do.

'Am I ever going to become a solicitor again? I don't know. Until three or four months ago, I would have said that is definitely where I will end up. For the two years before I finished playing, I thought I would go back into the law and become a solicitor. Now with the role that I have [as director of operations], I'm fully committed to Ulster and trying to achieve in the short to medium term what we want. It's not going to happen overnight. It's going to take a period of time and I'm planning to try to drive Ulster back to compete with the Munsters and Leinsters of European rugby.'

* * *

FROM HIS earliest days, David Humphreys was an out-half. He says he could count on the fingers of one hand the number of games he has played elsewhere on the rugby pitch. He insists that 'a ten needs to play in that position all the time because it is so hard to drop in and out of that position. That's why I have great admiration for James Hook and Paddy Wallace; you have to play there regularly and I think you'll find that the tens who have been around for a while always played in that position. Ballymena was a good place to learn, we got to two Schools' Cup semi-finals but came up against Methody in their prime and never managed to crack them. The school was very supportive of sport, they pushed us to be involved and I represented every team that would pick me. Every day after school, that is all I looked forward to and what kept me going through my school career. Of course I grew up in awe of Syd Millar and Willie John McBride. When you grow up in Ballymena, you are very aware of their huge history and the huge number of players who came through afterwards. Every Saturday morning we played rugby at school and in the afternoon we went to Eaton Park to watch the big names, the likes of Trevor Ringland, play for Ballymena. You see them play there and watch Ulster ... it's what you wanted to do. It wasn't a career, you did your work, you went to training and it was a bit of fun.

'I played for Ulster and Ireland Schools and went to Queen's with a little bit of a reputation as a rugby player, although it's not a good indicator that anybody who has played at a high level at school is going to make it. I'm a big fan of university rugby, it's good for players, not just in the rugby sense but good for them to meet people of their own age and have to take responsibility. It's easy to go into a club where there are lots of players who have been there for ten years. Especially when you are playing out-half, you have to make decisions, you have to make calls, organise the team and help people. I think it's a good life experience as well as a good rugby experience. I sometimes think it's something that is missing from young professionals, not just rugby players but sportsmen in general. Gary Longwell was there at the time but we didn't have anybody else who played for Ulster … Jonny Bell was there for about three days and changed his mind and moved on to Loughborough! We had a great team and a great time … I spent four years there and loved every minute of it.

'I made my first Ulster appearance in 1992 when I was at Queen's, away to Cumbria. We won easily. It seems such a long time ago, and then I came on for my first inter-pro against Munster in Limerick. I replaced Peter Russell, kicked two penalties and dropped a goal. We won that day and I haven't won too often in Thomond Park since then. My brother has won there twice and he talks about it plenty! At that stage, I was playing in a team of Ulster players who had been there for a long time, people like Bill Harbinson, Maurice Field, Colin Wilkinson. And I felt very much out of my depth.

'It's funny the way things work out. I left Queen's, went to Ballymena for a year and a half, and didn't play well at all. About 1993, I made my Ireland A debut and was probably closer to an Irish cap at that point when Eric [Elwood] made his debut the following day against Wales. But I just wasn't playing well and that's why I decided to go away to university in England. I went to Oxford University for a year to play rugby. It was fabulous, I played in the Varsity match and scored a few points, but we lost [in fact David went 'through the card, try, conversion, drop goal and three penalties' for a personal contribution of nineteen points – two fewer than Cambridge managed]. It was a massive occasion. It was the first real experience I had of professional rugby. Tyrone Howe was the captain and we trained so hard. Tyrone was the reason I went across. I was sitting in the solicitor's office one day when he phoned me and asked if I would like to go to Oxford. I said I would love to but probably couldn't get away. I spoke to Mike Gibson and he was very supportive and that's why it happened. There were 60,000 people at the Varsity match, but even then the occasion was definitely losing its significance because it didn't have the international players that it had in the past. There were still some very good players but it was dropping down a bit. For somebody like me who had done nothing at that stage, it was still a massive, massive game and such a wonderful experience to get away from Belfast and home for a year. I had never been away before. I rediscovered something over there and three months after the Varsity match, I was capped for the first time against France in February 1996, largely on the strength of that Varsity performance.

'After Oxford, I joined London Irish. Clive Woodward came up at Christmas, had lunch, and said two things to me – within a year rugby union will be professional and the second, within ten years, it will rival professional soccer. Unfortunately, the second one of those was wrong! About six of us from Oxford joined London Irish on the basis of what Clive said. We went down there in January; Irish were in the second division at that stage, we played an unbelievable standard of rugby and were promoted. We had pretty much become the Irish team and the following season, 1996/97, I went professional. I could take you through the team ... people like Conor O'Shea, Niall Woods, Justin Bishop, Rob Henderson, Niall Hogan, Victor Costello, Gabriel Fulcher, Kieron Dawson, Jeremy Davidson, Gary Halpin, Justin Fitzpatrick, Malcolm O'Kelly. The problem was we didn't realise how good we were because we still had this psychological thing, we were playing against English teams and they were better than us.

'It wasn't until the success of the provinces that it changed. I believe that is one of the fundamental differences and why Ireland has begun to dominate England at international level. The success they have had at provincial level means that it's no big deal when they step on to the pitch against these guys that they've beaten regularly in Europe and in the Magners League.'

* * *

DAVID HUMPHREYS came back to Ulster in 1998 and the following year he captained them to a famous victory in the European Cup. It is, of course, an occasion that will stand in the memory of everybody from the province and indeed throughout the Irish game. People turned up at Lansdowne Road that day from every corner of the country. But David is one of many who believes it is time to move on.

'I met with Harry Williams, our coach at the time, the other night and we agreed how much we would love to win it again simply because we're sick and tired of everybody talking about 1999,' he declared. 'Don't get me wrong. It was a fantastic few months. We had come home the summer of 1998 and we didn't have great players and none of us pretended that we did. But we had a great team, we didn't have any injuries, we had a lot of luck and a lot of really good characters. We were on a bit of a run and a lot of strange things happened. We beat Toulouse twice, we beat Stade Français twice. It should never have happened but we managed to grind out wins. In some ways, though, it almost held us back for ten years.

'There is no question it kicked professional rugby off in Ulster. We started off that season playing in front of 500 people in the inter-provincials. We could have sold 150,000 tickets for the final. That's how it captured the imagination of the public. People say it was one of the starting points of the European Cup. If one of the French teams had won it again, it might not have taken off the way it did. Munster and Leinster saw what had happened and they wanted a bit of it and have just dominated European Cup rugby for the past decade. If you ask any of us who were involved, it's without doubt the defining moment of all our rugby careers. It didn't matter about the rugby, all we had to do was win. There were 50,000 people at the final, it was a wonderful day and a wonderful occasion, and to see so many out there supporting Ulster rugby was a first step along what was a route to professional sport.

'It wasn't a nerve-racking time because we actually believed we were going to win the final. Colomiers were not as good as Stade Français, they were not as good as Toulouse. The Stade Français semi-final stands out for me, a beautiful sunny day in front of 20,000 people at Ravenhill. We played rugby against them, as good as anything that Stade produced. They came expecting to beat us by fifty points. They were the aristocrats of French rugby, but we won 33–27. It was a great day, but just one of a number of great days and nights against Toulouse, Stade and the rest … people talk about that final, but for me it wasn't about just that one game. It was a sequence of games that transformed Ulster rugby into a competitive element.'

Nevertheless, it was one of the most remarkable days in the storied history of the old Lansdowne Road. It certainly captured the attention of the English media, even if none of their clubs took part that year, and Tim Glover of the *Independent* described the atmosphere delightfully. 'The poor French didn't have a chance. The sky fell in on Colomiers, a satellite of Toulouse, almost as soon as they heard the final was to be held in Dublin – Christians, lions and amphitheatres came to mind. A capacity crowd of 49,000 filled Lansdowne

Road. All but 3,000 were Irish and at times Colomiers probably felt similarly outnumbered on the pitch.[1]

'By train, car and plane, the phenomenal support was transferred to Dublin. Colomiers, not as well equipped as Toulouse and Stade Français, were overawed. Ulster won comfortably with Simon Mason kicking six penalties from six attempts. David Humphreys, another key figure, dropped a goal and Colomiers inadequate reply was two penalty goals by Laurent Labit.

'Nothing was going to deter Ulster from what the supporters believed was their day of destiny and at the final whistle thousands of Ulstermen, nearly all draped in red and white, engulfed the ground and almost the cup itself.'

* * *

HAVING WON that first cap against the French in 1996, David Humphreys went on to become Ireland's regular at No. 10 for quite some time, even if he didn't realise that a future nemesis by the name of Ronan O'Gara was making his mark a couple of hundred miles or so away down south in Cork. David really was a classy out-half blessed with a golden pair of hands, an educated boot and the vision to spot a gap and go through it in a twinkle. Ulster fans drooled as they watched and inevitably likened him to greats of the past like Jack Kyle, David Hewitt and Mike Gibson.

---

1   ULSTER – S. Mason; S. Coulter, J. Cunningham, J. Bell, A. Park; D. Humphreys (capt.), A. Matchett; J. Fitzpatrick, A. Clarke, R. Irwin (G. Lesley, 73 mins), M. Blair, G. Longwell, S. McKinty, T. McWhirter (D. Topping, 75 mins), A. Ward.

'International rugby is the pinnacle, ask any rugby player, any young player, and they want to play for Ireland,' he stresses. 'I grew up wanting to do that. There were stages when I didn't think it would ever happen, probably 1994–95, I thought my chance had gone. The Irish team I first came into was very different from what it is now. I believe it's a long time since Ireland had so many good players in so many positions. When I first came in, we probably had one or two world-class players like Keith Wood, we had four or five international players and then we had ten who could be of international calibre occasionally, but not week in, week out. Now we have ten world-class players, probably twenty international players and that is how the game has changed and why professional rugby has been huge for Ireland.

'Everyone says the game was better in their day. I just think of the game I played in 1999, the game I played in 2005, and I think it's so much better today. It's a much better spectator sport and a better game to play. It's faster, there is more entertainment, there were so many games back in my time when the score lines were 6–6, 9–6, and the skill levels now are massively higher. I know some people will claim that is not the case, but you only have to watch re-runs on ESPN to see the difference. OK, it's impossible to compare players across generations; it's also impossible to compare the game because it changed not just over a five year basis but a year to year basis the way the rules are interpreted.'

David laughs at the suggestion that he would have earned even more than his seventy-two caps had Ronan O'Gara not been around. 'He would probably say the same thing. There was a rivalry between us but it was a friendly rivalry and I've said it so many times now …' David's voice drifts away in a direction that makes you believe that no matter what he says, people will see it in a different light. If so, they should take due note of what Rog had to say on the subject in his autobiography: 'He is such a gentleman and such a gracious fella that you could never hate Humphs for taking your place. In a way, it would have been easier if I didn't respect him so much.'

Well, David and Ronan did swap the No. 10 jersey around between them quite a lot, sometimes during the course of a game. O'Gara talks about the foot and mouth delayed matches eventually held in September 2001. He had a poor game against Scotland but hoped that a man of the match performance for Munster in the Heineken Cup before Ireland played Wales would help to redeem him. So how did Humphreys respond? He went and scored thirty-seven out of forty-two points for Ulster against Wasps, an individual record in the Heineken Cup and it was away from home as well! Rog accepted: 'With a player like Humphs around, I couldn't afford the kind of cock-up against Scotland.' Indeed. In that same Welsh game, David went out and had a 100 per cent record, with a nine out of nine goal-kicking record, as Ireland won 36–6 at the Millennium Stadium.

He now recalls: 'Rog and I spent a lot of time together, kicking and doing things, so what was the point of not being on good terms? We both wanted to play – he was a little grumpier than I was when he wasn't picked and probably still is. That is what makes him so formidable. You look back at his record – what he has won, what he has achieved – it's unrivalled. It's that competitive nature that has driven him on. At the end of my career, I was probably happy to sit back and let him play. But he's not happy to let Jonny [Sexton] play and that is what has made him the player that he is.

'The rivalry between Rog and me and now Rog and Jonny is a good thing. It's what we need. You look at the New Zealanders. They have a rivalry that probably goes three or four deep in every position, if you except Carter and McCaw. If we're serious about winning World Cups and competing for Grand Slams year in, year out, you've got to have three or four players in each position, such is the attritional nature of rugby union. You are always going to have injuries and it's how you deal with injured players that determines whether your season is a success or not. Some people make out that it's not good news to have people competing. Rubbish. You want four world-class players competing. That's what you pay the coach for. He has to make that call. You want to make that call as difficult as possible for him. Ireland have moved a long way, but if they want to be up there with the top teams they have to get better and they have to increase the popularity of the game.'

There are those – and not all are from the northern end of the country – who maintain that Ian Humphreys should be afforded a better chance to make the out-half duel a three horse race. David is as objective as a brother who also happens to be Operations Director of Ulster Rugby can be on the subject. 'I think Ian has shown a consistency in 2011 that he hasn't shown in previous years,' he mused. 'Everybody knew he was capable of producing good performances as he did for Leicester down in Thomond Park. But the secret at No. 10 is producing consistency week in, week out. Yes, you can produce very good games but you cannot produce very bad games. There has to be a level there that will deliver results. In previous years you could get away with it a little more and his performances were a little up and down over the last few years. But when there are jobs and so much money resting on the outcome of these games, you just cannot afford to be in and out. Ruan Pienaar has been a massive factor in not just him playing well, but in helping young players coming through. He is a world-class player and has made a huge difference.

'The future of Ulster? You don't want to make predictions because so many things change, but I would say it's much brighter than was the case twelve months ago. We are in a much better position on and off the pitch than we were at that point. We compare ourselves week in, week out, to what Munster and Leinster have done. We sometimes forget – what our supporters also forget – that Munster and Leinster are two of the best sides in Europe. Closing that gap doesn't happen overnight. We've closed it a lot quicker than I thought we might in terms of our results this year – but arguably not, because every time we play Munster and Leinster, we get hammered by not quite their second teams but their changed teams and that's the quality that they have. We aren't there yet, but we have young players coming through. We haven't been able to produce the Kyles, the Hewitts and so on. If you bring in international players, you want them to have a huge impact both on and off the pitch. You want them to be the first people picked on your team sheet every week and that hasn't been the case. Over the last eighteen months, we have tried to address that. The foreign players we have brought in have been of top quality and top quality people as well. Added to that, our academy has started to produce better players – we had five backs on the Ireland under-20 squad this year, three of whom will certainly go on to be international players at the top level. So things are improving, but we're aware that there's an awful long way to go to be able to compare ourselves with Munster and Leinster.'

* * *

To CLOSE, let's reacquaint ourselves with that Ireland–Wales game at Wembley in 1999 that meant so much to David Humphreys. It was played at Wembley which Wales used as their 'home' venue during the redevelopment of the Cardiff Arms Park. Ireland won 29–23, not least because David contributed nineteen points with three penalty goals, two drop goals and two conversions. Keith Wood and Kevin Maggs were the try scorers and the Irish team was Conor O'Shea; Justin Bishop, Kevin Maggs, Jonny Bell, Niall Woods; David Humphreys, Conor McGuinness; Peter Clohessy, Keith Wood, Paul Wallace, Paddy Johns, Jeremy Davidson, Dion O'Cuinneagain, Eric Miller and Andy Ward. Replacements were Victor Costello, Justin Fitzpatrick and Mick Galwey.

SIMON AND GUY EASTERBY

Simon Easterby is an unsung hero.

Ireland back row colleague David Wallace

TIME WAS when mention of the Easterby name immediately conjured up images of the famous horse-racing family from North Yorkshire. More recently, though, it has become synonymous with Irish rugby through the exploits of Simon and Guy Easterby, who between them amassed an impressive ninety-three international caps, while Simon was also a highly successful tourist with the British and Irish Lions in New Zealand in 2005.

Simon and Guy never imagined that such an array of honours in an Irish jersey lay in wait as they grew up in Yorkshire, even though they were aware from an early age that their mother, the former Katherine Doyle, was an Irish hockey international of considerable stature and that the land of her birth was very close to her heart. She came from Blackrock in Dublin and played for Pembroke Wanderers before meeting and marrying Henry Easterby, a member of the renowned horse-racing dynasty. The boys went to school at the famed Ampleforth College, but it was the amount of holiday time that they spent in Dublin that nurtured their love for Ireland, so much so that Simon proudly proclaimed, 'I was always completely comfortable wearing the green jersey.'

And there is little doubt that their close connection to Mick and Peter Easterby – and later Tim – helped instil in them their durability and toughness on the rugby pitch, a strong competitive spirit and a keen sense of humour. Mick Easterby is a cousin of their father and one of the great characters of the racing world. His conquests include winners of the 1,000 Guineas (*Mrs McArdy*), Gimcrack Stakes (*Wiganthorpe*) and the July Cup and Nunthorpe Stakes (*Lochnager*) and as he entered his early 70s, Mick was as active as ever. Money, he would contend, was never an object, although he did concede, 'I'd love to scoop the National Lottery and get those Camelot chappies to pay me in tenners. I'd hoard every note and get more pleasure from counting it rather than spending it.'

By all accounts, he is still waiting for his numbers to come up!

* * *

THE GUY and Simon Easterby story begins in the market town of Tadcaster in the Selby district of North Yorkshire. It's located some fifteen miles east of Leeds and ten miles west of York and one of its greatest claims to fame is the Samuel Smith brewery! It was a place that the Easterby brothers, and their older sister Deborah, learned to love almost from their birth as they grew up on the family farm nearby.

'There are actually three big breweries in Tadcaster with massive underground wells and they all tap into them,' Guy explains. 'We had a stud farm. My grandad, Walter Easterby, was the one who started the training dynasty. My dad was not that interested, but his brother's kids, Peter and Micky, ended up doing fantastically well. Our stud farm was just for racehorses, that was the main business, along with the arable side of the farm. It was about 150 acres of grass for the horses and a few hundred or so for arable crops as well.

'It was an enjoyable upbringing. We went to the local primary school until the age of ten and then it was off to Ampleforth, a famous catholic boarding school in North Yorkshire which was about an hour away. We went there as boarders, me first and Simon about four years later. We did eight years there and it was a great place for rugby. Believe it or not, they had twenty-two pitches, so you either liked rugby or you had a tough time of it. Luckily enough for us, we loved it from the start. The head coach was John Willcox, the former England and Lions fullback, and he certainly instilled a great deal of discipline into the rugby side of things. We were all really rugby mad.

'I also became a pretty serious cricketer. I captained the school, but funnily enough I struggled a bit at the rugby. When I got to my top years, the year above me had five players in the England Schools team, one of whom was a scrum half and his father taught at the school. He did badly in his A-levels, so they allowed him to stay over another year which was the first time that had ever happened and that put a stop to my career. I ended up playing in the second team and enjoyed a season with Lawrence Dallaglio, who was a year behind me. He was a No. 8 and I was scrum half.

'The situation is different now, but in those days there was nothing like the Leinster Schools' Cup, nothing competitive. Basically you just played all the big schools around you. It was all about protecting a record that ran for a couple of years in my time of never being beaten, just a case of rivalry between the schools rather than any cup or league system – I guess bragging rights during holiday times or something like that. Some would see it as a good way to go, although you could look at it both ways ... the cups in Ireland are so important, but you could be drawn against a good team in the first round and lose and then your season is over and the games you played beforehand don't count for anything. I do like the interest the cup here generates, the fanaticism that makes for some very young heroes.

'Our big match was against Sedbergh. Will Carling and Will Greenwood were there in our time. On one day every year, we had seven senior XVs playing them and then under-16s, 15s and 14s A and B as well – so thirteen fixtures in the one day against the same school and that was always a massive, massive fixture. That was our huge derby – they hated us and we hated them.

'Simon was four years after me. There are ten different houses at Ampleforth named after patron saints. When I was in my final year, he came into the same house as me in the bottom year. When I was younger, I struggled with being away from home but he loved it. Of course, he knew everything, where everything was, because of the number of times he had been to visit me. He thrived, and loved the outdoor activities and his sport and that gave him a great head start. When he came into my house, I was a school prefect and I was probably harsher on him than anyone else, but I suppose that was probably the big brother thing and trying to look out for him in a perverse kind of way. It was good having him there.

'Simon was a hooker right through until his top year. Again, he was good but wouldn't have been a stand-out. It was like being a professional rugby player ... as a senior, you were training five times a week, line-out practice during the break; they were way ahead of themselves, not in a bad way but you could become consumed by it all. Simon was in the first team for a couple of years but didn't earn superstar status if you know what I mean.'

In their time at Ampleforth, England Schools picked several players from the college but neither of the Easterbys was deemed worthy of the call, although in Guy's final year, five of the team were picked. And, lest you imagine the place was all about rugby, there were a few other demands – as you would expect of such a distinguished Benedictine-run academy! 'I wouldn't be the most religious person in the world although obviously I come from a big Catholic family in Ireland,' says Guy. 'Religion was a little bit forced upon you at Ampleforth, you had to do prayers, morning and evening, and it was probably a little over the top but that's the way it was then. You did what you were told and went to Mass two or three times a week. For young kids trying to make up their minds what they liked about stuff, it was probably a little too much, but it was a small price to pay.

'Ampleforth is an hour north of York on the edge of the North Yorkshire moors and absolutely in the middle of nowhere. You could not escape. But there was an amazing relationship with the local villagers – when you were sixteen at Ampleforth, you were allowed to go to the pubs on a Saturday … two pints and a meal was the rule, although there wasn't a meal to be seen, only plenty of pints! You drank the £10 or whatever you had. It was very weird, a sort of agreement with the local area and to their cost quite a few times, with lads rolling drunk. But it was also a sort of way of giving people a bit of responsibility. So as much as Ampleforth were restrictive in some areas, they had other ways of teaching guys to grow up, although sixteen years of age and alcohol are not a great mix!'

* * *

HENRY EASTERBY and Katherine Doyle met on a skiing holiday in Austria, duly got married and Deborah, Guy and Simon were the happy result. While home was in Yorkshire, much of the summer months were spent in Blackrock in Dublin, along with every second Christmas. The youngsters loved staying with their grandparents and all this meant that they were always very conscious of their Irishness. 'Our grandparents were a typical Irish Catholic family and had strong values which they instilled in us,' says Guy. 'They were great times and we definitely felt that we were always half Irish, which might not be the case for other people. As Mum was an Irish hockey cap, we would go around every Saturday afternoon and watch and run around the place. She still comes to Dublin and Pembroke and meets a lot of her old pals. Dad was a good rugby player and had he been born at the same time as Simon and me, it might have been a different story, whereas in his time there was no hope of a professional career, especially as you can't be off playing rugby on a Saturday afternoon when running a farm. But he was very sporty – when we were growing up he would kick the rugby ball as high in the air as he could and do deals with you, fifty pence if you caught it and that kind of thing, and that probably had an effect on our rate of progress.' All very nice and normal, of course, but the Easterby brothers went to a rugby playing school in England, grew up there and lived most of their lives there. So you would think it would be in the white jersey rather than the green that they would have seen their futures should international glory beckon. As it happened, the big question was asked of Guy in the most clear-cut manner when the issue could no longer be put on the long finger.

'I was picked for England A and Ireland A on the same day, I think it was 1996,' he recalls. 'England were playing Otago [a New Zealand side] and I cannot remember who Ireland were playing. I was left with a straight decision, but for me there was no decision to actually make. I knew what I wanted to do and didn't think twice about it. Why? A good question. I don't know. It was in my subconscious that I always wanted to play for Ireland. Was that because Mum had played hockey for Ireland and Dad had not played for England? I don't know. But there wasn't a moment's hesitation … and, you know, at under-21, I was involved with England, I played for North and they were sort of England trials, but then the Irish Exiles got involved. That was Phelim McLoughlin. I was playing for my local club, he came to watch someone else and I obviously did okay. So he asked me if I had any Irish blood in me, which I obviously had, and that is how it started. Simon very quickly got into the Irish under-21s and Phelim has been brilliant ... he became very friendly with my parents through being at games, he's very enthusiastic about the Exiles and for us he was a vital cog in getting us to where we got.

'I honestly don't remember going through the process ... all I remember is, right, Ireland A have come in for me and that is where I want to play. From then on, Dad decided he was half Irish and half Yorkshire rather than English and became the biggest fan of all. He passed away a few years ago, but he had the most fantastic time travelling to World Cups and to the Lions and all the internationals and was a huge fan of Ireland ... I suppose you would be, if you had two sons playing international rugby.'

* * *

IT WAS on a fine if rather chilly February afternoon at Twickenham in 2000 when the death of Ireland as a force in world rugby was widely proclaimed. Losing to England at any time is a dreadful experience for the Irish, but when the scoreline reads 50–18 against, one can only imagine how the whole country was plunged into mourning!

Radical action was demanded and the response was quick and forceful. It was time to scrap much of the conservatism that had traditionally overridden imaginative thinking in the game for the previous 120 years. New Zealander Warren

Gatland (now the boss at Wales) was Ireland head coach at the time and he had the guts and the freedom to bite the bullet. He brought in five new caps – Ronan O'Gara, Shane Horgan, Peter Stringer, John Hayes and Simon Easterby – for the visit of Scotland to Lansdowne Road. This was not the Irish way of doing things and 'Gatty' was on a hiding to nothing. He needn't have worried ... his young tigers came up trumps and when all of the quintet finally hang up their boots, they will have banked close to an incredible 500 Ireland caps between them!

Ireland defeated Scotland by double scores, 44–22, with the following team: Girvan Dempsey, Shane Horgan, Brian O'Driscoll, Mike Mullins, Denis Hickie, Ronan O'Gara, Peter Stringer, Peter Clohessy, Keith Wood, John Hayes, Mick Galwey, Malcolm O'Kelly, Simon Easterby, Kieron Dawson and Anthony Foley. It was a red-letter day and not just for Simon Easterby but also for Guy, who sat on the bench for the first time along with Frankie Sheahan, Justin Fitzpatrick, Jeremy Davidson, Trevor Brennan and Rob Henderson. It's an era that Guy recalls with considerable satisfaction.

'Simon and I had been picked to play against England A at Northampton. We won that game and it was on the next day that England beat Ireland by fifty points at Twickenham. There were all those changes that we still remember so well and I came on to the bench when Tom Tierney dropped out completely and Peter Stringer moved up one. That was it, then, we were stuck there for five or six years between us. Strings and I were battling away and he certainly won that battle. There was rivalry and sometimes it was hard to deal with because he got himself in there and did well and even if he did have a poor game, I didn't really feel that I was ever going to get a clear run.

'It was disappointing, but at the same time I understood the decisions and there was also a good friendship between Strings and myself. There were a lot of times when I sat on the bench [twenty-one out of twenty-eight caps] but they were great times, too, made all the more enjoyable because Simon was there. He dropped out a few times before cementing his place. He was on the edge really for the 2003 World Cup and wasn't guaranteed his spot. We both played in the UK. We lived together for a while in Cardiff when he was already a year in Llanelli and I was at Ebbw Vale before joining him. I loved the life in Wales and the people there. They are rugby mad and made life very interesting. Llanelli was a small town. If you won, the town was on fire, if you lost, it was in mourning. The passion they have for the game is unbelievable.

'Where the Irish place was concerned, no, we were not off the radar to any great extent. There were a good few of us over there ... Kevin Maggs, Kieron Dawson, Justin Bishop ... not like the last five years when they want all the players to be in Ireland. That wasn't the case then because professionalism hadn't really kicked in and there were lots of people playing in different places and they always made the effort to come and see us and pick up a couple of games before announcing squads. They were good at keeping in touch with coaches.

'Post 2003 World Cup, I went home for a year and played with Rotherham. I decided I wanted to go back to the farm, but Rotherham was in terrible trouble, I spent the whole of every game just tackling. Simon, meanwhile, was flying, and then Declan Kidney, who was with Leinster, asked, "What are you doing next year?" I was thirty-two and I just couldn't pass up such an opportunity. It was the best thing I ever did. You always felt like you were going home, even though it was not your home. Yorkshire was always our home but coming over to Ireland was also very special. It was not like I was going anywhere new.

'By that stage, of course, Simon was firmly established and then came the Lions call to New Zealand [in 2005]. Lawrence Dallaglio was the number one choice and it was probably right not to pick Simon originally. But Lawrence broke his ankle in the first game and I knew when Simon got out there that he had the ability to raise his game to that next level and be ready when the Test call came. You had one Ampleforth boy replacing another. A Lions tour is the pinnacle of any players' career and I think Simon and another replacement Ryan Jones were probably the two best players. I'm unbelievably proud of that.'

While sympathetic to Dallaglio, Simon was determined to make the best of his belated opportunity and did so even though it wasn't the happiest of tours and is possibly best remembered for the spear tackle in the first Test that ended the adventure for Lions captain and Irish team-mate Brian O'Driscoll. Simon's commitment, work rate, fearlessness and line-out ability were recognised by his selection for the second and third Tests. He scored a try in the first of these and was to be voted the player of the Test series ahead of the All Black

Jerry Collins. He was described as the 'most consistent Lion on tour'. Simon was never less than outstanding. He looked very much at home in the Test match arena and helped to settle the wonky Red line-out.

* * *

THE CONVINCING defeat of Scotland in 2000 may not have exactly launched an entirely new era in the fortunes of Ireland as a major force in world rugby, but the Twickenham disaster was quickly pushed to the back of the mind, if not exactly forgotten. The new millennium saw Ireland win four Triple Crowns and a first Grand Slam in sixty-one years. The Easterbys were a part of a lot of these great times and earned the respect of their coaches, their team-mates and the fans, not only for their skill and expertise but also for their honesty of effort and commitment to the cause.

Warren Gatland and later Eddie O'Sullivan also acknowledged Simon's value to the Irish team and he repaid their faith in spades. He touched down for eight tries in his sixty-five appearances in the green jersey, retiring from the international scene at the end of the 2008 Six Nations series. Sadly, Ireland were well beaten by England in Simon's last match, but acting captain Ronan O'Gara still noted in his autobiography that 'everyone suspected it would be his last day in an Ireland jersey. I had a quiet word with him and he confirmed that he was retiring but didn't want any big deal about it. At the meeting, I could not let it pass. Simon made his international debut on the same day as me and he had been a huge influence in our dressing-room. I told the players that I wanted this game to be a fitting end for Simon. With the affection and respect he commanded in our group, I knew that would strike a chord with everyone.'

It seems that, without exception, every single member of the Ireland squad had nothing but good to say about Simon Easterby. In the build-up to the Heineken Cup quarter-final against Llanelli at Stradey Park in April 2007 (which the Scarlets won fairly decisively), his long time team-mate David Wallace was warning his fellow Munster players that they faced a massive threat from Simon. 'The Scarlets came out of their pool against teams of the strength of Toulouse, Ulster and London Irish, and Simon Easterby had a huge amount to do with that. He is an unsung hero who is in the form of his life so stopping what he does best will be crucial to our chances. He will be firing into our faces from the start, something he does very well, and you can imagine how much he will relish doing that. We have won our second Triple Crown together and he was outstanding throughout. He seems to get better and better.'

Guy laughs, 'Simon was never going to score a try from seventy yards, but he might do something to win the ball to help somebody else to score. That was the way he played the game and he was pretty good at it in fairness. I broke my jaw twice and he picked up numerous head knocks and I'm sure my father and mother went prematurely grey having to watch him being dragged off and stitched up. I hated watching him play because of being worried about him getting injured and thank God he's not playing any more, so I dread to think what my parents went through.'

Guy certainly was not exaggerating. Simon did pick up a lot of injuries, sometimes because he was too brave for his own good, sometimes when, as his Scarlets colleague Gareth Jenkins claimed, he was 'cynically targeted' during Heineken and Powergen Cup matches against London Wasps in 2005. In one of those games, Simon suffered a split eyelid and a scraped eyeball, and in another was knocked out by a punch and had to be put in the recovery position by team-mate Mark Jones after he swallowed his tongue. In another game against Wasps, Frenchman Raphael Ibanez was handed a four-week ban having been found guilty of stamping on Simon. Throw in injuries to his knees, Achilles tendon, hand, etc., and he took more than his fair share of knocks throughout a glittering career.

Simon is nowadays the defence coach at the Scarlets, a club he has served superbly both as player and staff member. Having been captain for five successive years and played more than fifty matches in Europe, he retired entirely as a player in 2010. Looking back, he mused: 'To have played in a Grand Slam would have been nice but you cannot change what has happened and I wouldn't have changed my decision to play for Ireland rather than England. My international career was tremendously enjoyable!'

Having signalled his intentions, Simon was offered and accepted the job as defence coach at Scarlets with the admirable philosophy that 'I would never ask players to do something I wouldn't do myself.' He is married to Sarra Elgan Rees, a daughter of former Wales and Lions three-quarter Elgan Rees. A fluent Welsh speaker, Sarra is a television presenter and they have two daughters, Soffia and Ffredi. They live between Cardiff and Bridgend and Sarra is more than a little relieved that her husband has finally hung up his boots.

* * *

WHEN HENRY and Katherine Easterby decided to send their two sons to Ampleforth College, they would have had a different career in mind for them. Professional rugby union didn't exist at the time and even had it done, it would hardly have figured high on the list of priorities. However, Guy – Leinster's manager since the beginning of the 2010/11 season – and Simon – Scarlets' defence coach – insist they have absolutely no regrets about the hand that life has so far dealt them.

'I didn't turn pro until I was twenty-four and had worked a bit on the farm,' Guy points out. 'I was training hard for rugby anyway and to be paid for doing something you enjoyed and for the love of the game was an unbelievable opportunity. Guys coming in now have never had that feeling. For them, they see it as a job option, but when I was twenty-one it was not an option, you just got on with your everyday life and at night you went training. It opened so many doors friendship-wise. It was a massive change and of course you have ups and downs within your career and there are times you're not playing well and taking flak. But when you stand back and look at the bigger picture, it's amazing and you would be crazy to pass it up.

'Now I am manager of Leinster. When Michael Cheika

was here, he wanted to set up a network of scouts in an effort to pick up players not playing in Ireland who might be Ireland qualified. I was doing that, then the manager's role came up and they asked if I would be interested in going for it. At the time, Dad was quite sick and the farm was there and I had been away for twelve years and I didn't want to learn all the new stuff. But I thought I would regret not taking this job even though I have no interest in coaching whatsoever. I'm still passionate about rugby and Leinster rugby in particular. I'm pretty honoured to be in this position and to be able to help in any way I can feels pretty good. It's busy and it keeps you on your toes but I'm enjoying it. Maybe in ten years time and maybe with children and stuff, I'd rather go back to the big, open spaces where the kids can run for miles instead of being in the middle of Dublin. But I haven't had time to think about it and as long as I'm enjoying it and we're winning, I'm very happy here.'

PETER AND GER CLOHESSY

Ask me what was the highlight of my rugby career, it was the full-time whistle in the AIL final.

Peter Clohessy, capped fifty-one times by his country and a legend
of Munster and Irish rugby

THE MAN thcy call 'The Claw' is Peter Clohessy, a prop forward of legendary proportions who places his achievements
with his club, Young Munster, ahead of anything he achieved
with Munster or Ireland or even being chosen by the British
and Irish Lions. He simply smiles quietly when reminded
that he found a place in 'The Ultimate Irish Team' chosen by
George Hook and Gerry Thornley and published in *The Irish
Times* in December 2010. Winning the All-Ireland League in
1993 meant everything to him, not least because his brother
Ger was captain of a side that will forever hold a special place
in the hearts and minds of Young Munster supporters and
those who live in, come from or regularly frequent the Careys
Road-Parnell Street part of Limerick city.

* * *

ON 6 February 1993, Young Munster and St Mary's College

defeated Garryowen and Cork Constitution respectively in the penultimate round of the AIL, a competition that dominated the Irish rugby scene at the time. Those results left Mary's just one point ahead of Young Munster at the top of the table and by a quirk of the draw, the clubs were due to meet in the final series of matches at the St Mary's grounds at Templeville Road on the following Saturday. However, that left Young Munster with a problem on two counts. They realised that the Templeville ground had no chance of coping with the vast support they would be bringing with them to the capital. And then there was the announcement of the Irish team to play France seven days after the final. Their prop forward, Peter Clohessy, had been chosen to make his initial appearance in the green jersey and the tradition of the time dictated that new caps were 'rested' by their clubs on the week before their international debut.

Solving one of the problems was simplicity itself – but many words were spoken and written and countless hours expended before a solution was found to the other! First and foremost, Peter Clohessy didn't see any dilemma. He was playing for his club in the AIL final and that was very much that. However, switching the game from Templeville to Lansdowne Road, was to prove a different matter altogether! Some people today may well wonder what all the fuss was about. After all, the AIL hasn't made much of an impression on the national radar for several years. But back in the 1990s, before the advent of the professional game, it came second in significance only to the international arena and light-years ahead of anything the provinces could come up with.

Club grounds all over the country were packed from week to week and even the old Thomond Park with its capacity in the region of 14,000 struggled to cope for one or two big matches. Several clubs enlisted the support of leading players from the southern hemisphere and St Mary's were no exception. Central to their success was New Zealander Brent Pope, and he was to prove a major figure in that 1993 decider!

Furthermore, Cork Constitution and Garryowen brought the trophy to Munster in its first two years and Munsters did not fancy being the poor relations. And that's why Peter Clohessy insisted on being in the thick of the battle against St Marys on the big day and why his brother, club captain Ger, was also determined to be part of the action in spite of being troubled by injury.

Club rivalry is nowhere as intense as in Limerick and that's one good reason why their clubs boast an unrivalled record in the AIL. In the days when the Munster Cup and later the AIL assumed greater importance than anything else in many rugby people's minds, things frequently reached civil war proportions as brothers took on brothers and mothers and fathers frequently found themselves in opposite camps as well.

* * *

PETER AND Ger, and to a lesser extent another brother Des (who was good enough to play three European Cup matches for Munster), were to make a substantial mark on the game and bring considerable honour on the family.

Peter Clohessy recalls with a wry smile how his rugby career began, not in the black and amber of his beloved Young

Munster but, whisper it, in the light blue of Garryowen! 'We were living in Ballykeeffe across from the shopping centre in Dooradoyle and all the lads I was knocking around with went up to the local rugby club and that was Garryowen,' he says. 'We played under-12s, 13s and 14s and our coach was Paddy Reid [a member of Ireland's Grand Slam-winning side in 1948], but having gone to Crescent Comprehensive that put the kibosh on the club scene. I was lively then and played at scrum half in the Schools Junior Cup. I left school after the Junior Cert and didn't play at all for a year. And then Jim Brislane asked me to join Young Munster and Ger was playing with them at the time and so I did.

'By that stage, I was in the back row, No. 6 or No. 7, and doing nicely as captain of the under-20s. We had only one prop and Roy Grant was the coach and one day he told me, "You'll have to go into the front row." I said, "I'm not going in there" or words to that effect, and he replied, "It's like this, either you go in there or you're not playing." So that is how I ended up in the front row. I played a bit of thirds and junior and my first senior match was against Shannon in the Munster Senior League final. Johnny Murphy was the captain but he had the flu so I was picked and never looked back after that, even though we lost the game. Jim Brislane was a Munster selector and I was on the verge of the team for a couple of years and I was always giving out to him about not getting on. My first game for Munster was against Ulster in 1987.

'There were only a couple of hundred going to the inter-pros at the time. They were dead, there was no interest and the big match always was to beat Leinster. The games did matter to the players, though, as they were a kind of Irish trial with all the selectors looking on. The difference between then and now is absolutely huge. The most you would have was four or five Munster matches in a season and the same number of training sessions.

'I was knocking on the door for a first Irish cap for a year or two as I was doing well with Munster and the club. I remember the day we were above again in Lansdowne Road and as usual the team that was likely to be picked was given a set of white jerseys and the others trained in their own gear. We were togging out in the dressing-room and Paul McCarthy was a tighthead at the time. Willie Anderson was the forwards' coach and he turned to Paul and told him to give Clohessy that jersey. It was the first indication that I was going to be picked against France. I was delighted with myself and a couple of days afterwards the team was picked and I was in for the game against France.'

It was to be the start of an international career that saw him pull on the green jersey on fifty-one occasions and pack down with equal facility on either side of the scrum. One of the disappointments of an Irish career that extended – with some breaks – from 1993 to 2002, was to miss out on a Six Nations Championship title, but Peter was regarded by players from all the other countries as an outstanding practitioner of the art of front-row forward play and as one of the hardest men they ever came up against.

* * *

EIGHTEEN YEARS after Young Munster defeated St Mary's College to decide the outcome of the AIL, two of the heroes of the day sit on a couple of barstools in Peter Clohessy's bar on the riverfront in Limerick to recall that famous occasion in the history of their club and their rugby-mad city. Ger Clohessy captained Young Munster that day, his brother, Peter, aka The Claw, was the talisman.[2]

They look back with unconcealed pride and total recall on every single thing that happened before, during and after a game that attracted approximately 20,000 spectators to Lansdowne Road, at least two-thirds of whom had travelled from Limerick. Peter opens the conversation by outlining how, in the traditions of the time, he might not have taken the field that day.

PETER: You did not play for your club the week before your first cap and I was due to make my debut against France the following Saturday. But it was never a conflict for me. I was never not going to play in the AIL final. It was like the Heineken Cup to us at the time. It meant so much to everybody in Young Munster. The club had got me to where I was to be selected for Ireland and so it was never going to

---

2 *Young Munster* – G. McNamara; N. McNamara, F. Brosnihan, N. O'Meara, J. McNamara; A. O'Halloran, D. Tobin; J. Fitzgerald, M. Fitzgerald, P. Clohessy, R. Ryan, P. Meehan, G. Clohessy (capt.), G. Earls, D. Edwards. Replacements – D. Mullane for G. Clohessy, M. Benson for F. Brosnihan.
St Mary's – A. White; A. Gillen, B. Cunningham, G. Lavin, D. Wall; N. Barry, M. Thorne; B. Keane, M. Corcoran, D. Dowling, T. Coughlan, S. Jameson (capt.), K. Potts, B. Pope, K. Devin.
Referee – Dave McHugh.

be an issue whether I played or not. I always wanted to play that match unless I was told I couldn't play by the IRFU.

GER: There was never a question of him not playing because quite simply this was a massive match for Young Munster. Con had won the league, Garryowen had won it and we wanted it badly. There was no injury problem with Peter but there was with me … I had a back problem and they were treating me for a hamstring and that wasn't damaged at all. The back cleared up. We went for a training run out in Howth on the morning of the match and I passed all the tests, but five minutes into the match it was gone again.

PETER: There was a big fuss throughout the week as to where the game would be played. It was supposed to be in Templeville and not Lansdowne Road, but I think Mary's got the gate at the end of the day because it was a home fixture for them, so it was probably the money that swung it. They probably didn't want to play it there but with the amount of money they were getting, they had to.

GER: Yeah, Mary's were saying the maximum they could hold at their own ground was 6–8,000 but we would have had that and more on the first number of trains leaving Limerick. They asked if we would accept 2,000 tickets and raffle them or spread them around the best way we could, but of course we shot that down. There was a rule at the time that if the match was postponed because one team refused to play another, they wouldn't receive full points but just one point

... and if that was the case and Con won the last match, they would have won the league. That also had a bearing on the proceedings, although in the end it was just common sense. It had to be Lansdowne Road. Had it been played in St Mary's, there would have been carnage.

PETER: There was pressure on us to keep the AIL in Munster – it hadn't gone out of the province at that stage and wouldn't do so for a long time afterwards.

GER: The other thing was that we were representing the city as well. We didn't have *that* many supporters from Young Munster, so people from all the other clubs travelled, while those who had only just learned about the AIL and the excitement of it over the previous two years decided that with all the hype they were also going to make the journey. We certainly didn't expect as a team that big of a crowd when we ran out onto the field.

PETER: Did we expect to win? I think we did. We always knew it was going to be close and it could have gone either way. It was very close.

GER: We scored first. There were two penalties, they got one back, and then we got Ger Earls' try. Aidan [O'Halloran] missed the conversion but got a drop goal only for them to come back into it with a try and they had a penalty near the end to win the match.

PETER: We were only two points ahead but it hit the post. And as I turned around, I was hit on the side and got a dead leg. With a dead leg, you're thinking your leg is broken and there I was thinking, Jaysus, that's next week gone out the window, but thank God it was grand two days later and I forgot about it.

GER: It was a fiercely competitive match. Brent Pope was sent off about three-quarters or so of the way through the first half.

PETER: It might have got their rags up. When a fella is sent off, going down to fourteen men will very often lift the rest and it can go against the other team. He gave Brossy [Francis Brosnihan] an elbow into the jaw – but not half hard enough because he got up again!

GER: The ref was Dave McHugh. He said he was left with no other choice. He tells the story about how the touch judge said to him, 'I don't think it's a sending-off offence' … this is only a story now, obviously … McHugh said, 'Are you joking me, if I don't, I'll never get out of here, look at the size of the crowd' as he pointed at all the black and amber in the terraces and in the stands. In the end, I suppose, luck was with us as we survived by the width of an upright.

The incident happened so fast, none of us saw it. It was only when they showed it on the TV later that we saw what happened. The match was not shown live, it only came on that evening. I lasted only five minutes because of my injury and had to go off and it was worse to be on the sideline, especially with the result hanging in the balance and how much it meant to us. I know it meant a lot to St Mary's as well but to us it meant everything. Losing was not an option … I have played a few matches in Lansdowne Road but not in front of that amount of people. With a full stadium, the noise must be unbelievable and I remember saying to the lads as we went out, 'We just can't lose this match today, no matter what happens.' The singing of our club anthem on the West Stand at Lansdowne Road at the presentation will live with us all forever. Willie Allen belted it out in fantastic fashion. 'Beautiful Munsters, beautiful Munsters' never sounded so good and piles and piles of grown men were crying openly and without shame. I have never experienced such emotion and such joy. Willie was always very close to us and he loved to sing 'Beautiful Munsters' like Frankie Flynn sang 'There is an Isle' for Shannon. Great characters and you had them in every club. In those days, it was better than Munster … your club was number one. It was only after the game went professional that it started to turn around and Munster became the number one as opposed to the clubs – which had to happen for us to progress to where rugby is today.

PETER: The noise and the atmosphere were unbelievable. 'Twas probably as noisy if not noisier than a full house because you had genuine rugby supporters, you didn't have any of the corporate stuff with half of them interested in drinking their gin and tonics rather than watching the match. So it was like playing an international. Every minute of it was nerve-racking. It was so close and so intense, you were afraid of your life that you would lose the game. Usually, once a match gets started, you get into it and forget about it, but that match was so big for us from start to finish that you were on edge all the time.

Compare that day with the biggest international occasion? To this day, the happiest time of my rugby career, and I played a lot of matches, was when the full-time whistle went that day. That was the best thing I ever got out of rugby. That was so important ... ask me what was the highlight of my rugby career, it was the full-time whistle in the AIL final.

GER: It was the same for all of us ... the delirious supporters ... the passion that was there ... I remember the late Clem Casey [a huge Young Munsterman, former Mayor of Limerick and President of the Munster Branch] came up to us. He had to listen to the match outside the ground because they told him his heart couldn't take watching. He was crying, sobbing like a two-year-old and he wasn't the only one. That really summed it up for us. He said, 'Can I hold the cup, please?' It was his as much as it was ours. You can only imagine what it meant to us. I look back on it sometimes and the hairs still stand up on the back of my head and this is eighteen years on. I could be driving the car or be anywhere in the world and I think about that day. Every time you meet someone, they reminisce about it, the great team that we had, what we brought to the club, what we brought to the city, the crowds, the passion ... club rugby at the time was immense. Every week before the matches, it was like a build-up to an All-Ireland and that's just what it was to all the teams. When you were playing Garryowen or Shannon or Con or the teams down from the north or Dublin, everyone in the city was so looking forward to Saturday afternoon, to breathe all that passion and we lived off it as well … it was absolutely fantastic, without doubt the best time of our lives.

PETER: I missed the homecoming because of the Ireland game the following Saturday. We came together the night of the league final for training on the Sunday and I missed all the parties. We had a couple of pints in Dublin, no Young Munstermen to share them with, but myself and Gaillimh [Mick Galwey] – and he was half Munsters anyway – and we went on a bit of a rampage. I made up for it when I got back on the Sunday night.

GER: The homecoming was fantastic. To be honest, we were all so exhausted mentally that the team bus was very quiet on the way back. Everybody was just knackered. We stopped outside Portlaoise or Kildare, I cannot remember which, because another bus had broken down. When we got out, we realised it was a supporters' bus and they were waiting for a replacement to come from Limerick. I said to Tom Ryan, an uncle of myself and Pete and married to my aunt Olive, 'What are the rules and regulations here?' and he said, 'There will be no rules tonight, get them on.' So we piled them all on to our bus and as they were getting on, they didn't realise this was the team bus. So you can imagine the excitement on their faces ... from there on, they were singing and having a few drinks and this broke the journey for us. We slowly but surely got into it and then we hit the outskirts of the city. It started at Herbert's pub, the Hurlers in Castletroy was the same, the traffic lights at St Patrick's church and the area around the A1 Bar, the people were all out on the streets. So as we moved into town, we realised what it meant to everyone. It was really a Limerick thing ... driving up O'Connell Street, turning up Glentworth Street – one big party. We got out at the station and mixed with the people and they were just so happy to see us, jumping up on our backs and kissing us and hugging us.

PETER: It went on for weeks – I think some fellas are still celebrating!

The late Karl Johnston – a Limerick man – summed up the day beautifully in the *Irish Press*: 'If rugby was played like this, and if rugby had followers like these in every town and village and city in Ireland, our national team would be up there with the Australians, New Zealanders and South Africans and England.'

* * *

THE CLOHESSY brothers enjoyed many other great rugby days together, most notably the Munster clash with the reigning world champions, Australia, at Musgrave Park in 1992. Although professionalism in the game was still frowned upon, attitudes were changing where preparation of teams was concerned and it was with total focus and intent that coach Garrett Fitzgerald (now CEO of Munster rugby) made his plans for the Wallabies visit.

'Maybe once every three years you'd get a big touring team coming here and they were huge games where you could prove you were good enough to go on to the national team, and I would say it was on the strength of that game that I got picked by Ireland,' says Peter Clohessy. 'When you look back on the two teams, they were far better rugby players than us. We were just hungrier and more determined because it meant more to us. When it came to games like those, everybody knitted together as if we were playing together every week.'

Ger takes up the story: 'Our team was composed of players from the top AIL clubs. There was no inferiority complex. We never felt that we could not beat them. OK, these guys are more professional than us and this, that and the other, but we knew we could do it in the hour and a half on the day and that a few of us might never get the chance again.'

Peter is back in like a flash: 'Gaillimh was sent off that day – disgraced the province again! But, seriously, the referee lost it. Gaillimh should never have been sent off and neither should your man [Australian Garrick Morgan]. If that was the case, the two teams should have been sent off, there was a bit of mayhem for five minutes or so and the referee lost all control.'

Jimmy Galvin came on as a sub at out-half for Dan Larkin who had been injured by a roughhouse Wallaby tackle and with the sides level at 19–19 and time almost up, here is how I described the winning score in *The Murphy's Story of Munster Rugby*: 'Brian Walsh found a majestic seventy-yard touch, Ben Cronin won a great line-out on the Wallaby throw, Derek Tobin reached Jim Galvin with a quick, crisp pass and the Shannon super-sub split the posts with a perfect drop kick.'

Looking back, Peter acknowledges, 'The crowd that day were brilliant. They half won the match for us. Once we got our noses in front at all, they went mad and that gives you extra energy, you would find energy out of your socks to keep going. We got a vital penalty try as well that day. It came early on and to be honest, it was soft enough.'

Ger agrees: 'There were three infringements and the referee was straight away under the posts. We didn't expect him to give a penalty try although we were looking for it. You know, the usual, as we were getting up, we were shouting at him, they're dropping it, they're dropping it, penalty try, penalty try and eventually he listened to us.'

Peter was also surprised: 'A lot of refs wouldn't have given it against a touring side playing Munster. They would have thought that Australia were superior and the penalty might have gone the other way.'

So another great day in the history and traditions of Munster rugby had to be celebrated. A short few months later, Young Munster were All-Ireland champions and Peter Clohessy was setting out on a distinguished international career that would see him recognised as one of the finest tight and loosehead props in the world. But the game was also changing utterly. Professionalism made its uncertain arrival in 1995, although The Claw did not embrace it entirely until the opportunity arose to play in what was then the Super 12 with Queensland in Australia in 1997.

'That was a big move for me at the time,' he says. 'Anne [his wife] talked me into it for a finish and I'm delighted she did because I would be a bit of a home bird and humming and hawing about going or not. But she said, "We'll definitely go." She was mad to go. We had Luke at the time, he was only a little fella, and it was fabulous. It was a great decision not just for the rugby but for family life as well. It's so laid back over there and the weather was fantastic, getting up to sunshine every morning.

'I came home early and finished with Australia because I was picked for the Lions tour to South Africa. I reached as far as London but got a back injury and lasted only two days and never even made it to the plane. Of course it was a big disappointment but probably wasn't so bad because I was [on a high] after coming back from Australia and having a great twelve months between playing here and over there. It was disappointing, but it wasn't the end of the world. Wally [Paul Wallace] went instead of me and did very well and they won the series. I was only home a day from Australia and was happy to be at home … if I hadn't been in Australia, it would have been a lot worse. I never went back but it was a very happy part of our family's life.

'After that it was mostly about Munster and the Heineken Cup. The real turning point for us came when we won down in Bordeaux against Toulouse [in 2000]. We weren't going to be the bridesmaids any more. It wasn't expected, but we always believed we were good enough to do it. We had always been good enough all right but we'd run out of steam because we weren't fit enough as we weren't professional long enough. We would usually fall away in the last twenty minutes but that day we were different, if anything we actually got stronger.

'We reached the final and of course it was a huge disappointment to lose it. It was gutting. Of the two finals I played in, that's the one we should have won, against Northampton, whereas Leicester two years later were better than us. That was the day of the "Hand of Back", when Neil Back illegally put the ball into the scrum. I had actually gone off by the time that happened; Marcus [Horan] had come on instead of me with ten, fifteen minutes to go. I saw what happened on the screen but, look, even if he didn't do that, who is to say we were going to score. There was no guarantee of anything. If he was playing with us, he would have been a hero for getting away with something like that. I have no sense of grievance about Neil Back. What happens on the field stays on the field and that's the good thing about rugby. You can box the head off each other for forty minutes or an hour but when the game is over, it's all forgotten about.'

* * *

PETER ACKNOWLEDGES that he was fortunate to enjoy both the amateur and professional side of the game. 'The amateur was more fun, there was more craic after matches and indeed on Tuesdays and Thursdays when you'd go for a few pints with the lads after training,' he says. 'But the rugby is much better now while it is also a lot harder on the players. For a full-time rugby player, it's a tough job. There's no going out for a pint on Tuesday and Thursdays although I suppose that is their job now. People might think you have it handy and you're paid good money ... yeah, you're paid good money but you have no life with it. Your life is rugby, but I have no regrets. The game got better, faster and everyone got fitter and it was definitely better for the game.

'I was a tighthead prop for much of my career but loosehead was easier so as I was getting older, it was easier for me to go over to that side because you're not under as much pressure in the scrum. Tighthead had been easier but then they changed all the rules. A lot depends on the way you are built as to which would suit you but you wouldn't be under as much pressure at loosehead.

'Of course the game is an awful lot better. Look at old matches on tapes and you'd be laughing at some of those fellas trying to jump in the line-out without being lifted and getting about three inches off the ground and floppy old floating passes and that kind of stuff. It's just a different game.'

Ger joins in on Peter's side: 'Look at the guys now, they're bigger, stronger, faster ... I wouldn't say more skilful but these guys are training on drills and skills and have to be good ball-handlers. To be fair, we recently watched the videos of the 1993 AIL final and the Con match and the Munster match in which we beat Australia and I was thinking, they weren't bad matches and were good to watch. We were getting fitter and the AIL was bringing us on and we were putting more effort into it.'

Peter interjects: 'Of course, they'd have been very intense matches and it's different watching something you're playing in yourself.'

Many have played more often for Munster, but the records indicate that Peter pulled on the famous red jersey seventy-three times, often in the company of brother Ger, and always enjoyed the full respect of those he played with and against.

* * *

THE CHAT was so entertaining that I could have sat there all day and listened. The boys had so much more to tell – like the week Peter was given no chance of playing for Munster in the 2000 quarter-final of the Heineken Cup against Castres in Beziers, having suffered severe burns in a household accident. But they had reckoned without the fierce heart and raw courage that burned within the heart of The Claw. It was not for nothing that Ronan O'Gara observed in his autobiography that 'every team was afraid of Peter Clohessy. You could see that other teams never messed with our front row or any of the forwards when he was playing. In many ways, he was the perfect rugby player. He was an animal, he was hardy, he was able to mix it and he would just say it as he sees it, bang, bang, bang.'

Keith Wood, beside whom he scrummed down alongside for Munster and Ireland, regarded The Claw in a similar light: 'He was one of the most important characters in the team. He wears his heart on his sleeve and is the embodiment above and beyond the rest of them of what Munster rugby – and I suppose Limerick rugby – is about.'

Peter Clohessy lived up to those words that sunny day in Southern France. He wore a special arm guard to protect him and played a major role in a great Munster victory. There are so many other stories that one could relate about The Claw … but they would fill an entire book in themselves!

WHAT OTHERS SAID ABOUT PETER CLOHESSY AND YOUNG MUNSTER

ANTHONY FOLEY: 'They were a frightening bunch including the Clohessy brothers, Peter and Ger, Paco Fitzgerald, Ger Earls and so on. If you got in their way, they'd run over you. Basically, the Cookies [Young Munster] bullied their way to an AIL title and fair play to them. There are a few ways to win a league and that's as good as any.'

MICK GALWEY: 'You're always happy to go out on the field with Claw. You know he'll fight his corner. He'll always give you 100% and you know he'll always do something good in the course of a match. You often come across players who dish it out but can't take it back but you could never say that about Peter.'

DANNO AND MICK HEASLIP

Billy Glynn was such a good tackler, he could stop
the 4 o'clock train.

Danno Heaslip

FRANCIS BRENDAN Heaslip? Never heard of him, you might
well say. However, change that to Danno Heaslip and eyes
will immediately light up in recognition. You see, the little
fellow from Knocknacarra, Galway, was happily scampering
around the house, back in the early 1940s, when somebody
remarked that he was the spitting image of Danno Mahony,
a famous wrestler of the time. The name stuck immediately
and has lived with one of the most popular and recognisable
characters in the western capital ever since. Indeed, Danno
and his brother Michael became synonymous with Galway's
sporting and business life and they not only glory in their
exploits on the rugby field and in the financial world, but
also in their status as owners of the winner of the Champion
Hurdle at Cheltenham in 1982!

As nippers, the three Heaslip boys – the eldest, Jimmy,
was to make a considerable reputation for himself as an
oarsman with Galway Rowing Club before emigrating to

Canada – concentrated mainly on Gaelic games and soccer before graduating to St Joseph's College, Nun's Island, known to one and all as The Bish. Rugby, and even springboard diving, captured the imagination of the sports-mad Heaslip boys before their father's business brought them to Limerick and Crescent College. It was there that the rugby bug took hold in earnest. Schoolmates included Terry Wogan of broadcasting fame and politician Des O'Malley, and it was an academy that rated the oval ball game almost on a par with educational priorities!

'My first serious game of rugby was a junior cup match for Crescent with guys like Des Moloney, Don Reddan, they'd be of my vintage,' explains Danno. 'Micky was actually captain of the senior team in the college.'

Yes, but was he any good?

'Well, he was always a hooker, not much good, a little sluggish if you like,' said Danno with a wicked grin that for once reduced Micky to a disbelieving silence!

'In 1954, we played Pres in the junior cup and the man standing beside me at scrum half was a certain Thomas Kiernan. Tom went from scrum half to out-half to centre, to fullback and all sorts of honours and we have been great friends ever since.

'After that it was back to Galway and the Bish. There were only three rugby-playing schools in Connacht at the time – Sligo Grammar, Garbally and the Bish, so the Connacht selectors spread the captaincy around for each of the inter-pros. They made Tony White, a fullback and Roscommon footballer, captain for one match, Brian Siggins, a very good centre from Sligo the next and I was captain for the third. It was the first year that we beat Munster and Leinster, but we lost to Ulster when David Hewitt dropped a goal in the last minute. Éamonn Maguire, who later played for Ireland, was a member of that Connacht side.'

Danno was already being earmarked for a very bright future and he actually played his first game for Galwegians while still a schoolboy. He recalls with pride being 'a member of the great Wegians teams ... Johnny Dooley, Seán Calleary, Tony O'Sullivan and so many more including, of course, Micky! There was no Glenina [the location of Crowley Park, the club's headquarters since the 1960s] and our base was the Great Southern Hotel. A man called Brian Collins was the manager and we had a free run of the place. After a match or training, we came in covered from head to toe in s-h-i-t-e and went up to our allocated bedrooms and fellas got into the baths and the showers before heading back downstairs and into the bar. We played all our matches at the Sports Ground and all that was there for changing at the time was an old shed.'

Danno spent two years in London where, like every rugby-playing emigrant, he joined London Irish and was very happy to serve as understudy to Andy Mulligan, a remarkable character and an Irish and Lions scrum half of the highest quality.

'I played on the second team known as the "Wild Geese" and fortunately Andy was away a lot of the time and I got a few games on the first team and also had a few matches with the Public School Wanderers,' he recalls. 'London Irish had twelve teams at the time and it was a great club. I loved my time in London. I didn't drink or smoke until two months before I left for home, although I suppose some would say that I have made up for it since. We all went to a pub called the Queen's Elm on the Kings Road, and I would have a club orange and go home. I was working as an ordinary trainee clerk in an insurance company, not much bucks, saving up to go home all the time.'

Danno and Micky love to tell the story about a Public Schools Wanderers tour on which Danno spotted one of the alickadoos reading the racing pages. Danno expressed an interest and was quietly informed by his new friend that 'I have a horse that will win the Cambridgeshire'. So he came home to Galway, told Mick and the whole of Galwegians his story, and they all put more or less their life savings on this particular animal.

'We had a hundred each way, Danno and myself, and that was a fair amount of money at the time,' says Micky. 'Trouble was, the race was run at the same time as we were playing Ballymena in the Sports Ground. They had come down the night before as well and they were also on this horse. During the game, Danno was putting the ball in the scrum when John Moore shouted from the sideline, "The horse won!" The players on both sides stopped playing, we were all dancing around and everybody watching was wondering what was going on. So when the scrum settled again, Danno said, "The horse won, coming on the left, NOW." We got a fortune that day, it was an awful lot of money to us. You have to remember, he was 12 to 1, and a pound each way gave you almost £20 and that was the equivalent of a week's wages.'

Oddly enough, Danno has few happy memories of playing

for Connacht. He thinks he might have pulled on their familiar green jersey six or nine times, while admitting that he was never on a winning team. It was a different matter where Galwegians were concerned. From that first appearance as a schoolboy, he figured in the senior team over a twenty-three-year span and picked up no fewer than eleven Connacht Senior Cup medals.

'I was a member of a great team and winning the cup was a bit of a formality for us,' he admits. 'The big enemy at the time were Athlone. Corinthians were a cakewalk and the same with UCG. We were used to winning it because we had such a cracking team. Tony O'Sullivan, a truly great No. 8 forward and close friend, was worth two men. If he was playing today, he would be unique. He had pace and he had football. He played soccer at a high level. They called him the "Green Ghost" when he pulled on the Irish jersey, which he did fifteen times. I can see him taking the ball at the end of the line-out and kicking ahead at a time when a No. 8 could never kick the ball. We had a great fullback, Seán Calleary, although he won his Connacht caps under the name J.J. Kelly … the GAA ban, you know. We also had Billy Glynn, soon to be president of the IRFU. He came to us as a schoolboy. He was a champion sprinter, really quick, and he was such a good tackler that he would stop the 4 o'clock train. I couldn't say enough about him as a player, the only reason he didn't get a cap was his size. He was only about ten stone and when he played against Old Belvedere he would be marking Tony O'Reilly who was fifteen stone. We had a terrific sevens team, all great runners, and we won our own

Blake Sevens, Dolphin, Old Belvedere … they were very big competitions at that time.

'Micky was hooker on that team. We had a lot of fun and good teams and it was really only when we moved outside of Connacht to play the likes of Ballymena, Garryowen, Blackrock, Highfield, or whatever, that we could measure ourselves against the best in the country. Very rarely do I recall walking off after we had been beaten.'

* * *

DANNO AND Mick Heaslip were indeed privileged to play in the same sides as not just Tony O'Sullivan but other outstanding performers such as Dickie Roche, Johnny Dooley, who was also a brilliant soccer player, Brendan Guerin and Seán MacHale. Indeed, in 1966 Danno was a member of a Connacht team that contained eight internationals … Johnny Dooley, Mick Molloy, P.J. Dwyer, Mick Leahy, Éamonn Maguire, Locky Butler and Ray McLoughlin, a remarkable achievement given the way the national side was chosen at the time and for many years before and after. 'The selection committee – or "Big Five" – consisted of two members each from Ulster and Leinster, one from Munster and not a soul from Connacht,' Danno reminds you forcefully. 'You had to be eleven out of ten to get a sniff of an Irish side. It was very hard. I had a personal thing about Johnny Quirke, who is now a judge. I used to think he took caps off me. I fancied myself to be better than he was. He came on as a schoolboy. He was only seventeen and there I was playing my heart out for Wegians and Connacht and I didn't get a smell. We had no selector ... no voice. I got a trial for Ireland and from our point of view, that was nearly as good as a cap. But all they were doing was kowtowing to us. The attitude was, "Give your man a trial and that will keep him quiet.'"

Then there was the late and much esteemed former IRFU President Bobby Deasy who was a very useful wing-forward but on one fateful day was pressed into service in the front row. His reservations fell on deaf ears and as Danno puts it, 'For months afterwards Bobby was hardly able to talk. He was a great friend.'

Ralph O'Gorman in his book *Rugby in Connacht* extolled the virtues of the Galwegians team that completed a record five-in-a-row in the Connacht Cup: 'The remarkable run started in 1956. So many of the team were household names. Dickie Roche, Johnny Dooley, Brendan Guerin, Tony O'Sullivan and Seán McHale played for Ireland. Seán Calleary, Seamus McEvoy and Billy Glynn had final trials. Rynal Coen, Laurie Noone, Henry Forde, Joe Tyrrell, John Moore, Seán Healy, Joe Costello, John Callanan, Tom Browne, Danno Heaslip, Dermot Lovett and Michael Heaslip all played for Connacht. This Galwegian team not only recorded a five-in-a-row Senior Cup success, but made it a five-in-a-row Senior Cup and Senior League double. What a pity the Bateman Cup was long discontinued.'

And O'Gorman later noted, when referring to Wegians 1975 victory over Ballinasloe, that 'it was the final that allowed Danno Heaslip to collect his tenth Connacht Senior Cup medal, seventeen years after his first!'

* * *

DANNO HEASLIP is blessed with an impish and often self-deprecating sense of humour and loves to recall his wife Mary's first dalliance with Galwegians and Galway rugby. 'I met her only the week before at the wedding of my great friend Billy Glynn and invited her to the Galwegians dress dance on St Patrick's Day in the Great Southern Hotel. I told her that on the way into town she should drop in to see our game against Corinthians. So she did and leaned up against the rails and asked the guy beside her, "Which is Galwegians and which is Corinthians?" So he told her and there was a pause as she looked around all the guys in the blue jerseys before asking, "And where is Danno Heaslip?", as there was no sign of me on the pitch. And he replied, "That is him over there on the sideline with Paddy Flynn, they have been sent off for fighting." Not very auspicious from Mary's point of view, but of course I convinced her I suffered for retaliating.'

The lady in question and Danno's wife-to-be was, in fact, Mary Murphy of the popular RTÉ *Home Truths* programme. A Wexford girl, she excused this particular transgression (and, you have to suspect, one or two more over the years) and they married shortly afterwards and now have a fine family – Simon (a member of the Connacht Professional Game Board founded by the IRFU in late 2010), Justin, James, Mary and Kate.

The brothers' love for all things Galwegians and Connacht also played a major part in helping Warren Gatland to become a major figure in northern hemisphere rugby. During the New Zealand tour in 1989, Michael Heaslip was in London when he happened to bump into a couple of All Blacks. One of them was prop forward Craig Dowd and Heaslip asked if he knew of any tourist who might be interested in coaching in the west of Ireland when the tour was over. Dowd made a few enquiries and when the Kiwis arrived in Galway for the game against Connacht, Mick, an influential figure in the game in the west and especially in the Galwegians club, contacted him and was introduced to Warren Gatland. The AIL was about to become big business and Wegians wanted to be a part of it. They made him a worthwhile offer to come and coach their players and Warren and his wife Trudy were enthused enough by the proposition that they packed up their teaching jobs in Waikato and set off for Ireland. Gatty quickly feared he might have made the biggest mistake of his life. Player attendance was poor, many arriving well after the stipulated hour, and they were hardly the most skilful in the world. Patience hasn't always been regarded as one of Gatland's virtues but he stuck at it and with such success that the club won two Connacht League titles and were duly promoted to the AIL in 1992–93.

Michael Heaslip was his keenest supporter and even though the Gatlands returned to New Zealand after four years at Glenina, they were lured back in 1996 to take over the coaching role at Connacht just vacated by Eddie O'Sullivan. The professional game was stuttering uncertainly into life at the time but Warren worked his players hard, got the desired response and achieved the near impossible by coaching Connacht to victory over Bordeaux Bègles and then Northampton Saints at their home ground of Franklin's Gardens to qualify for the knock-out stages of the European

Conference in 1997. He was on his way to the top job with Ireland, an alliance that unfortunately ended in tears, and nowadays is with Wales, with whom he won a Six Nations Grand Slam. And it might never have happened without the initiative and foresight of the brothers Heaslip.

If there was a ball to be kicked or struck, the Heaslips were never far away. And when it came to horse-racing, they enjoyed a very special place in the pantheon of great Irish achievements. Their interest in the 'sport of kings' was sparked when they lived within a stone's throw of the old Limerick race course at Greenpark.

'We used to get in over the wall, pick up the discarded tote tickets and usually made a few bob,' says Micky. 'Also, my mother loved a punt and would have a half crown or so on a horse most days. Later on, we had a few horses together – *Birthday Suit* was the name of the first one – and then had a bit of a run with Paddy Prendergast Junior. The next thing, we met Michael Cunningham and he told us about this lovely horse he had. That was *For Auction* and we were ecstatic when he won at Fairyhouse. At Christmas, we went to Leopardstown and won the Sweeps Hurdle, a huge race at the time, by a short head. He was 12 to 1 that day.'

And there was a lot more besides. Micky and a friend, Tony O'Mahony, bought a half share in a sweepstake ticket and it proved to be worth £25,000 when *For Auction* was first past the post. A few weeks later, *For Auction* travelled to Newbury where he finished fourth, a performance that hardly suggested that victory could be attained in the biggest race of all, the Champion Hurdle at Cheltenham. The brothers, however, were enthused by the comment of the jockey, Colin Magnier, who told them after Newbury: 'None of those horses will ever finish ahead of me again.'

Micky Heaslip goes on: 'I had £300 each way on *For Auction* at 33 to 1. Michael Cunningham had £100 each way on the day at 50 to 1 and he was returned at 40 to 1. He won by seven lengths with an amateur jockey on board. *Broadsword* was second and *Ekbalco* third but *Ekbalco's* rider was so sure of winning a long way out that he turned to Colin and asked if he was coming with him. Did he what! *For Auction* cruised home, Galwegians colours and all. The prize money was £33,000 and you can only imagine the celebrations. John Mulholland played the piano all night and we didn't stop for many a day afterwards.'

If you imagined that this wasn't exactly a vintage Champion Hurdle year, you would have to think again. *For Auction's* immediate predecessors as Champion Hurdlers were three legends of the sport, *Monksfield*, *Sea Pigeon* and *Night Nurse*. You could hardly ask for more illustrious company! The Heaslips mastered the art of combining business with pleasure to a remarkable degree and this is one reason why their company is respected and enjoyed no matter the milieu in which they might find themselves.

SIMON AND RORY BEST

I was in no man's land so I went as hard as I could to get out of the road.

Rory Best talking about the seconds before Ronan O'Gara won the 2009 Grand Slam for Ireland

IT WAS a warm, pleasant afternoon in Bordeaux on 26 September 2007. Simon Best was strolling the streets with his good friend Paddy Wallace, quietly enjoying the many delightful aspects of this elegant French city and putting rugby to the back of his mind for a couple of hours. For a few good reasons this would not have been particularly difficult, given that the Rugby World Cup campaign on which Ireland had embarked with such high hopes a short few weeks earlier had turned into something of a nightmare. They had scraped wins over Namibia and Georgia and been heavily beaten by France. The only result against Argentina the following weekend that would guarantee them a place in the quarter-finals was a win by eight points but they also had to score four tries in the process. It was a virtually hopeless scenario, but where there is life, there is hope and publicly at any rate the Irish were not conceding defeat just yet.

Sadly, however, Simon was to be left with other far more important matters to concern him after the happenings of that fateful Wednesday afternoon. To his consternation, he was suddenly afflicted by a loss of feeling down his right side, a mild headache and a slight difficulty with his speech. Not surprisingly, Paddy Wallace was shocked by the sudden change in his friend. He quickly raised the SOS and Simon was whisked off to the city's Pellegrin Hospital and from there to the Leveque Hospital for further tests. The local medics and Ireland team doctor Gary O'Driscoll maintained a close watching brief but it was already apparent that Simon's World Cup was over and that his capacity to continue as a front row forward of world class was very much in jeopardy.

Brother Rory was also a member of that Irish party and indeed the replacement hooker for the clash with the Pumas. Obviously, he was particularly worried by the shock development, but by the time Simon's wife Katie and parents John and Pat arrived less than twenty-four hours later, the news was a whole lot better. The diagnosis was an irregular heartbeat and was to end Simon's rugby career, but otherwise leave him in rude good health and looking forward to the full if not quite so active life that stretched ahead.

Simon Best retired at the age of twenty-seven with twenty-three Irish caps to his credit. He captained the side on two occasions during the 2007 tour of Argentina and represented Ulster on 124 occasions. He made his first appearance in the green shirt as a replacement against Tonga in 2003 and his first start was against Wales in August 2003. The World Cup defeat by France at the Stade de France in 2007 was his last time to represent Ireland. And he was badly missed, not just for his ability as a strong, committed and honest scrummaging forward, but also for his positive, forthright attitude in the team room.

'Simon was an incredibly honest, talented and hard-working player in every aspect of his participation in the game and was a model professional,' commented Irish coach Eddie O'Sullivan after his retirement was officially confirmed in February 2008. 'In addition, he was and still is an extremely popular guy with all the players and it's very unfortunate that his career has been cut short by this condition when he still had so much more to offer Irish rugby.'

Simon accepted the situation with typical grace, stressing that he was 'grateful to have had the opportunity to work with coaches, management and players that I have had the utmost respect for and I have formed lifelong friendships with many'.

One can only imagine, however, how brother Rory felt when the news of Simon's illness was broken to him after he had just completed a game of golf near Bordeaux.

'I got into a taxi and noticed there were a couple of missed calls from Gary O'Driscoll,' says Rory. 'He said there was no need to panic, Simon had been taken to hospital not feeling very well. It wasn't that much of a shock because of the way Gary said it … I believed it was just a bump from the previous game or that he had been sick and it wasn't really a big thing. Gary met me at the hotel and told me it was the heart, it's not brilliant, but the bottom line is that he's safe, he's conscious, and everything was going the way they wanted, even though he hadn't been in a great way for a while. I then went to the hospital and it was not particularly nice to see Simon like that. He was very much struggling with his speech, it certainly wasn't a hundred per cent. It was scary to see someone who was older than you, who was always bigger, always stronger, the big brother, to see him affected by this, lying in a hospital bed … it was a bit daunting. That was really when it sank in that he mightn't be out of here tomorrow and ready for the game at the weekend.

'Gary and I talked about how we would tell the parents. I said, "Listen Gary, there's no point in me phoning them because they'll start asking me questions and I'll probably make it out to be worse than it is." So he phoned first and then I chatted to them. The IRFU, to their credit, did everything they could to get Dad, Mum and Katie, his wife of only two months, out on the first available flight. They were very worried and the worst thing was being so far away and having to travel. I was very concerned but I talked to the doctors and they laid a lot of my concerns to rest. His long-term rugby future wasn't mentioned once. All everyone was worried about was his health and nothing else so I left the hospital slightly happier. Gary O'Driscoll [now with Arsenal] is a brilliant doctor. His bedside manner was fantastic, not so much to defuse the situation but to make everyone feel slightly more comfortable that Simon was going to be all right. You couldn't give him enough credit for that.

'Simon is never one to lie down and let everyone feel sorry for him. He wouldn't have enjoyed lying in a hospital bed and fought very hard to get out of there. At that stage, I think he just wanted to get home to his own place and house and judge everything by how he felt instead of everyone pandering to him. He doesn't particularly like being told what to do. He was disappointed to leave the World Cup the way he did and never to be back to another one, but at that time all he wanted to do was assure everyone he knew that he was okay and not to be worrying too much about him.

'Simon is great now. He's doing a bit of coaching with Banbridge, he's coming up and down working on the farm, he's got a couple of kids, everything is going well for him. He obviously misses the big games, the Heineken Cup at Ravenhill, the internationals; at the same time he gets to do what every rugby player wishes they could do when they're playing but at the same time don't want to because they want to be involved, and that's to go down with your mates and watch the games. And he does that. When the big games come around, you want to play in them but there are parties going and it's a lot easier to go with your mates and enjoy them. He goes to most internationals, has time to go skiing, things you cannot do when you are playing. We talk most days … there's always something needed by one of us from the other.

'Obviously he'd still be very friendly with Girvan Dempsey and Humpf [David Humphreys] although a lot of the guys he played with have also retired and gone on. Everybody goes about their life – if they see each other, they see each other … I suppose it's like leaving any job or company, you might not see everyone and when you do, you catch up. It's just the way it is.'

Rory Best has had many health issues himself arising from his rugby career. Like almost every front row forward worthy of his crust, he has had more than his fair share of injuries. He was ruled out for long stretches by serious knocks to the ankle, rib and eye, but a neck injury, an extremely dangerous area where rugby hookers are concerned, was a far graver matter. Given what had happened to Simon, Rory might also have considered calling it a day. He is quite philosophical on the subject, simply pointing out, 'Once Dr Niall Eames at the Ulster Independent Clinic advised me that I'd be better off in future if I had an operation, it was a no-brainer, even though there was no guarantee I'd play again. He admitted there was a slim chance, but I had it in my head to be back in January of 2010. I had just turned twenty-seven, was out for just short of five months, and got the all clear on my birthday. I felt ready and comfortable. I suppose my mum and my new wife Jodie [they married in July 2009 and now have a son Ben] were worried about the operation and then going back to play. It was very difficult for Jodie. We had been together since we were sixteen, she had seen a lot of highs and lows, but never anything like this. But she gave me a lot of support and it was something you just had to get on with.'

* * *

SIMON AND RORY Best grew up on the 900-acre family farm near Poyntzpass, coming under the influence of their dad, John, and his love for rugby from an early age. Rory was to actually play alongside John in the Banbridge front row, although all three never scrummed down together in the same side. 'There were three young boys in the house and, of course, my dad, while my grandfather lived not very far away,' recalls Rory. 'So we would have spent Sunday afternoons playing rugby on the lawns of the house. My father John and grandfather Don played for Banbridge and that became a Sunday tradition from the time I was four or five years old. Winter memories are of four- or five-man matches in the garden after *Rugby Special*, boots, full-on scrummaging, fists and all.

'When we got a small bit older, it was into Banbridge Rugby Club on Saturday mornings. It's about six miles from home and where my grandfather and father played and all three of us grew up playing probably from five or six right up through to fourteen when we went to Portadown College. It wouldn't have been one of the more elite rugby playing colleges, although every now and again it would have a very good year. There have been some good teams without being cup favourites or anything near it, the sort of team, if you like, the favourites wouldn't have particularly fancied travelling away to without being overly scared at the same time.

'Simon, who is four years older than me, and Mark, who is in between us, travelled the same route. Mark was a scrum half, my grandfather an out-half and my father a prop … Dad, Mark and myself played in the same team and Mark, Simon and Dad also, but with me being four years younger than Simon, by the time I got to be of a legal age to play in a senior game, he was a professional and couldn't take the risk at the end of the season to be playing in a fourths game for Banbridge.'

The potential of the Bests was flagged from an early age. Simon played for Ireland Schools and also at under-19, 21, 25 and A before graduating to the national side. Rory enjoyed a similar level of recognition and Mark's caps came his way largely at under-age. Simon did three years at Newcastle University and was also in the Falcons' academy. He could have stayed or returned to Ulster, but his ultimate choice was inevitable for such an enthusiastic and promising forward.

'He wanted to play for Ulster, it's where his heart and soul were and it wasn't about money,' explains Rory. 'Mum and Dad had been very good at taking us to all the Ulster games and we wouldn't have missed too many home Ireland games either. So all we wanted to do was to go Ulster–Ireland, that kind of progression. And thankfully, that's the way it panned out.

'We had one start together for Ireland against Scotland when we won the Triple Crown. Obviously, we had loads and loads of matches together for Ulster. I suppose I have 110 caps or something like that for Ulster and over 50 per cent would have been with Simon. I came in in the 2004/5 season and we would have played together until his career came to an end at the 2007 World Cup. We had been scrummaging down together since those days back in the garden as kids and it certainly was a massive help for me at the start. At the end of the day, we came from a very small village, went to very much a non-rugby school, had played a little bit for Banbridge and so, if you like, were in very comfortable surroundings, playing with boys we had grown up with. Suddenly, I'm into Belfast Harlequins and Ulster and it is very different. You obviously recognise all the faces, especially the older ones at that stage like Tyrone [Howe], Andy [Ward], Gary Longwell and Humpf, these guys you had watched all the way through and suddenly you are in the same squad. So, for me, it was very nice to have someone like Simon who, there's no doubt about it, did a lot for me, keeping an eye on me and making sure I was settling in well. It made it slightly more comfortable to be in those surroundings because while I wouldn't necessarily be intimidated, I had a lot of respect for those players. Sometimes, you wonder if the younger guys coming through now are all that fazed by it.

'Simon's presence was probably even more helpful when I came down to the first Ireland squad session. I found it very daunting. At that stage, Ulster was struggling and we had minimal representation, so there was no one I knew very well. A lot of the guys were strangers to me. From my point of view, a lot of them were from very successful teams and I would have watched them growing up. But they were all great guys, all very welcoming. It has been a great experience, a lot of highs and a lot of lows, but that's just the way it goes. The fact that you were rated among the top thirty to thirty-five players in the country was not lost on me. And, of course, it was competitive. Nobody was going to roll over to let me in. Denis Leamy, with whom I had played at Ireland Schools, was in there and that helped, and obviously Simon was very good. Like everything, over time you get to know them, what they like and don't like, and find a lot of common ground. I'm from a farming background and I'd have conversations with John Hayes about what's going on at home and so on … I've sort of followed the same route as him, moved home, bought a few cattle and played rugby as well and got away from it by looking after the stock at home.

'Simon is still living up in Holywood since he retired. He travels up and down to do a bit of work at home. Dad is still the boss and will be for a long time. It's something we both enjoy, being out and about looking round the stock. Simon probably enjoys the arable side more than I would, the cereals, the oats, the wheats, whereas I have always enjoyed looking after the cattle and walking about through them and that sort of thing. That's where we are slightly different and that suits as well. As I have said, it helps you to get away from rugby and really that is the release for me. We farm just around 1,000 acres so there's plenty for everyone … Dad doesn't push you to do anything you don't want to, but he expects that when you do something, that it's done and done well and done tidily … he loves to keep the place neat and tidy and if it's not done, then there are issues.

'I have some cattle and have moved home from Belfast and live quite near the family home on one of the holdings. My father and I keep some pedigree Aberdeen Angus cattle … we have a half share each. I would look after them from day to day and he'd do likewise if I'm away.'

* * *

THE BEST BROTHERS Simon, Mark and Rory, and their sister Rebecca grew up at a time when the Troubles in Northern Ireland were raging. There were countless atrocities throughout Northern Ireland and rugby people were not spared. On 25 April 1987, Nigel Carr, David Irwin and Philip Rainey were on their way to Dublin for an Irish squad session before the inaugural World Cup when a bomb was detonated at Killeen on the border. The IRA had targeted Lord Justice Maurice Gibson, a Northern Ireland senior judge, who was returning from holiday with his wife, Lady Cecilia. Both were killed and while the rugby players, who were on that stretch of road at the time, avoided the same fate, Carr, an openside wing-forward of world-class calibre, suffered such serious injuries that he never played again. He was twenty-seven at the time.

Naturally such a tragedy would have registered high on the minds of the rugby-mad Best family, who did not live all that far away. Fortunately, though, as Rory recounts, they avoided much of the mayhem caused by the strife and tried to live life as normally as possible. By and large they succeeded.

'I was born in 1982 and by the mid to late 1980s, it was beginning to settle down and wasn't as intense as it had been in the late 1970s and early 1980s,' says Rory. 'But bits and pieces did happen. Poyntzpass is a very small village and everyone mixes with everyone. There's no real divide but there is one thing I do remember. When I was about fifteen, two best friends, a Catholic and a Protestant, were shot dead in the local pub. You thought things had settled down and then you heard something like that especially so close to home and it came as a shock when you knew the families so well. The whole village was in a state of mourning for a very long time. For the people who were in the pub, it's obviously a very touchy subject to this day. Nobody wants to be reminded of it.'

The victims were Damian Trainor, a twenty-six year-old

Catholic, and Philip Allen, thirty-four, a Protestant. It was a Loyalist Volunteer Force gun attack on the Railway Bar and the belief is that Trainor had just asked Allen to be best man at his wedding. Other than that, however, Poyntzpass (located on the Dublin to Belfast rail line and on the border between Counties Armagh and Down and named after Colonel Charles Poyntz from Gloucestershire who defeated the forces of Hugh O'Neill, 3rd Earl of Tyrone in 1598) was a peaceful place in which to grow up.

'We were very much taught to get on with life, to work your day's work, and at weekends go out and have a few pints and go home and do the same all over again,' says Rory. 'That incident in the pub was the only time it directly affected us. Everyone gets on well with everyone.'

* * *

WHILE SIMON AND Rory are the high profile members of the Best family, Mark also made his mark and indeed caught the attention of coach Declan Kidney who called him up to his Ireland under-19 team.

'Mark went to university in Edinburgh and just sort of enjoyed the social aspect of the rugby and really loved to play sevens,' Rory explains. 'He's in London now and has a good group of friends who also moved from university in Edinburgh to London to work. He just enjoys the craic. They go away to sevens tournaments like Carrick and Kinsale. The Ireland under-19s experience hurt him a bit because he'd been in the squad all the way through, played in the friendlies, and then was one of two people cut just before the World Cup.

He had put a lot of work and effort into being in that squad and when he didn't quite make it, he would never let on to you, but I think it hurt him a bit and he just decided that he enjoyed the social bit so much that he would nearly prefer that to putting himself out there again ... he had enough going on without that.'

Simon and Rory Best also flew the family nest for a time to study at Newcastle University but by this stage the lure of professional rugby was becoming quite consuming for two young front row forwards who believed they had a lot to offer. Rory was given a place in the Newcastle Falcons academy but did not really enjoy the scene, largely because he was being switched too often between prop and hooker when the No. 2 jersey was all he wanted. And when Allen Clarke at the Ulster academy approached him, Rory did not hesitate. Clarke later enthused: 'Rory has raw strength and aggression and is a tremendous scrummager with a great knowledge of all front row positions. His core skills are excellent and he's brilliant at the break down.' At this point, he also came under the influence of the outstanding South African coach Andre Bester and was appointed captain of the Belfast Harlequins AIL team at the age of twenty.

The emphasis was very much on getting the basics of forward play spot on. Each Monday night, they would do something like sixty scrums and forty mauls so his father had no real reason to worry when he saw Quins take the field for an AIL game against Garryowen in 2003. To John, it looked very much like a case of men against boys, but Rory recalls how that day they were awarded a penalty try and scored a pushover try and scrummed not just Garryowen but most teams into the ground! Not surprisingly, Rory's first contract came along under Mark McCall and Allen Clarke in time for the 2004/5 season.

* * *

ULSTER'S FAMOUS European Cup triumph in 1999 was a massive boost for the province and inevitably proved a major incentive for the up-and-coming contingent to emulate the great achievement of David Humphreys and co., who had decisively defeated the French side Colomiers in the final in front of a packed, red-and-white-bedecked Lansdowne Road. Simon Best was doing his finals at Newcastle that year, Mark had just left Portadown College and Rory was in his second-last year in school.

'A group of us from school travelled down in the bus and had a good old day,' he recalls. 'The big thing you remember was the stream of buses. We parked in the RDS and walked to the game in the floods of Ulster shirts. At that stage, I had been to many Ulster games with the parents and family, but it had never struck me as the same spectacle as this day. It seemed that the whole of Ulster had gone down to Dublin for the day and even coming back, it was bumper to bumper but nobody cared because we had won the thing.

'It was a very special day even though I was a bit younger then. The European Cup hadn't exploded to the extent that it has now, but you still remember being down there while probably not realising just how special it was going to be while still acknowledging it was a big, big thing. The scenes at the end certainly made you want to play for Ulster, to get to big occasions like that.'

Having distinguished himself with Ulster, Rory made his first appearance for Ireland as a replacement for the injured Frankie Sheahan against the All Blacks in 2005, a matter of minutes after Simon had also been drafted into the side. He doesn't have many happy memories of the occasion, admitting, 'The score wasn't overly flattering and while it was nice to come into the same front row as Simon and I'm sure it was nice for my mum and dad as well, the team didn't do very well.'

Simon and Rory were due to start against Romania shortly afterwards, but an injury to Rory intervened and after that he admits to enduring a tough Six Nations. Jerry Flannery had become the preferred choice at No. 2 and after some frustrating times during the summer tour to New Zealand when he didn't see any action at all, Rory knew it was time to change his attitude to the whole thing.

'I got fifteen, twenty minutes towards the end against Australia and it was then that I made the decision, look, it took a lot of hard work to get where I was and I just couldn't relax. I needed to work a lot harder, to change my body shape and lose a few kilos. I worked very hard that summer and in the off-season to be sure I was in good shape. Instead of starting the pre-season at ground zero, you had a bit of a head start over everyone. I started two of the three Tests that autumn against Australia and South Africa and benched against the Pacific Islanders only to come on and score my first international try. I started off the games in the Six Nations, for sixty minutes or so, before Jerry came on, and that was nice.

'We had the tour to Argentina when most of those who started in the Six Nations were rested. On the one hand, it would have been lovely to go with Simon as captain as he had captained Ulster so many times, but on the other, it gave you a nice feeling that you were one of the fifteen that would get an extra push at the pre-season, it was a nice feeling that you were one of the fully established players. And then it was on to the World Cup ...

'It was a very odd experience. One of the first things I noticed was getting on this really big jet and there's only the team on it. We didn't even go through the normal security. The bus literally drove us to the steps of the thing and dropped us off so we could walk on to the plane. This was something completely unheard of for me and it was great. Everything was provided for us. Sadly, once we got off the plane, though, things started to go downhill from there. It really wasn't nice to be involved in it. There had been so much expectation leaving and by the end there was so much pressure on us that we needed to perform, that we needed to do this and that and we couldn't do it. It was very unfortunate but hopefully you live and learn from that. You realise that World Cups don't come round too often, that you have four years to wait before proving the last one was a blip. At the time, you sort of think, ah, it's just another game, but it's not.'

* * *

THERE WERE disappointments but also great days as well – led by that amazing March afternoon in Cardiff in 2009 when Ireland bridged the sixty-one year gap since they had completed the Grand Slam of beating all other countries in the Five/Six Nations Championship. Rory Best did not start that game – but he came precariously close to eventually playing a key part in its outcome! The dramatic climax, during which Ronan O'Gara dropped the decisive Irish goal and Stephen Jones' penalty shot to give Wales the victory dropped short, will forever be a part of Irish rugby folklore.

'When the drop goal went over and the penalty dropped short, it was something very special,' says Rory. 'It was a surreal moment and took a while to sink in. O'Gara loves to spread the rumour that I might have dropped his goal instead! Basically, we threw into the line-out and mauled it and were trying to get it closer to the posts, we just went "runner, runner, runner coming infield". When I was just about to come in the corner, I noticed Ronan hadn't sat back in the pocket just yet and I was thinking we were going to hit one more. But suddenly he goes back at a rate of knots and Peter Stringer is about to pass it. So I am in no man's land and I went as hard as I could to get out of the road – the last thing I wanted is one thrown at me. I looked up and Ronan's drop kick went over … it wasn't the prettiest drop goal ever but it didn't matter.

'Then there was Stephen Jones' penalty. I was beside Paddy [Wallace] in that melee and he tried to blame me for it! I knew it was in and around Stephen's range. You try not to think about it. You never really wish for someone to miss but that's as near as you would come. It would have been such a travesty to have lost out on everything including the Triple Crown. It meant so much to everyone and I realised that very quickly when I saw Paul O'Connell sprinting towards me after the whistle sounded. To see how important it was to a player who has achieved as much in the game as he has really brought it home to me.

'It meant a lot to have Jack Kyle present. It was huge for me. I met him that day and a couple of times since. From talking to Jack, you knew how much it meant to him that he was able to see another Irish team do the Grand Slam. He was happy that it took a few years because he got an extra bit of credit, but he was very happy to have been one of the few of the 1948 side to have seen it. I would have heard of Jack Kyle from a relatively young age. You would have heard people like David Humphreys being compared to him and it didn't take a genius to ask the question – what did Jack Kyle do? My grandfather would have been a massive fan so we were well aware of who he was for a long time.'

At the end of the less successful 2011 Six Nations Championship, Rory Best had already gained forty-seven Irish caps, but undoubtedly this number will rise before the end of a brilliant career in Irish rugby.

THE DEPARTED

A LOVE for rugby has been an integral part of Irish families ever since a crooked ball was first kicked in anger. Parental influence has been considerable, a fact never more forcibly demonstrated than by the three generations of the renowned Cork Constitution Murphy dynasty: N.F., first capped in 1930, N.A. in 1958 and Kenny in 1990, who have all worn the green with distinction. Then you had the Collopys and McKibbins who provided a father and two sons to the cause, while the most recent case of father and son achieving the distinction was provided by Gordon (who first played in 1954) and Keith Wood (1994).

However, my brief in this book has been to highlight the sets of brothers who have distinguished themselves at international, provincial and club level and in this chapter I look back at some of those who performed the exceptional in days gone by and have since departed to that great rugby stadium in the sky.

* * *

ONE CRUCIAL fact must be underlined from the outset when discussing the O'Flanagan brothers, Kevin and Michael. Michael is still very much alive, hale and hearty and living in South Dublin. But Kevin has passed away and I felt no book of this nature could be published without due reference to their unique claim to fame.

All that said, an unfortunate date of birth and a remarkable level of versatility almost certainly combined to deprive the remarkable O'Flanagans of even greater recognition in the sporting arenas of these islands. And, yet, it has become increasingly unlikely over the years that they will ever be deprived of one outstanding achievement: they remain the only brothers to win international caps in both rugby and soccer.

Kevin O'Flanagan was born in 1919, twenty years before the outbreak of the Second World War. As hostilities erupted, he was on the cusp of becoming All-Ireland champion in the 60 and 100 yard sprints and the long jump, and as such was a virtual certainty for the Irish teams in the 1940 and 1944 Olympic Games. Neither, of course, took place, and while this was obviously a keen disappointment for the young Dublin medical student, he did not really have a whole lot of time to worry about it.

When he was not stuck in the books at UCD, Kevin found time to indulge in his three great sporting loves: soccer, rugby and athletics. Throughout the 1940s, he was arguably the most gifted footballer in the country and undoubtedly the quickest. He captained Bohemians, an amateur club at the time, to beat Belfast Celtic, in the final of the Inter-City Cup contested annually between the top clubs in the two cities, his sense of satisfaction all the greater because brother Mick netted the winning goal.

At the age of eighteen, and already studying at UCD, Kevin made his international debut against Norway in a

World Cup qualifier at Dalymount Park. He picked up four soccer caps and played in an all-Ireland team in a game that marked the first appearance of the great Jackie Carey. Mick won his soccer cap in 1946 and became part of a very famous group of rugby players two years later.

On graduation, Kevin was offered a position as a junior GP in Ruislip, Middlesex. On arrival in London, he signed amateur terms with Arsenal, where he was warmly welcomed not just for his footballing qualities but also for his delightful personality. The Gunners official history to this day refers to him as the 'charismatic' O'Flanagan. In the transitional post-war season 1945/46, he scored eighteen goals and in his subsequent time at Highbury he played sixteen first team games, fourteen in the league and two in the FA Cup, once scoring the only goal in a crucial encounter with Stoke City. All the time, he was attending to the demands of his medical career and coping with a troublesome ankle injury that eventually forced him to bow out in 1949.

Then there was Kevin's rugby career to which he attended as assiduously as possible, despite all his other commitments. In 1942, he had played on the wing for an Ireland XV against the British Army at Ravenhill and again appeared in the unofficial international against France at Lansdowne Road in 1946. His first official cap followed against the touring Australians in 1947, before brother Mick's chance came later in the Triple Crown and Grand Slam year of 1948, when he appeared in the centre in the 6–0 defeat of Scotland.

Unique is an adjective easy to use when describing the O'Flanagans, and it certainly applied to Kevin. He played rugby for Ireland on one Saturday, soccer for Ireland against Scotland the following Saturday and would, in fact, have played international rugby again the next Saturday except that fog delayed the boat-train from London to Holyhead and he was unable to get to Dublin in time to turn out against England.

A chance encounter with Stanley Rous, the then Football Association chairman, opened further doors for Kevin. It led to his appointment to the British Medical Commission and he went on to become a pre-eminent sports medicine specialist in London. He was doctor to the Irish Olympic team for sixteen years until 1976 and he was on the Irish Olympic Committee's drugs panel from 1977 to 1979 and was later made a lifetime member of the IOC.

Kevin O'Flanagan returned to Dublin in the early 1950s and again demonstrated his remarkable versatility by becoming a low handicap golfer at the Milltown and Portmarnock clubs and a very proficient tennis player at Fitzwilliam. He died on 26 May 2006.

* * *

BACK IN the days when international teams played, at most, five games in any one season, the Stephenson brothers from Belfast, George and Harry, set a record that was to stand for many years by appearing together fourteen times in the same Irish shirt.

Perhaps just as significantly, George, who was first capped in 1920, went on to represent his country on forty-two occasions until 1930, a record for any country until it was overtaken by Wales' Ken Jones, and it remained an Irish record up to 1958 when it was equalled by the great Jack Kyle, who went on to pick up four more caps.

Even though George would eventually be regarded as one of Ireland's greatest ever players, he got off to a slow start and could hardly have had a more difficult baptism as he lined out against France at Lansdowne Road that fateful afternoon in 1920. He had been a mere third team player at Queen's University twelve months previously although he had improved to the firsts by 1919. Ireland had lost the first two games of the 1920 campaign by the time France came a-calling and things got even worse when they went down to their visitors for the first time ever.

This horrific run of results could have heralded the end of most of that squad, but the selectors in their wisdom stayed loyal to Stephenson, a policy that proved well justified. Although frail of build, he was a superb defensive player and a prodigious goal kicker, talents that served him and Ireland well in each of those forty-two games. In all, he made thirty-six consecutive appearances for Ireland until dropping out of the Scottish game through injury in 1929 and this, at the time, was also a record.

The 1920s and 1930s were significant for the number of brothers and sons of famous fathers who wore the green. Billy Collopy's father had been capped in 1891 and was joined in the national side by his brother Dick, as was George Stephenson by his sibling Harry. Frank and Tom Hewitt, also from Ulster, were key men in a side that grew in stature with every outing, while Tipperary provided Ted and Victor Pike, two of the eleven children of a clergyman, to the national team. Three other sons of the reverend also represented Leinster and subsequently three became bishops, with Victor serving in that capacity at Sherbourne in Salisbury, Rhodesia (now Zimbabwe).

In his book *The Men in Green*, Sean Diffley regales us with the following: 'Victor's opposite number in Rhodesia was the Catholic bishop, Dr Moloney, who was also a noted rugby player in his younger days in Ireland. It was said the reason that the Bishops Pike and Moloney made uncertain progress in the ecumenical movement in their diocese was that those close friends talked so much rugby when they met that they had no time left to discuss any less important subjects!'

Frank Hewitt was a schoolboy when making his debut in the centre against Wales in Cardiff in 1924 but, like his brother Tom, called it a day very early in what was obviously a burgeoning rugby career. One worthy who tried to dissuade Frank from making this decision optimistically pointed out that he 'wouldn't be finding Jesus Christ on the rugby pitch'. Frank considered this for a moment before replying: 'Maybe not, but you hear an awful lot about him!'

The Hewitts were a massive loss to the Irish cause with Frank regarded as good enough to be spoken of in the same breath as George Stephenson. Shrewd judges recalling this era regarded the Irish back division against England in 1926, which consisted of Ernie Crawford at fullback, a three-quarter line of Denis Cussen, George Stephenson, Tom and Frank Hewitt, and half-backs Eugene Davy and Mark Sugden, as one of the best in the history of Irish international rugby. That was the unit when Ireland bridged a fifteen year gap by beating England in a marvellous match by 19–15 at Lansdowne Road in 1926, the clinching try touched down by Frank Hewitt. The Arms Park, Cardiff, 1924, provided another famous occasion for the family when Frank, making his debut, and Tom became the first brothers to score tries for Ireland in the same game.

The Hewitts certainly were a very gifted rugby family as another of the clan, Victor, earned six caps as an out-half in the 1930s and cousins John and David (a son of Tom) and Gerry Gilpin were all capped in the 1950s and 60s. At seventeen years, five months and five days, Frank Hewitt was the youngest of the (at least) six schoolboys to have been capped by Ireland, when he lined out against Wales in that Cardiff game in 1924. Just slightly older was Johnny Quirke in 1962 and the others were: G. McAllan of Dungannon High School in 1896; Aidan Bailey from Presentation College, Bray, 1934; F.M.W. Harvey from Ellesmere College, Salop, in 1907; and J.B. Allison of Campbell College, Belfast, in 1899.

Although a side of considerable talent and formidable spirit Ireland failed to win a Triple Crown in the 1920s – they provided great entertainment only too often to lose with a great deal of honour. At the time, too, the Lansdowne Road stadium was being developed, but the 1927 game against Scotland went ahead before the roof had been put on the East Stand. As it transpired, it was a dreadful day, fiendishly cold with lashing, icy rain, so bad that two Irishmen, George Stephenson and W.F. 'Horsey' Browne, collapsed and had to be helped off the pitch!

Stephenson wasn't long in recovering and he and his brother were rated very highly at the end of their respective careers by Sean Diffley in *The Men in Green:* 'George Stephenson is considered one of the finest rugby centre three-quarters of all time,' Diffley wrote. 'Tall and frail-looking, his appearance was deceptive. Harry played fourteen times between 1922 and 1928, wing three-quarter to his more famous brother, and was an excellent performer in his own right. But the fame of George naturally tended to overshadow the more pedestrian excellence of Harry.'

In his *Irish Rugby History, 1874–1999,* Ned Van Esbeck graphically recalled the February afternoon in 1929 when Ireland at last laid the Twickenham bogey to rest: 'It was a victory achieved against a background of misfortune in the shape of an injury in the early stages to George Stephenson, who fractured several ribs. Always magnificent in defence, he won the game for Ireland with a great saving tackle in the dying minutes despite his broken ribs.' Ireland somehow held on to win 6–5 and a newspaper report told of how the result caused 'a spate of uninhibited hibernianism'. Seat cushions were thrown high in the air and pillow fights took place with the result that the occasion was dubbed 'the Twickenham battle of the cushions'.

* * *

THE INFLUENCE of a whole sequence of other families such as the McVickers and Beamishes from the northern end of the country and the Collopys from Bective Rangers all contributed handsomely to Irish teams pre-Second World

War. Air Marshal Sir George Beamish was a magnificent forward in the best Irish tradition and gained twenty-five caps between 1925 and 1933 while his brother, Charles E., picked up another twelve from 1933 to 1936.

The ancient art of dribbling the rugby ball has long since been discarded but back in those days, forwards and backs who could control the ball at their feet were invaluable members of any side. Green-jerseyed Irish teams seemed to master it better than most and they were an awesome sight in full flight. It was a brave man indeed who tried to stop them!

* * *

WHEN OLD BELVEDERE was granted senior status in 1937 on the back of two successive victories in the Metropolitan Cup, not even the club's most ardent supporters could have foreseen the glory that lay in wait. Their elevation led to the return to the fold of Belvederians like the brilliant scrum half George Morgan, Paddy Quinn from Clontarf and Vinny Aird from Bective Rangers, and coincided with the arrival on the scene of several other members of the Quinn family who were to be at the forefront of the club's amazing achievements over the next decade and beyond. After a chastening first appearance in the Leinster Senior Cup in 1938, the following year revealed distinct signs of the potential that was about to be realised throughout the 1940s. George Morgan, who had toured with the Lions in 1939, captained the 1940 side that captured the cup by beating Clontarf in the final. It also included Des O'Brien, another who would tour with the Lions and be a key member of Ireland's Grand Slam-winning side in 1948, along with Gerry, Paddy and Frank Quinn and the unrelated Brendan Quinn.

Incredibly, Belvo went on to win the coveted title in each of the next six seasons to set a seven-in-a-row record that eclipsed Lansdowne's five successive wins in the 1920s and created a mark that surely will never be broken. All the time, the Quinn brothers were very much to the fore and in fact they were joined by another member of the clan, Kevin, who was arguably the most talented of the lot and represented Ireland on five occasions. They picked up twenty-eight medals between them, in a family contribution without parallel in the Irish game. Paddy (who had the distinction of winning the cup with three clubs, Old Belvedere, Clontarf and Lansdowne) was the successful captain in 1941, Gerry led the way in 1944 and Kevin in 1951 when the title was regained after a five year hiatus. It was retained in 1952 when Kevin was again a key member of the side.

Belvo had the happy knack in that era of producing outstanding players at the most opportune moments and among those to share in the Leinster Cup medal booty were the legendary Karl Mullen, captain of Ireland's Grand Slam triumph in 1948, Paddy and Jack Belton, both lord mayors of Dublin, and the versatile and richly talented Des Thorpe, who ranks foremost in the list of 'best players never to play for Ireland'.

After Belvo lost to a Jack Notley drop goal in the 1947 final against Wanderers and so were deprived of the eight-in-a-row, Arthur MacWeeney in the *Irish Independent* still felt moved to observe: 'One cannot let the occasion pass without a reference to the losing team who played great rugby throughout their long period of dominance and set an example of skill and sportsmanship which can be followed but which will not be excelled.'

The Quinns were not just great rugby footballers, they were also dedicated Old Belvedere people as exemplified by Paddy who acted as honorary secretary for fifteen years between 1951 and 1968 and was president of the club in 1964–66.

* * *

Nowhere in Ireland does a love for rugby burn so brightly and the traditions of the game are more respected than in Limerick. The city has produced many great players and its famed Thomond Park stadium has hosted some memorable games, most notably, of course, the 12–0 defeat of the otherwise undefeated New Zealand All Blacks in 1978. Family contributions have been as fulsome in Limerick as in so many other parts of the country and in this respect the O'Connors from Athlunkard Street are as worthy of acclaim as any other.

I recently happened upon an old cutting from the then *Cork Examiner* in which Dermot Russell quoted from a letter he received in 1975 from the remarkable Shannon RFC and Limerick man W.W. Gleeson, detailing their remarkable exploits on and off the rugby field: 'The O'Connor family, seven boys and a girl, were born at 11 Athlunkard Street in the second half of the last century. All the boys, Mick, Charley, Jack, Thade, Joe, Bryan and Jim, played rugby, junior with Shannon, senior with Garryowen. It is on record that on one occasion when Garryowen played Shannon, all seven brothers took part, four with Garryowen, three with Shannon.

'The boys shared forty-seven Munster Cup medals between them. Jack (11), Thade (9) won the most and a son of Jack's, Mick, won two himself to make the family total forty-nine. Jack, who played at centre three-quarter against Scotland in 1895, held the Munster 220 and 440 yard track record at the same time. Joe, who played in the out-half position in 1909, had a promising career cut short through a series of injuries resulting in his death in March 1910. His funeral was recorded as one of the biggest and most representative ever in Limerick.

'Jim, who captained the successful Garryowen team in 1913–14, won the All-Ireland 100 yards championship at the GAA sports in Clonmel in 1912. An objection was lodged, and sustained, on the grounds that he had played a foreign game (rugby) previously. However, years later better relations existed and he duly received his medal.

'It will not be out of context here to mention that Bryan was captain of the Athlunkard Boat Club for thirty years during which time the IARU (Irish Amateur Rowing Union) cup, senior (twice), junior, maiden and inter-provincial championships found their way to the parish club. Also, it's right to record that Mick Kelly, father-in-law of Paddy Reid, shares with Thade O'Connor the honour of holding nine Munster Senior Cup medals.

'Thade would in all probability have worn the green jersey but after selection for a final trial, a damaged cartilage forced him out of rugby for the best part of that season. Indeed, Thade's grandson, Billy Casey, captained the Cork Constitution side which lost to Garryowen in the final of this year's [1975] Munster Senior Cup. Billy himself has won three Munster Cup medals with Constitution.'

'Whack' Gleeson – as he was known throughout a colourful life during which he traced the family tree and history of countless people in his native city and invariably showed it all off with flowery handwriting in green ink – was too much of a gentleman not to recount what became of the only female in the remarkable O'Connor clan. 'As a young girl, Mary O'Connor joined the religious life as a member of the Mercy Order. In later years, as Mother Mary Dominic, she spent the greater part of her life in Mountrath and later in Birr where she died recently in her 100th year.'

EPILOGUE

Meeting the people who are the subjects of this book was a great privilege for a rugby fanatic like myself, who had covered the exploits of the majority over the years and would have been awed by many of their achievements.

To a man, they gave of their time willingly as they recalled the many memorable moments, the matches won and lost, the joy of victory, the disappointment of defeat. Great deeds were re-enacted; the wonderful characters who have personified the unique ethos of this remarkable game for well over a century stirred the emotions and revived memories of many famous days.

Just as it was a privilege to reacquaint myself with some of the greats of the past, it was equally rewarding to discuss the many changes that have overtaken rugby union, especially since the switch from amateurism to professionalism in 1995, with the stars of the modern game. The change came out of the blue and many at the time regarded the Irish Rugby Football Union as one of the tardiest in accepting the tsunami in favour of an entirely new structure. If so, the Union adjusted as it had to until today the way it handles the elite players is the envy of most other nations. That it has come through many difficult and fraught times to remain a cohesive thirty-two-county body makes the point graphically and that is why the Irish game can look to the future with complete confidence.

Family tradition, of course, has played a major part in the evolution of the game. Time was when sons followed fathers into the national side and brothers togged out together in the green. Just as rugby itself has changed, so, too, has family life and the number of siblings representing Ireland has dropped with the passing of the years. But let's hope it will never cease altogether and if it should, hopefully this book will help to recall some halcyon days!

INDEX